The Survivor's Journey

Celia Williamson, PhD
& Lisa Belton, MSW

DEDICATION

The Survivor's Journey is dedicated to all of the survivors of intimate partner violence, sex trafficking, sexual assault, and child abuse that were brave enough to share their story and courageous enough to work on their recovery.

CONTENTS

ACKNOWLEDGMENTS

Thank you to all of the interns, students, survivors, and direct service workers that supported this book. Much gratitude to the highly competent Human Trafficking and Social Justice Institute team & interns that because of their competence, allowed this book to be possible.

Williamson & Belton

Foreword

"Walking, I am listening to a deeper way. Suddenly all of my ancestors are behind me. Be still they say. Watch and listen. You are the result of the love of thousands." ~ Linda Hogan, 1947 Native American Writer

We wrote The Survivor's Journey and developed TNT groups to help those that have suffered trauma because of violence, abuse, and exploitation. We know society has ignored you and not given you the kindness, concern, and effective healing you need to put the pieces of your life back together. Through the victimization you suffered, and because of the lack of appropriate societal concern and support, you went on to treat yourself in ways that haven't been kind. On a personal note, we have some feelings around this. We feel that someone has hurt and continues to hurt our friend, someone we deeply care about and love. You have been unkind to yourself, and we also have some feelings about that. Stop hurting the person we love. That's our friend that you are putting down, hating, and treating badly and we love you. Quite frankly, we are a little pissed off and kind of frustrated about the way you have treated yourself and the way others have treated you, and we are coming for you to make it right. The Survivor's Journeys get right to the heart of the matter to bring you the healing you need and deserve. No more bullshit. No more abuse. No more exploitation. No more excuses. No more drama. No more trauma.

PART I:

The War You've Been Through

"We all take part in fattening the pig, but then hate the butcher"
~ Celia Williamson, PhD

Surviving War

The Art of War is a famous 1500-year-old Chinese text which outlines strategies and tactics related to warfare. The art of war involves many components, but a critical component to making war is the creation of soldiers who will fight for your cause. The strategy involves not only creating and training soldiers, but the "art" is to create *loyal* soldiers who will do anything they are asked to do without question and to risk their very lives to do it. The making of a soldier first requires they are isolated so there are no other voices and perspectives dominating their lives except their sergeant at boot camp. The military demands unquestionable loyalty and the love of country, even to one's own personal detriment. Providing consistent messages, beliefs, and activities designed to gain compliance, commitment, and ultimate loyalty is the plan, because if the mind can be controlled, so can the body. In boot camp they provide the solider with an intense environment requiring they get up at dawn, engage in extreme and extensive exercise while a sergeant's voice and intense manner overwhelms their sense of individual identity and opposition. Individual identity is replaced with complete loyalty to the one who will give the orders. Any

1

military around the world can take a once independent individual and make them go to another country and kill another human being they have never met. The solider is willing to make the ultimate sacrifice if it is needed. However, for some when they return home, what they did, what they believed, who they became, and what they saw and experienced becomes hard to live with and process.

A survivor of violence; whether it is via the military, child abuse or neglect, sexual assault, sexual exploitation, domestic violence, or is the result of violence, gang violence, or other means; has suffered a level of trauma. The trauma experienced can be significant and if left untreated has the potential to alter an entire life.

Post-Traumatic Stress Disorder (PTSD) is an illness first discovered in soldiers returning from war. PTSD is a mental health condition that is diagnosed by a professional. PTSD happens when someone has experienced or witnessed a traumatic event. Some individuals diagnosed with PTSD might experience intrusive nightmares, flashbacks of certain events, depression, anxiety, and more. When someone has PTSD, they are not simply having horrific memories, they are reliving their experiences over and over. However, not everyone who suffers from trauma will be diagnosed with PTSD. There are numerous debilitating physical, behavioral, and emotional symptoms associated with those who live with untreated trauma. People living with untreated trauma can also become addicted to drugs, get involved in abusive relationships, and participate in other self-destructive types of activities including a persistent self-hatred, shame, and self-blame. Inside themselves they are living with someone they loathe, and they are trying to kill the part of themselves they hate. Without help, some returning soldiers live their whole lives in misery with a few days of happiness and contentment. The same can be true for some survivors of violence, abuse, and sexual exploitation.

Unlike war time, when someone is caught up in an abusive and violent situation, the controller may use kindness, support, and love and then use fear, manipulation, violence, threats, to hold your feelings and thoughts hostage while they overtly or covertly gain your commitment, compliance, and then your complete loyalty. They work to take away your freedom to think your own thoughts, feel your own feelings, and behave in your own true nature. Often the controller makes their victim believe what they are doing is right or necessary. In exchange they leave their victim with heartache, shame, and self-hatred.

Perhaps in the beginning they made you feel like you were the most important thing in their life. Maybe they spent a considerable amount of time with you telling you and showing you how much you meant to them and how much what you were doing meant to them. Then they taught you, mentored you, and trained you until what you believed was what they believed. Sometimes this type of experience didn't even start with your latest abuser, maybe it started with the childhood abuse you experienced or the vulnerability created when you didn't have enough to live on, or enough love to grow you into a strong and healthy human being. Because of our lack of the essential elements we needed in our early years, we became susceptible to people who controlled us, or to drugs that controlled us, or we became susceptible to self-destructive activities. Someone or something was in control, and they led us to put aside who we really were to satisfy the needs of someone or something else. And it cost us.

Just like a soldier leaving a war leaving your dysfunctional situation may leave you feeling ashamed, blaming yourself, and struggling with the demons inside you.

If you have been a victim of any form of prolonged, abuse, victimization, or violence, make no mistake about it, what your mind, body, and heart went through was equivalent to surviving a war. You may not think of it like that, but just like a solider may have experienced trauma, you have experienced trauma. Having had to survive behind enemy lines, you're not sure who you are anymore. Because what happened to you and what you've seen and done, you experienced traumas that greatly affected your mind, body, and spirit. Some of what you've experienced would bring the most hardened of us to tears. Each time something happened that you didn't want to happen it was an act of emotional violence to your psyche. Yet you survived with mixed emotions about your past and the people involved. And just like soldiers in war, you did what you had to do in order to survive. Some of what you had to do is something you never want to talk about again and you have tried to bury it and shove it deep down inside, so deep that even you might not remember it. But as you try and forget it, the body keeps score and remembers what happened.

And just like soldiers at war, you believed in things and saw things you know today wouldn't be understood by everyone. And just like soldiers, you sometimes find it hard to forgive yourself and others for what happened to you. Many soldiers survived their experience, but when they came back to a peaceful country they just didn't feel like the same person they used to be. Some victims of violence, abuse, and/or sexual exploitation have that same feeling. They confuse what they had to do to survive with who they are today. They blame themselves for what they felt, thought, and did at the time. They started hating themselves as a result of what they were forced to do and who they thought they had become. They blame themselves for what others manipulated them to do. Just like soldiers, survivors of violence, abuse, and/or exploitation suffer from depression and anxiety. Some are given a diagnosis of PTSD or another diagnosis, but all have suffered a level of trauma.

The Set Up

Being able to survive emotionally and physically violent experiences is a feat of great strength, a force of nature, a miracle, and is sometimes against all odds. Individuals that survive violence, abuse, neglect, sexual exploitation, rapes, beatings, gang membership, or domestic violence and/or a combination of these experiences should be seen for what they are, "heroes" because they fought for their lives and got to keep their lives.

The truth is, at our darkest most vulnerable moments in life, no one was there to help us and to save us. The fighting we did to survive involved the use of our survivor skills. Thank God for those. We used our survival skills to get through what we experienced in order to survive it. Just like on the show "Survivor", we used what we had and did what we could to survive. We have been to hell and back. And when we think back at what we had to do, what we had to say, and how we had to behave in order to survive, we shouldn't be ashamed. Understand that everything we did and didn't do, helped us survive so we could be here today to focus on our healing.

As a survivor you showed valor and courage making it through your circumstance, but just like soldiers of war, you didn't leave your experience behind. Many survivors suffer PTSD and have the symptoms of depression, anxiety, and hyper-vigilance, to name a few. Many suffer drug addiction, a lack of trust, have inappropriate boundaries, dysfunctional relationships, and lack the ability to experience true joy and a fulfilled satisfying life. However, unlike war where you never leave a man behind, almost everyone that purported to love you left you behind to suffer in silence.

Even though over 70% of those in the U.S. will experience a traumatic event at least once in their lifetime, trauma is rarely talked about. The crippling effects of trauma have been well documented in psychological and sociological studies and in numerous government reports. That's why society's silence about the lifelong effects of trauma is baffling. It seems in our society, if we can't touch a problem in physical form, or if we can't see it, hear it, or easily explain it, we like to pretend it doesn't exist.

Trauma can be debilitating and can affect the quality of our lives. Indeed, trauma is a silent killer. When you are emotionally traumatized it's like being shot. The bullet rips through your internal self. As it travels through your body it damages your ability to feel safe again. Once you suffer from trauma, it becomes difficult to emotionally invest and be vulnerable again. Trauma twists your thoughts and perceptions making you feel suspicious and hypervigilant. It warps your perception and becomes the driving force behind your decisions. Trauma often dictates your behavior. It destroys your hopes, dreams, and causes you to give up on your goals. It can destroy everything in its internal path. It wreaks havoc and steals your internal joy. Traumatized people no longer feel carefree to learn, love, and grow. They are enslaved by their trauma.

Trauma can make you go against your own best interest to convince you to stay in physical, emotional, and psychological places that aren't good for you. It can prevent you from living the life you were meant to live.

If you have been a victim of violence, abuse, or exploitation, the criminal justice system is designed to initially respond. However, the best you can hope for from this system is to pursue and receive procedural justice through the courts. When it's done through the courts, the perpetrator can face criminal charges. You may also have an opportunity to sue for damages. If the criminal justice system is successful, they say they hope to have given you "closure".

But what does "closure" mean? Does it mean because someone went to jail or you received money through a civil suit that now you are all better? Does it mean the internal pain you suffer will somehow magically go away? In reality, that message seems to encourage you to close part of yourself off, stuff it down, and pretend to move on.

"Closure" does little to soothe your internal pain. The problem is, trauma doesn't go away because someone was punished for a crime against you. Trauma doesn't go away on its own. It festers like a toxic poison and permeates throughout your thoughts, feelings, and behaviors. Trauma steals your joy. It robs you of trust. Trauma can prevent you from getting the job you want or remaining successful at the one you have. It destroys the potential for future healthy relationships and from becoming the parent you want to be. A court system cannot help you to heal internally from the pain and suffering that was caused. Only trauma work can heal internal pain and the damage caused from internal trauma. The system sets you up to believe that some form of procedural closure will somehow magically heal your internal trauma. It will not.

To add insult to injury, most often when you are in need of help from the social services system, they assist you to meet your external needs. For example, if you have been a victim of intimate partner violence, this system will help you find a safe place to live and will help you set up a new life free from violence and control. However most often this system also doesn't focus on healing the trauma that was caused. We skip over the part requiring intensive internal healing and we call you a "survivor." Once again you've been set up to believe the external resources and services they provided somehow helped to heal your internal pain. But this is just another set up.

Perhaps you are one of the lucky ones and you find your way to counseling through the mental health system. All counselors are not alike. Many miss your need for intensive trauma treatment and/or are not trained and certified to provide the needed and most effective trauma treatments available. Many will focus on the symptoms and triggers of trauma and will treat those, while missing the elephant in the room, which is the need for trauma-focused treatment. They may tell you that you have an anxiety disorder, major depression, anger issues, substance use disorder, or you are simply suffering from learned helplessness. They may send you to anger management classes, substance abuse treatment, or counseling for depression and anxiety. In other words, they will treat your symptoms and may fail to treat the core issue, which is trauma.

In reality, trauma is a risk factor or root cause for nearly all behavioral health (mental health, well-being, and behavior) and substance use disorders.[1] Unfortunately when legitimized systems fail to acknowledge and treat trauma and prefer to treat the symptoms of trauma instead they fail to serve their clients effectively.

When powerful systems fail to treat your trauma, it leads you to conclude you are unique and there is something inherently wrong with you. Despite all of their structure, building, degrees, and professionalism, they failed you. Typically, the lowly person who doesn't receive healing rarely concludes the systems are ineffective. Instead, they conclude they themselves must be defective. When their clients don't get better, their negligence causes victims of trauma to blame themselves. When systems treat the symptoms of trauma instead of trauma itself, we inadvertently tell clients their failure to get better is their fault.

---

[1] Substance Abuse and Mental Health Services Administration (SAMHSA) (2022). Understanding child trauma. https://www.samhsa.gov/child-trauma/understanding-child-trauma - :~:text=Trauma is a risk factor, important role in their recovery.

The Silence and Suffering

Because society's criminal justice, social service and mental health systems set the standard for practice and recovery, their silence and subsequent failure to acknowledge and treat trauma sends the subliminal messages to the sufferer of trauma. The first message is that we brought our best knowledge and practices to support you. If you failed to improve, it is your fault. Second, because the sufferer assumes others have gotten better as a result of the services received from the systems, they believe there must be something different about them that is beyond help.

The sufferer buys into the silence resigning themselves to the fact they are unique and their unique problems prevent them from living a normal, fulfilled, and joyful life. This *grand collusion of silence* keeps both the professional and client communities from acknowledging, normalizing, and treating trauma.

The result is we continue to suffer in silence from a very similar and prevalent affliction called trauma. We may even be diagnosed with all sorts of different symptom-related problems e.g. depression or anxiety. We may have physical symptoms that physicians acknowledge, label, and treat. We may experience a series of dysfunctional and abusive relationships or non-loving relationships. We may succumb to alcohol and drug addiction and receive treatment for our addiction. But what we fail to realize is all these misfortunate experiences are symptoms of trauma. These symptoms can be very common across people and populations. Trauma left untreated will continue to permeate and destroy us.

Finally, when professionals tell us our symptoms are indeed the problem, we treat our symptoms alone. However, we continue to get involved in dysfunctional relationships. We continue to backslide on the progress we made and we continue to be traumatized. Over time our mental health meds aren't working as well as they should. We have to up our dosage. The doctors and the social workers lead us to believe we just aren't working hard enough at our own goals and recovery. We are led to believe it is our lack of motivation or our lack of will power and hard work causing the stagnation. We indeed believe it's us. We are the only ones who can't seem to be happy and be fulfilled. There is something unique to us causing us problems. We are alone in our pain and there is no one else quite like us who is experiencing what we are experiencing. There is no one else that is failing like we are or that is bankrupt inside. We don't even really have words to describe our dissatisfaction with our lives. Suffering in silence is the only way we know to move forward in life. Perhaps we feel like we are asking for too much out of life. But why do other people seem to experience genuine joy in their lives and we don't? Are they pretending like we are pretending? Their joy seems genuine. We know we aren't genuine. What we portray to the world is not how we really feel. It must be us.

What silence does is it convinces us that no one else in the world is like us. It encourages us to suffer in silence. What we don't know is that we are dead wrong. We are not the only ones that feel this way. There are thousands and millions of others who have suffered from long lasting trauma that have been misdiagnosed and left unattended. What we don't know is we are in the company of many living in our own community that are experiencing the same feelings and thoughts as us.

Sharon's Story: I had no words for understanding or addressing that feeling of overall trauma so I had to invent some words. I created an outer self, one that everyone would see, but it wouldn't be me. It would be the one who looks invincible and can handle anything. I talk and smile and act like I am a part of something or even a part of anything – but it wouldn't be me. The real me would be sitting back, way back inside myself watching the others. I would be praising myself on how much of a good actor I am. At the same time, I hate myself. No one can tell that I'm not really here. I hate that I'm not real. I'm so ashamed that I'm hurt. And I'm hurt that I'm so ashamed. I'm mad that I can't come forward. I'm sad that I can't be real and show people my pain. No, it's better to sit back. It's safer to stay here. I watch everyone and they seem normal. They seem to actually be presenting their real selves, but not me. My real self is wounded, scared, hurt, and in pain. If I showed my real self they would run in horror. They would be ashamed for me and worse they would be ashamed of me. It's better to hide. They don't know that sometimes I'm even outside of my body watching me interact with others. None of what I talk about is real. None of what I say I feel is real. It's all an act. I wish I could be real."

Surviving the past should be held in high esteem and immensely celebrated. However, living a life as a survivor does not suggest all of the healing needed after surviving traumatic experiences has been done. When asked "How are you?" and someone answers "I survive" or "I'm surviving" does not suggest they are truly living the life they want to live. Being a victim, survivor, or thriver are action words. Just as "victim" shouldn't remain your identity, neither should "survivor". If every day you operate as a victim, then you are being taken advantage of and not attending to your own true needs. You see yourself as a victim and you act accordingly. If you are a victim then almost everyone is a perpetrator taking advantage of you at every turn. "Surviving" is also an action word indicating that you remain in survival mode with a survivor's mentality. Just as no one likes to be called a victim, no one's identity should remain "survivor". Survivor is but a rest stop on the highway heading somewhere else. Your destination is thriverhood and all it entails.

No One is Coming to Save You Except YOU

It is a harsh and sad reality, but it's true. Some people may make you feel like they are going to save you, but the truth is, only you can save you. Others may have compassion for you. A good case manager or advocate may support you by helping you link up with services you need. A good therapist may help you sort through some of your internal issues. A good lawyer may help you win cases for the crimes committed against you. A compassionate, intimate partner may help you along your journey; however, even they can only help you so much.

- Only you can commit to changing your life, living the life you want, and being the person you want to be. And only you can feel better about you as you go into your future.

- Only you can commit to stop self-medicating with drugs.
- Only you can come out of denial and see your life for what it really is.
- Only you can choose friendships and relationships that are healthy.
- Only you can create the future you want. And only you can change your life in ways that make you feel better and be better long term.

No one else can do it. The few people who support you right now need you to get it. If you get it, you'll be ready to take the Survivor's Journey. If you don't get that simple yet powerful reality, you'll forever be bitter, angry, uneasy, confused, apathetic, and mad at the system and your life, and will forever blame others for the lack of change that's in you. That decision is up to you.

Even though you may no longer be connected to your exploiter, or perpetrator, until you do your internal work, you remain a victim, or "prisoner of war." You may be physically free, but you are still trapped in the emotional chains of your experience. The Survivor's Journey is a love-based journey to help you face critical truths in your life. Weekly Survivor's Journey groups provide you with the tools and support you need to transform your life and live the life you truly want to live.

Whether or not society recognizes and validates your victimization, vulnerability, and trauma, you carry the internal wounds and scars inside. You indeed survived your experience but brought out of your war with you a personal wreckage, that of which no one might see but you. In some cases, there were others that validated your experience and attempted to help you process through it and heal. There are others that don't recognize or validate your traumatic experience and may have even stigmatized or blamed you, not taking your vulnerability or victimization into consideration. Perhaps you haven't even realized what you may have gone through in your life was traumatizing and damaging to you. Perhaps you hid your internal pain and pretended you are alright. You put on a face and acted like the person everyone wants to see. You want the strong person that can survive anything? You want to see the hero? The bad-ass? The image of a well-put-together strong person that survived it all? Here I am.

Victim, Survivor, Thriver Defined

Along the Survivor's Journey you will travel through 12 Journeys, each of which are outlined within the 12 chapters of this book. These 12 Journeys move you through a process of recovery from victim to survivor to thriver. The definitions of each are provided below.

Victim

A victim is a person who experienced trauma via destructive or injurious, acute or chronic, emotional, mental, and/or physical victimization derived from real or perceived threats or actions. The victim may continue to be involved in their traumatic experience or may no longer be involved. The victim continues to suffer trauma manifested in some or all of the following ways: continued dysfunctional professional or personal relationships, living in or experiencing reoccurring crises, continued necessity for basic needs, lack of adequate attention to health, an unwillingness or inability to engage in reflection or insight into their life and situation, a lack of meaningful movement toward recovery or change, and significant deficits in positive and pro-social informal and/or formal support systems. Victims have the opportunity to work through Survivor Journeys 1 through 5.

Survivor

A survivor is a person who suffered trauma from destructive or injurious, acute or chronic, emotional, mental, and/or physical victimization, derived from real or perceived threats or actions, and because of these circumstances, suffers distress. They are actively involved in recovery services but are fragile and may be re-traumatized and/or re-injured emotionally. A survivor may shift in and out of victimization and victim-survivor status as they may return to their abusive and/or exploitative situations and continue to be impacted by the abuse, violence, or exploitation. Survivors may be involved in some or all of the following: some relationships in their lives are dysfunctional and some are positive. Survivors recognize their circumstances and issues and are actively working on them. They experience periodic crisis and basic needs may be occasionally needed.

Acute conditions are resolved immediately, and chronic conditions are addressed under the care of a professional. There is meaningful reflection and/or insight by a survivor about their life and situation. Meaningful movement is occurring toward recovery and there are some positive and pro-social informal and/or formal support systems in their life. Members have the opportunity to work through Journeys 6 through 9.

Thriver

A thriver is a person who suffered trauma from destructive or injurious, acute or chronic, emotional, mental, and/or physical victimization, derived from real or perceived threats or actions. A thriver no longer suffers, or minimally suffers, from the trauma related to the violence, abuse, and/or exploitation they suffered. They may or may no longer be involved in recovery services, however, they continue to work to maintain emotional, mental, spiritual, and physical health. Thrivers feel empowered to make healthy decisions about their lives and people involved in their lives. They actively pursue and are engaged in positive and prosocial informal and formal support systems. They work toward goals and have attainable objectives to reach them. Most meaningful relationships in their lives are positive. Thrivers consciously monitor their emotional, mental, physical, and spiritual health and attend to it. Thrivers live their lives intentionally and purposefully because they choose to. They experience periodic crisis but can recover using the resources they have or the knowledge they have about how to obtain the resources they need. Thrivers engage in meaningful reflection and/or insight into their lives and situations and make plans to maintain or enhance those positive aspects. Recovery is something a thriver holds dear, invests time in, and places importance on. Thrivers empathetically reach out to others in need because they can do it without being easily re-wounded or triggered. Finally, thrivers understand boundaries and balance, and work to achieve both. Thrivers have the opportunity to work on Journeys 10 through 12.

It's time to stop pretending. It's time to do the work to live the life you want to live. It's time to take back control and focus on healing. The

Survivor's Journey is best suited for those that have experienced domestic violence, commercial sexual exploitation, child abuse and/or neglect, sexual assault, emotional or physical violence and control through gang affiliation, or any form of violence that has negatively impacted one's life.

Considering Whether to Take the Journey?

To achieve the life you want to live, it will take hard work and commitment. We've taken the time to develop this program because we know you're worth it. Your facilitator is taking the time with you because they know you're worth it. We hope you are ready to take this Journey because you know you're worth it. We want to begin by asking you three simple questions:

1. Are you not where you want to be in your life because of the victimization you suffered?

   If you believe you are where you want to be in life, close this book. It is not for you. Hand it to someone who could benefit from it. You are living the life you want to live. If not, keep reading and coming to The Survivor's Journey group.

2. Is it possible for you to obtain the life you want on your own?

   If it were possible for you to obtain the life you wanted on your own, you'd be living that life right now. Ask yourself if you are living the life you really, truly want. If so, hand the book to someone who could use it. If not, keep reading and coming to The Survivor's Journey group.

3. Are you, on your own, able to heal yourself?

   Given your experiences in life, do you feel good about yourself? If you do, you are on top of your world and healthy internally. Be kind and give this book to someone who you know could use it. If not, keep reading and coming to The Survivor's Journey group.

Translations: For those of you who have been greatly harmed and are deserving of love and support to live the life you want to live, but have been in survival mode so long you may feel undeserving or are hardheaded, we provide a version of the above questions for you:

1. Are you fucked up?

   If you believe you are not fucked up, close this book. It is not for you. Hand it to someone who could be fucked up. You are living the life you want to live. If not, keep reading and coming to The Survivor's Journey group.

2. Could you not be fucked up?

   YES! Absolutely and most certainly. You can live a happy life and the life you want to live, but if you are totally fine, hand this book to someone whose life is fucked up. If not, keep reading and coming to The Survivor's Journey group.

3. Are you, on your own, going to unfuck yourself?

   Working on your own has gotten you where you are today. This is your evidence you might need to try something new. You will not be able to think, feel, or behave your way out of your trauma on your own. The victimization or abuse you suffered was not your fault, but your recovery is your responsibility. With support from others and an openness and willingness from you, it is possible to live the life you want to live. If you are all good, hand this book to someone who knows they aren't going to unfuck themselves on their own. If this is you, keep reading and coming to The Survivor's Journey group.

The answer to all these questions above lies your salvation.

PART II:

The Survivor's Journey

1

1st Journey: *The victim comes to believe they are not living a life of choice and freedom, but a life filled with internal traps and external trappings, but this can change.*

1st Truth: *I have been internally and externally trapped by trauma and am not living the life I want.*

1st Transformation: *I have the power to choose to change my life.*

Trigger or Validation:

For some, the material in this Journey may be triggering. If it triggers you, reach out to your support system and/or engage in some self-care activities. For others, this information will be validating. In those cases, use the material to help validate you and affirm what you are or have been experiencing is real.

CHAPTER 1: AWARENESS AND EXPECTATION

"If you don't know where you're going, any road will take you there."
~ Lewis Carroll

When someone has suffered trauma from abuse, violence, and/ or exploitation, their life can be altered. While the physical body survived the victimization, the internal self has been damaged. Left unattended, this damage can alter the way we see and interact with the world.

Many people don't connect what happened to them days or years ago as trauma. Even though psychological trauma is common following victimization, society really doesn't acknowledge it in any meaningful way. We don't typically teach survivors about trauma and the potential long-lasting and life-altering effects of trauma. Even though rapes, beatings, shootings, domestic violence, human trafficking, and child abuse happens every day; we haven't figured out that we need to make trauma-focused care a well-known and necessary ingredient to recovery.

Indeed, trauma is very real, and it can be debilitating to the person that suffers from trauma. There are approximately 80 or so different emotional, mental, behavioral, and health related symptoms we can experience when we suffer from trauma. We discuss trauma in more detail in the 3rd Journey. However, when we don't understand that we have been traumatized and don't receive treatment for trauma, we often begin to blame ourselves for the trauma related symptoms (Note: for a peek at the trauma-related symptoms you can experience, look at the chart in the 3rd Journey). When we aren't able to simply bounce back, we believe we are weak or somehow at fault. When we don't have an explanation for why we feel, think, or behave a certain way long after a trauma, we psychologically attribute it to some deficit or dysfunction in ourselves.

Trauma does not discriminate. There is no exclusive ownership of trauma. Indeed, there are many individuals that suffer trauma from a range of various traumatic experiences. When someone experiences life altering trauma, they can become trapped in their trauma. When they become trapped, their feeling, thinking, and behavior is altered and filtered through their trauma. Once significantly traumatized, the victim of trauma is no longer internally free. Life changes for them. They often don't genuinely and fully receive or give love because they don't' trust. They can't openly receive support from others because they are guarded. Their relationships aren't authentic because they don't deeply trust anyone anymore. This is because they fear being vulnerable and victimized again.

Often the victim of trauma doesn't realize that trauma is the root of their problem. Understanding their trauma and working through the trauma is the way to learn to love, trust, and experience internal health and authentic joy again. If you have been a victim of child abuse, child neglect, sexual assault, commercial sexual exploitation, physical violence, emotional violence, or any form of domestic violence, you may be suffering from untreated trauma. If so, you are not currently living a life of internal freedom. However, in working through your trauma, it is possible to experience joy instead of pain. It's possible to be vulnerable and to love and trust again. Your transformation lies in understanding your life can change for the better. Even though you survived your traumatic experience, we still refer to you as a victim. Why? Because you have not yet realized you are still internally trapped, and that trauma continues to victimize you.

Freeing yourself from the traps that trauma creates, understanding the external illusions that trauma produces, and untangling yourself from the dysfunctional trappings that have supported your continued enslavement in trauma is what The Survivor's Journey is about. Instead of taking your rightful place in the world with all its beauty, benefits, and responsibilities, you have suffered the consequences of a life controlled by someone, something, or the trauma.

Since there has been internal trauma, internal recovery is needed. Along the Survivor's Journey you will learn to use the tools provided in this book to understand certain truths about your life. These truths will lead to a number of internal transformations. We called this process the Truth and Transformation Process aka TNT process.

Truth: *"I have been internally and externally trapped and am not living the life I want".*

The victim's challenge in the 1st Journey is to understand those mechanisms in life that keep you trapped and from becoming internally healthy. Thus, to prepare to take the 1st Journey, you need to understand both the internal traps and external trappings in your life that serve to enslave your mind and heart. Internal traps are those feelings and thoughts, derived from your external experiences that have profoundly impacted your internal thoughts and feelings about yourself and your value in the world. Internal traps lower your self-esteem. These internal traps include being trapped by the invisibility of trauma, trapped by stigma and oppression, trapped in shame and more. External trappings are those material possessions we own that tell us and others our life is great. They include our car, our address, our clothes, our friends, and more. Other external trappings also include the way we falsely pretend we are fine, our relationships are fine, our children are doing well, and our friends and family are healthy. Indeed, we use the outward appearance of health and wellbeing to convince ourselves and others that our life is great. When this happens, we can even begin to deceive and delude ourselves. In hampering and clouding our ability to see the truth, we stay in denial about the reality of our current lives and how much our traumatic experiences have crippled us emotionally. We're being misled by both the internal traps and external trappings of our life.

Trapped in the Invisibility of Trauma

Victims of abuse, violence, and exploitation come in all shapes, sizes, colors, and genders. Our traumatic experience could have been physical, sexual, and/or emotional. The same traumatic experience can happen over and over, such as in the case of domestic violence or child abuse for example. One individual can also experience different types of trauma, such as being a victim of child abuse and then later a victim of sexual assault. Trauma can negatively affect our lives both internally and externally. While physical scars will heal, the emotional effects from trauma may last many years.

Trauma is a deeply distressing and disturbing experience. Any number of experiences can cause trauma. The Survivor's Journey focuses on trauma that occurred because of abuse, violence, and/or exploitation.

The terms violence, abuse, and exploitation are often used interchangeably, although societal understanding of each may differ. When we think of abuse, we think of child abuse and neglect. When we consider victims of violence, we think of domestic violence, physical assault, or sexual assault. When we imagine exploitation, we think of commercial sexual exploitation, or sex or labor trafficking. Because these experiences can cause trauma, we refer to all three throughout the Survivor's Journey. However, getting the technical terms and definitions right is not as important as understanding and validating the experiences of victims of trauma.

The common denominator among those that experienced abuse, violence, and/or exploitation is that trauma occurred. Most people don't understand trauma and the negative results on the physical, emotional, mental, spiritual, and social self. Instead, society focuses almost solely on the violent act itself, and doesn't understand much or attend to the internal trauma suffered by the victim. The energy is on ending the victimization and punishing the victimizer. However, an equal amount of energy should be spent ending the victimization, holding the perpetrator accountable, and ensuring the victim receives trauma-focused recovery services.

Even as victims of trauma, we don't realize we need to address our trauma. We don't understand our ability to move forward and become a joyful, well-adjusted, and healthy person relies on our ability to work through our trauma. We have no idea trauma, depending on how traumatic the experience, stays with us, and like a chronic disease, begins to destroy every aspect of our lives. We are unaware we have been trapped in a story of trauma that hasn't fully been understood nor embraced by society. Even though our trauma is very real, when society fails to recognize our trauma, they communicate to us the trauma we experienced isn't legitimate or important enough. People around us may not understand why we are acting a certain way or feeling a certain way. No one has clear and comprehensive answers for us. It can be debilitating and crippling, because we believe we are alone in this Journey and something is unique and unhinged about us. The real truth is that we have been a victim. We have unresolved trauma, and we need to be treated for trauma. Just as if we had a form of untreated cancer that eats away at our healthy tissue, we need to treat our trauma in a laser focused way so we can become healthy again.

However, instead of understanding and recovering from trauma, we are categorized and diagnosed with unflattering labels offered by doctors, psychologists, social workers, therapists, and others, while the problem really is unresolved trauma. We even expected to move on with our lives and forget what happened. We are dumbfounded when we realize we can't move forward or our trauma has manifested into depression, anxiety, persistent or sudden anger or we are no longer motivated, or no longer feel good about ourselves. We can't figure out what is crippling us. Since we don't talk about trauma as much as we should in society, we might feel like we are the only one experiencing this. Maybe we chalk it up to our own individual shortcomings.

Perhaps you personalize it, and instead of blaming the trauma brought on by someone or something else, you blame yourself. You keep quiet about how you really feel, and you fall deeper into depression, anxiety, anger, emotional isolation, and apathy and may use drugs or alcohol to cope or numb the pain. What you are experiencing is not any deficit you have. You have a very common problem that is not your fault and is not unique to you. However, just like untreated cancer, it may have metastasized or spread to your feelings, your thoughts, your behaviors, and your interactions with others to affect your motivation, your hopes and dreams, and your self-esteem.

This is the result of not understanding trauma and buying into the myth of time heals all wounds. In reality, time without trauma-focused treatment allows wounds to scar over, or become infected, but not adequately heal. While most victims understand abuse, violence, and exploitation is wrong and harmful, what they don't understand is the lifelong effects of unresolved trauma. They think once the abuse, the violence, or the exploitation has ended, the victim is free. What they don't realize is even though they may become externally free, without becoming internally free, they are enslaved.

Because trauma is largely invisible and not very well recognized by society, we tend to bypass the emotional trauma and instead treat the symptoms as if they were root problems. If someone has a drug or alcohol problem, we send them into drug and alcohol treatment. They may also begin a long and productive relationship in Alcoholics Anonymous or Narcotics Anonymous groups where they work the 12 steps associated with building character and maintaining sobriety. Likewise, when someone has an anger problem, we send them to anger management. When someone is obese, we give them a diet plan. We don't worry about why they are self-medicating themselves with food. What happens in a society that doesn't recognize trauma as a root cause? We don't attend to it. When victims don't get better, we cause them to shame and blame themselves for their weak character. We call that "shooting the wounded".

Jada's Thoughts: "I never thought of it that way. I just thought it was me. I was overly sensitive, or I was not as good as others at letting things go. Whatever it was, the problem was always me. I always felt different. I always felt like counseling and substance abuse treatment didn't work for me. I blamed myself. Why can't I stay sober? Why can't I feel better and be happy? Now I get it. It's my trauma."

What victims need to know, is that they've been trapped in the story that left out the part about focused healing and recovery. And just like cancer won't heal without specific interventions, neither will trauma. Being on the Survivor's Journey is like your chemotherapy and radiation treatments. Just like chemo and radiation, some Journeys will feel like they are weakening you at first because they are narrowing in on the trauma and the areas for recovery and interpersonal growth. Initially, the recovery work may make you emotional and maybe even physically exhausted, so it will be important to eat and sleep well and take care of yourself so you can continue to the fight to lower or eliminate your trauma and begin to fully embrace joy and your life again.

Trapped in Stigma and Oppression

> *"Privilege is when you think something isn't a problem*
> *because it's not a problem for you."* ~ Anonymous

To add insult to injury, there are some in society, because of stigma and oppression, are less likely to see justice in the court system. Those who are "marginalized" because of race, ethnicity, sexual orientation, gender, or nationality are especially viewed as having less value across all walks of life when compared to those who are "centered." Being marginalized means being denied significant involvement and equitable inclusion in mainstream economic, political, social, and cultural activities.

To further explain what being marginalized means, let's think of a sheet of paper. When you think of a sheet of paper, the important things you have to say are written clearly within the margins or center of the paper. Notes that are not central to the paper might be written on the side, or in the "margins." They may be smaller thoughts. When you are marginalized, you are not central to society. You are relegated to a less important position. You are an afterthought. In order to properly talk about marginalized people, we have to identify the center people. Center people are those in control of and dominate many of the world's critical institutions including the political, business, educational, religious, criminal justice, and health care systems, to name a few. Those center people in the U.S. are predominately white, male, heterosexual, able-bodied, Christian, and with access to money, means, and power. To be a member of any of those categories is to have an element of privilege. Privilege means someone has unearned social power given to all members of a particular group who put them at an advantage over other groups. Those with privilege are taught not to see it (e.g., white privilege, male privilege). In fact, "when you're accustomed to privilege, equality feels like oppression." Not to be a member of one of the center elements means you likely have suffered from oppression identified as negative beliefs about you (stereotypes), negative attitudes and values about you (prejudices), and actions (discrimination) against you and others that look like you. Not surprisingly, those who are marginalized also happen to be those statistically more likely to be abused, victimized, and exploited.

Many people have elements of both oppression and privilege. White women have privilege because they are white but suffer elements of oppression because they are women. White males have privilege, but suffer elements of oppression if they are gay, or if they don't have access to means/money and live in poverty. When you're not a member of the center group, you experience the consequences of oppression. Oppression is displayed on a personal level, positional level, and institutional level.

On a personal level, when you are marginalized because of who you are, you are seen as less valuable and as having several negative attributes. As a result, your victimization may be rationalized and/or you may be blamed. Such comments as "she was asking for it," and "men can't get raped," are some of the ignorant comments meant to minimize you and your experience. They are rooted in beliefs by those who stigmatize others. Other comments meant to blame the victim are "why did she even go to that place alone anyway," "she should have known better," and "well look at what she was wearing," are other comments intended to particularly blame female rape victims and women in the sex trade. Comments like "she was always a fast little girl anyway," "she seduced him," and "how could he help himself around a teenager like that," are some sentiments of the ignorant and oppressive.

If you are gay, transgender, or nonbinary, you may have overheard comments like, "well look at how sexual they are," "they are an abomination and God is punishing them," and "that's what they get when they have no morals." All these prejudices are designed to blame and stigmatize the victim and justify why your experience is not worthy of care and concern.

Historic and systemic racism perpetrated against black, indigenous, Latinx, and other persons of color add to the trauma these populations face. When they are abused, victimized, or exploited it can be seen by the dominant group as less horrific and traumatizing. Because they have historically been seen as having less value, their victimization is more palatable to the larger society. They are sometimes seen as being able to tolerate more pain.[1] In reality, a diagnosis of PTSD in the U.S. is higher among blacks, Latinx, and Native Americans.

[2]The rape of women, defined as forced vaginal, oral, or anal penetration around the world remains high. In the U.S., One in six women are raped or experienced attempted rape; that's about 17.6% of the female population. That equates to 14,903,156 women in the U.S. One in 33 men have also been raped or experienced attempted rape.

The pain and trauma suffered by Indigenous peoples and Native Americans around the world is high. [3]Four out of five Native Americans and Indigenous Alaskans have experienced violence in their lifetime. Both Native men and women experience high rates of violence (81% and 84% respectively), while 56% of Native women have experienced sexual

---

1 American Psychiatric Association (n.d.). What is post-traumatic stress disorder-https://www.psychiatry.org/patients-families/ptsd/what-is-ptsd

2 Full report on the prevalence, incidence, and consequences of violence against women. National Violence Against Women Survey. National Institutes of Justice and Center for Disease Control https://www.ojp.gov/pdffiles1/nij/183781.pdf

3 National Institutes of Justice (n.d.) Five things about violence against American Indian and Alaskan Native women and men. U.S. Department of Justice https://www.ojp.gov/pdffiles1/nij/249815.pdf

violence.[1] In addition, Native Americans are three times more likely and African Americans are 2.6 times more likely to be killed by police.

[2]LGBTQ populations are almost four times more likely to be victims of a violent crime than non-LBGTQ populations.

At the same time, male perpetrators that hold more value and power in society are more likely to garner sympathy from the public. While some question the victim's character, they may be willing to give the accused the benefit of the doubt. When this happens, they say things like, "Well boys will be boys," "There are two sides to every story," "I don't believe her," "If he is convicted, this will ruin his career," and "He was drunk and didn't know what he was doing. That normally isn't him."

Negative thoughts about marginalized groups lead to racial jokes, racial slurs, objectification of women, jokes about the LGBTQ, developmentally disabled communities, and more. These negative beliefs and comments are designed to devalue marginalized groups, and to show others that it's alright to assign less value to them. Even when the law should be applied equally, the discretion and benefit of the doubt afforded to some people may not be afforded to people who society is biased against. The empathy shown to one group may not be shown to another group. The second chance some may get, may not be afforded to others.

Positional stigma takes place as social service, health care, and criminal justice focused organizations designed to help those who are vulnerable, see you in a different light. They begin to practice institutionalized discrimination. They are looking to treat the stereotyped version of a helpless victim. Prosecutors are looking to protect the stereotyped view of a victim. The judge and/or jury are waiting to convict the

---

[1] Belli, B. (2020). Racial disparities in police shootings unchanged over 5 years. Yale News. https://news.yale.edu/2020/10/27/racial-disparity-police-shootings-unchanged-over-5-years

[2] LGBT people nearly four times more likely than non-LGBT people to be victims of violent crime. UCLA School of Law. https://williamsinstitute.law.ucla.edu/press/ncvs-lgbt-violence-press-release/

perpetrator that hurt a poor, defenseless girl or woman; any variation of what doesn't fit their belief system dulls their sense of duty to protect.

Social service programs and health care facilities are also looking to support defenseless stereotypes of what they picture a victim should look like and what their history should be; when that doesn't jive with the "you" they see before them, there may be problems. When this happens, they may not view you as someone deserving of the best recovery services they have to offer. When this is repeated over and over, it shows up as institutional discrimination as they choose to support those that fit their stereotyped versions.

The result is discrimination on an institutional level, where oppression is manifested in widespread withholding of quality services, unconditional positive regard, and empathy from professionals providing services to those who have experienced violence, abuse, and exploitation. With oppression operating on a personal level, positional level, and institutional level, we see widespread failures across systems and an ignorance, invisibility, or refusal to serve all victims of abuse, violence, and exploitation with quality and effective services that support recovery.

Depending on the type of crime perpetrated against you, who you are in society, and your past, you likely have either been invisible or stigmatized. If your experience of victimization doesn't fall into the parameters of what and who a victim should be, you will not likely be seen as a human being deserving of all the rights, protections, and privileges afforded to a human being that has been victimized. It follows that your victimization will also not be seen as credible, traumatizing, or worthy of the best services your community has to offer. In fact, some in power may conjure up reasons why you are unworthy or why it's your fault or why you should have known better. In some cases, you may be the one to go to jail as a result.

Some victims of sexual assault face horrific and devastating stigma. If sexually adventurous, some of the stigmatizing comments might be "you can't rape the willing," "you deserved what you got," and "you shouldn't be putting yourself at risk." These are often widely held beliefs even by those charged with making sure every human being receives fair and just treatment, including the police, social workers, health care workers, and others.

Trapped in Shame

Some victims believe if they were to come forward and talk about their pain associated with their abuse, violence, or exploitation, or even worse, really feel their pain, they are not sure they would be able to handle it. Often there is so much toxicity inside us that we are afraid it will poison us even further than we already are. Instead, we have preferred to try and stuff it down, lock it away, or pretend it doesn't exist. This toxicity is called shame. What is actually happening is that we are internally poisoning ourselves with shame. There is a difference between guilt and shame. Guilt is what you feel when you've done something wrong. Shame is what you feel when you *are* something wrong. Somehow, we have twisted our experience of trauma into one in which we guilt, shame, and blame ourselves. And further, we can feel disgraced. We can feel dishonorable. We can feel embarrassed and humiliated.

We can beat ourselves up about what happened. We can obsess about it. We engage in self-loathing. We can't believe we allowed this to happen. In reality, we didn't have the power to have stopped what happened to us. In most cases, we could not have out-thought our perpetrator. We couldn't have changed the circumstances or undo what was happening. But shame will keep us hating ourselves about something we couldn't control. Even if we wish things could have been different, what happened already happened. We can't change the past. We can get so caught up in the shame that we want to disappear, to no longer be alive because of the unbearable emotional pain we feel. It's important you recognize this is only shame. Sometimes when something horrible has happened to us, we blame and shame ourselves. We need to know that when we are feeling shame, we can learn to recognize that it's shame. We can bring the feeling to our consciousness, take a look at it, label it, and tell ourselves that this is how shame is showing up in my life. You can tell yourself that shame isn't valuable to your life. Shame isn't reality. It's something we tell ourselves. When we go through the

Survivor's Journey we will have the support and people in our life who help us work ourselves into a place of internal recovery and joy. We need to suspend judgment of ourselves right now and know if we take the Survivor's Journey, we stand the best chance of not only surviving our life, but actually thriving and experiencing joy in our life.

Trapped in Your Own Beliefs

"Say goodbye to toxic, limiting beliefs. In fact, sometimes the thing you're most afraid of doing is the very thing that will set you free."
~ Reimaged from Robert Ten

We all have various beliefs about the world and ourselves in the world. Some beliefs were likely handed down to us by others in our family. We adopted these beliefs and took them into our hearts. These helped shape our core beliefs. Core beliefs are the most profound and deeply held beliefs about ourselves and the world around us. They are also formed based on our experiences. If we were abused or neglected, or experienced/witnessed violence growing up, it shaped our core beliefs. Some of our beliefs promote positive feelings about ourselves, those around us, and the world in general. However, we can get trapped by negative core beliefs about ourselves. These beliefs can encourage us to stay in a bad situation, even when it's obvious to everyone else that we need to leave. Our core beliefs become our truths for ourselves. They are the rules in our minds that are rarely questioned. Our beliefs about who we are supposed to be in life, what we are supposed to look like, what we are supposed to have, and who we are supposed to be with can trap us and make us stay where we are. Our negative beliefs can also manifest into what we believe we deserve. We can punish ourselves by only allowing ourselves to have what we think we deserve. In addition to the experiences we've had, our core beliefs about ourselves are also based on how others have reacted to us. What they've done or not done, and what they said to us or didn't say. Therefore, our beliefs about ourselves are informed by our families and earlier experiences, society's beliefs and reactions to our abusive or exploitative experiences, and our perceived value and place in society. When we get trapped in a negative core belief system, we refuse to live the life we truly want and deserve to live.

Trapped into Believing there is a Hierarchy of Acceptable Trauma

Some members of society believe there is a hierarchy of acceptable types of victimization and response. You may believe being victimized and having fought back for instance is somehow more noble than someone that didn't fight back. That would be wrong. Surviving the experience is what is most important. There are many victims who are not here today because they didn't survive.

You may believe because you were victimized by your significant other while trying to build a loving relationship and family is somehow better than someone who was victimized by a customer while involved in the sex trade. That belief would be wrong. There is no hierarchy of acceptable victimization and trauma.

In turn, you may believe your childhood abuse, domestic violence, rape, or victimization was more traumatizing or less traumatizing than someone else's. That belief would be wrong. Trauma is in the eye of the beholder. Which means only they can determine the impact, legitimacy, and level of trauma they experienced and how it impacted their lives and their recovery. To question someone's trauma, is to deny them their voice and human dignity.

In the Survivor's Journey groups, we work to find common ground, and in acknowledging our common ground, we can heal together.

Trapped in Seemingly Impossible Situations

> *"If you really want to recover you'll find a way.*
> *If you don't, you'll find excuses." ~* Jim Rohn

When you were abused, assaulted, violated, victimized, or exploited, you may have felt trapped in an impossible situation and believed you couldn't get away. Some of the reasons you may have felt trapped and stayed connected to your victimizer is because the various traps seemed impossible to escape. Some examples are provided below.

- *Physical Traps* – Being afraid to leave because of physical violence we will suffer if we do. Other physical traps include not being able to leave because of our physical location or physical isolation.
- *Emotional Traps* – Being unable to leave because we are emotionally cornered. We love our abuser or sexual exploiter. We may have children and are concerned with their well-being if we try to leave.
- *Social Traps* – Being unable to leave because of our mutual friends and the love and care we have for our social networks, loss of social status, and/or social embarrassment involved in leaving.
- *Financial Traps* – Leaving may mean leaving the financial security we have or our children will continue to have if we stay in this financial trap.
- *Family Traps* – Being unwilling to leave because of the family situation. Any attempt to be truthful or deal with problems may cause you or others to be victimized, ostracized, or blamed.
- *Cultural Traps* – Being unable to leave because it is culturally inappropriate and may bring shame to the family or harm to you or others.

Below are a few examples of some of the types of victimization those on the Survivor's Journey may have experienced.

Intimate Partner Violence

There are many ways an intimate partner can victimize and traumatize their partner. These include physical abuse, emotional abuse, sexual assault, financial abuse, using the children against their intimate partner, intimidation, threats, isolation, minimizing, denying, blaming, and other forms of coercive control.

Victims of domestic violence often work very hard to fix their relationship. Having tried and tried, some begin to find fault with themselves. Leaving an abuser can be dangerous, but necessary. Prior to leaving, many victims establish a safety plan. They make a copy of their important records and keep them in a safe place outside of the home. Some make duplicate car keys they keep hidden in the event they have to get away quickly. They pack clothes and keep them elsewhere in the event they have to leave right away. They notify others about the situation. They establish code words with friends so they can communicate information in a way that doesn't alarm their abuser. Some work with the court system to help them exit the relationship safely and equitably. Others leave quickly and swiftly when their abuser is gone from the home. And others may stay in their abusive relationships. Whether one stays or leaves, the effects from their traumatizing experiences can last a very long time. Without trauma-focused help, it can prevent victims from being able to experience deep happiness and joy, and may prevent them from experiencing love, trust, and being vulnerable again.

Childhood Abuse & Neglect
Child abuse may include physical, sexual, emotional abuse, or child neglect. Child abuse and neglect can damage a child's self-esteem and self-worth. In some cases, victims of child abuse and/or neglect have suffered trauma with self-esteem issues their whole life. The Survivor's Journey can help child abuse and neglect survivors to trust in themselves and others again.

Gang Members as Victims of Trauma
Gang membership or just hanging out with gang members provides many individuals with the connection they need to experience support, love, attention, and belonging. These are important elements most human beings are looking to connect to. Some gang members become like family. And just like families, they can abuse, victimize, and exploit. It's when gang affiliation becomes victimizing and traumatizing, that it becomes internally hurtful to the person being victimized.

Even though many people don't think of gang members as being subjected to victimization, exploitation, and trauma, it does happen. Often there isn't a place where these traumatized individuals can receive recovery.

Victimization in the Sex Trade

When we talk about trauma through abuse, violence, and/or exploitation, trauma through commercial sexual exploitation is one of the least accepted by society. In the Survivor's Journey groups we are not concerned about legal definitions and whether someone meets the definition of a sex trafficking victim. For the purposes of trauma recovery, we also do not engage in any political discourse around whether or not someone chooses or should have the legal right to choose sex work as an occupation. If someone has been involved in the commercial sex trade and was exploited, abused, or victimized as a result, the Survivor's Journey groups are the right place for them to heal and recover.

Sexual Assault

One in three women and one in four men have experienced sexual violence. In most circumstances, victims of sexual assault knew their perpetrator. They may have interacted minimally with this person or knew them fairly well before the assault. Part of the trauma that has damaged them is the act of sexual assault itself; the other part of the trauma is damage to the implied trust and faith they put into their perpetrator. Many victims never report their assault. They go through life walking wounded, traumatized, and never wanting to trust again. A part of the wonder of life has been taken from them because trust has been taken, their self-esteem has been damaged, and they begin to blame themselves for the crime committed against them.

Whether you were a victim of sexual exploitation, intimate partner abuse, childhood sexual abuse, or other types of abuses, these physical, psychological, emotional, social, financial, family, cultural, and other needs become traps designed to keep you exactly where you are, surviving in an unhappy, abusive, and unfulfilling existence.

Trapped in Earlier Trauma and Abuse

"Becoming free doesn't begin with opening the gates of heaven to let you in, it begins with opening the gates of hell to let you out." ~ Anonymous

Most victims of trauma have a pattern of vulnerability and abuse. Many victims who are no longer physically trapped, remain internally trapped. There are metaphorical chains wrapped around their minds and their hearts. For example, many victims of sexual exploitation do not experience being held in physical chains. Neither do victims of domestic violence or drug addiction. Their hearts, minds, dreams, and hopes are chained. For some this is a familiar experience, because the feeling of not being in control, having power taken by someone or something else, and being forced or manipulated into doing things and feeling things is psychologically familiar. These experiences don't feel good and are extremely damaging, but it feels familiar on an unconscious level because it likely has happened before. Without professional help, many people are doomed to create the same or similar experience again and again. Because it unconsciously seems familiar, the victim remains vulnerable to the familiar. They don't like it. It doesn't feel good, yet it is what's familiar.

We cannot and should not look at someone's victimization as a one-size-fits-all experience. Just as each person's story and victimization is unique, each person's recovery journey will be unique. We may have been a victim of earlier childhood abuse, neglect, or later sexual assault. We may have witnessed or experienced abusive relationships. In many aspects, these models presented to us became familiar. As we navigated through life, we may have been involved in systems that were not trauma informed and served to stigmatize us. Society ignored our vulnerabilities and treated us as invisible and our pain as unimportant. We have suffered long-term vulnerabilities and were particularly susceptible to being victimized. An abuser, an exploiter, or victimizer exploited the vulnerabilities that were already there.

Trapped in your Addiction

"My recovery must come first, so that everything I love doesn't have to come last." ~ Daily Sobriety Journal for Addiction

Many of us chose to cope with our trauma by numbing out on drugs and alcohol. In the face of an impossible escape, we chose to escape, if only temporarily, by using drugs and alcohol. We didn't care about the consequences. In order to survive, we needed that escape. These temporary escapes seemed fun, or at least less painful than living in our reality every day and every minute of the day. Over time we just couldn't function without being high. Life without being high was too hard.

When you are in active addiction, your life consists of drug seeking or drug using. There is little that happens outside of your need to find more alcohol or drugs. Every conversation you have, other than the occasional thought of ending it all, is about alcohol or drugs. In the back of your mind, you are always thinking about how you can get more alcohol or drugs. When you are wrapped in an addiction, your life becomes very dangerous. The risks you were willing to take to get more drugs and drink more alcohol goes against your better judgment. The intuition you used before to increase your safety is ignored. At this point, you may be one drink or one drug away from death.

Trapped Because You Can't Read Well or Don't Speak the Language

Some Survivor's Journey members may not read well or understand English well enough to receive the tools provided through the Survivor's Journey. Please make arrangements so you can understand all the group has to offer. Perhaps this book is being used in a different country and culture. Take your time with this book and with this group. Have others help you translate the words and meaning into your culture. The 12 Guided Survivor's Journeys are universal, and if applied, can help any vulnerable member make improvements in their life.

Trapped Because We Don't Believe it When People Show Us Who They Really Are

"Stop looking outside for scraps of pleasure and fulfillment, for validation, security, or love. You have a treasure within you that is infinitely greater than anything the world can offer." ~ Eckhart Tolle

Part of our vulnerability is we have a tendency to not believe people who continually tell us and show us through their actions who they are. We dismiss them because we look at them through the lens of our good nature and believe they have good intentions like us. This couldn't be further from the truth. Our good nature and kind hearts have us believe in people who don't deserve it and have us forgive and allow back into our lives people who haven't proven that they have changed or are trustworthy. This is our downfall. And it puts us right back in the trick bag every time. Forgiveness is noble, and if you have the power and ability to forgive, you have to understand forgiveness is for you. It's not for the person who hurt or harmed you. Forgiveness is so you have peace within your heart which enables you to stop being troubled by the experience. Forgiveness and having someone back in your life are two totally separate things. If you still want this person who wronged you in your life, forgiveness doesn't absolve them from their wrongdoing. Only real change over time can do that. If you want to avoid being victimized once again, set boundaries to protect you. When considering having someone back in your life, ensure they prove themselves to be trustworthy and respectful of your boundaries.

In sum, whether you are currently involved in continued abuse or you are no longer involved, without trauma treatment, in many respects you remain internally trapped. The longer your exposure to victimization and untreated trauma, the more likely you have convinced yourself being internally unhealthy is a normal way of being.

The External Trappings

> *"If outside validation is your only source of nourishment,*
> *you will hunger for the rest of your life."* ~ Unknown

External trappings are those outward appearances and possessions that tell you and others your life is going well. They are illusions which make you and others believe your life is fine when it's not. Your external trappings may include your material possessions such as your clothes, car, address, or your external beauty. They may include the appearance of a great relationship, loyal friends, or a loving family. Being genuinely honored with these gifts in life are not traps. They are blessings. They only become traps when they are not real. When material possessions are used to cover up the hurt and pain inside, they are not blessings, they are crutches. They help you convince yourself and others that you are healthy and your life is good when it's not. Remember, you can fool some people some of the time, but you will never truly fool yourself into believing everything is alright.

Wearing great clothes, buying new shoes, ensuring your hair and nails are done, and that you own the best Apple iPhone in town won't fix the brokenness inside. A dysfunctional and unhealthy relationship appearing to be so wonderful you are the envy of your friends, won't heal internal pain. These are just window dressings meant to cover up the pain inside from unresolved trauma.

Having the appearance of being strong, and invincible to others when you secretly suffer, may gain you the admiration you want, but inside you will still know the truth.

Being blessed with luxury items is a complement to a healthy, well-adjusted person, but they don't make a healthy person. There is nothing wrong with spoiling yourself with luxuries you enjoy. The problem occurs when you chase after exterior possessions and appearances, believing these make you a person of value. When someone assumes their value is based on owning external items, there is a serious problem happening.

Wearing designer clothes, having your hair done, getting a manicure and pedicure, driving a nice car, living in an expensive home – all these items complement a person; they don't define the person. These items can't give you genuine value. Value is internal. These items do not and will never replace your internal value. If you wrap someone of weak internal self-value with expensive trappings, they run the risk of self-destruction. There are many celebrities and rap stars who suffered early trauma and/or had experiences that inhibited their ability to grow emotionally and develop internally. Many of them ended up self-destructing through the use of drugs or suicide. No matter how hard they tried to give the appearance of success, they did not do the internal work needed to maintain a level of health and well-being. They leave us all wondering why they would do that when they seemed to have it all. What they had were the exterior trappings that made us believe they had it all.

Without the internal work first, it won't matter how much you own or how successful you look, it won't help you in the end. A person of value believes they are valuable. They work hard to maintain their internal health and well-being first, and they recognize the material possessions they own reflect their external success. And some who are highly successful, aren't concerned with material possessions or the outward appearance of success at all. They are most concerned with the success that comes from a healthy family, a loving relationship, and having friends who are healthy and care about their well-being. Healthy people have a well-rounded idea of what success would look like for them and they work to achieve and maintain it.

Triiana's Story: I had everything. I had the car, the condo, the jewelry. I made sure my man had. He was dressed. He drove an escalade. We had it all. I made it look like my man treated me like a queen when he didn't. I made money. I had bank accounts, but you know I was bankrupt inside. When it was all said and done, I didn't have any real friends. My relationship was messed up. My son was on drugs, and I didn't tell anybody. When I went to jail, there was nobody who really cared about me. My friends were around because I had some money. But when I got in trouble, like real caught up, nobody was really there. They just liked what I had. They didn't care about the real me. I don't think they even knew the real me because I don't know that I knew myself.

The outward appearance of healthy and successful relationships with an intimate partner, family members, and friends are other ways we show the world our lives are fine. Instead of telling the truth, we post pictures on social media of us looking great, our children doing well, our loving relationships, and our well-adjusted family members. Too often however, we can become confused and begin to believe our own lies. We delude ourselves with this fantasy and actually begin to believe our fantasy is reality. Instead of working through our problems, we hide our problems and stuff them down inside. The "appearance" of health and well-being becomes more important than our own health and well-being and the health and well-being of people we claim to love.

However, when we do our internal work by completing the 12 Journeys, we create the opportunity for true health and well-being. When we do our work, we acknowledge our dysfunction. That gives others we love permission to do their work.

Be-Do-Have, is a maturity continuum that appears in the book, "The Seven Habits of Highly Effective People" developed by Steven Covey. One of the messages in the book is this idea of Be-Do-Have. Based on who you are inside (your character, beliefs, thoughts, feelings), you DO. The question to ask yourself here is, "Who do I need to BE?" And based on what you DO (your actions), you HAVE (material possessions and positive relationships with friends, family, and intimate partners). In other words, who you are inside as a human being drives what you do and how you conduct your life. Based on what you do, or how you conduct your life, you have. People who have healthy, warm, positive, and supportive friendships and relationships have them because of who they are – or their "BE." How they conduct their life is based on who they are, how they treat themselves, how they treat others, what they spend their time doing and not doing, also known as their "DO." What they DO and don't do comes from who they are, and what they HAVE is the result. When you know who you are, the material items or possessions you have are luxuries. They complement who you are, but they don't define who you are. When you get caught up in the trappings and understand the material possessions or the façade of a good relationship to be who you are instead of a complement to who you are, you remain confused and trapped by your understanding of the external trappings. If you just want to "HAVE," but haven't taken the time to build who you are and what you will do and not do to get it, then you will end up lost. Once lost, you are willing to do anything to both obtain and maintain your external trappings. Because you have managed to define yourself by what you own, or a set of dysfunctional relationships cleverly disguised as healthy relationships, when they leave or are taken from you, you are left without an identity you can be proud of.

Mind-Fields: The Circumstances and Consequences

"A ship in the harbor is safe, but that is not what ships are built for."
~ Grace Hopper

You don't have to get caught up in the traps and the trappings. You don't have to live your life by circumstance or consequence. What is living a life of circumstance? When you believe you have no control over your own life and have no power to create change in your life, you live by fate. Unseen forces or other people are in control. You can't see or refuse to see it's the traps and trappings preventing you from taking control over your life and internal health. Life and what happens in life continues to be a big mystery to you and is outside of your hands. You may hope things get better, but you believe you have no power to make it better. It is what it is. This is because you suffered trauma. You no longer steer your own ship and navigate your own troubled or calm waters. You go with the flow and whatever comes you have little control over. People who live by circumstance believe they just have bad luck.

Living a life of consequence means even though you continue to believe you have no real control, you are blamed for the circumstances of your life, and you suffer the consequences. But in reality, if you suffered trauma, you had no control over the traumatic experience(s) that occurred. However, today, you are responsible for your life. It is your responsibility to take control. You decide through your thoughts, feelings, and actions, if your life will be a great hit or a flop.

More Truths

"I'm not telling you it's going to be easy.
I'm telling you it's going to be worth it." ~ Anonymous

The truth is you have been living a life of circumstance and consequence and you can change that. Getting clear with what you want out of your life is the most important. The beauty about your life is you can CHOOSE what your future will entail. You have the power to change your life and create the life you want. Dare to dream. We don't mean small changes; we mean big changes you want for your future. And we don't mean sort of live the life you want; we mean you have the power to create the exact life you want and one you deserve. We mean a happy and fulfilling life.

The challenge is to know your truth. You were divinely made to live a life filled with learning life's lessons and experiencing joy and accomplishment in living a life well lived. The truth is, your future is up to you. The past is just a collection of experiences, but your past doesn't dictate your future. If you take your power back, you get to decide what your future will look like.

Tools: Awareness and Expectation

"When we have hope for the future, that gives us power in the present."
~ John Maxwell

Now that you are aware of the traps and the trappings, it is our hope that you are teachable. Some people involved in Survivor's Journey Recovery groups remain unteachable. They already know *it all* and no one can tell them anything different. To those folks, the Survivor's Journey will not be helpful. Being teachable means you read the evidence about the ways you have been trapped or tricked, and traded your happiness and freedom to suffer in silence. If you took these realities presented to you to heart, then the explanation of the 1st Journey created a tipping point of awareness for you and you want to take back power and control over your life to create the life you want. Indeed, the tool you acquire in this Journey is "awareness". Creating a tipping point of awareness means we have filled-up your bucket so much with the reality of your life, it has started to lean over, and you are ready to empty the toxic waste you have been carrying around in your life bucket. You are ready to clean out the negative, toxic, and destructive experiences and fill it with a positive, hopeful future you control and own for yourself.

In reading and discussing this Journey you may come into awareness. Feelings are often attached to this awareness. We hope one of those feelings is anger. Because you should feel angry about how you've been treated and how you've treated yourself. The flood of anger you feel in reading how you've been mistreated and tricked is normal and healthy. Anger is energy. Channel that energy into your recovery. Get so mad that you decide you will take on the challenge to recover and live the life you want to live.

Awareness is a motivator. Get fired up about the possibility of living the life you want. Imagine it. Think about it. Sit with it. Dream about it because it's entirely possible. You're going to need your anger and your motivation as fuel to do the work you need to do to live the life you want to live.

Some people count success by the amount of money they have or the clothes they wear but remember, that will put you right back in the trick bag. We identify massive success as someone who is emotionally healthy and present for themselves first, then their significant others. Make a vow to become so massively successful you actually become a happier, healthier person.

In addition to coming into awareness about the internal traps and external trappings we wrapped our life in, an additional tool you need to successfully complete in the 1st Journey is the most important tool you'll need- that is expectation. Expect that if you work the 12 Journeys you will become more internally healthy and your life will change for the better.

Because you can't fix what you don't acknowledge, the key to the 1st Journey is to become aware of your internal and external circumstances. Once you are aware, if you expect your life will change, you are set up for success. It sounds simple, but this is the foundation upon which your house of health, happiness, and well-being will be built on.

Expectation is made up of two elements, hope and belief. Hope is to *want* something to happen. Hope is one of the strongest assets a person can possess. We want you to want change happen in your. Without hope, nothing changes. All of the Survivor's Journeys are built on the idea of hope. Hope calls forth an amazing amount of strength. Hope can appear in the most dire circumstances. Someone who has cancer, but who has hope, can muster the strength to fight it. Someone convicted to prison, and who has hope that someday they will be free, can survive it. When all hope is lost, the entire game called life is lost. Always have hope. Because without hope you are lost forever. Hope is vital to survival.

Belief is to think something is true without seeing proof of it. You can believe your life can change without having seen it happen yet. The difference between hope and belief is hope is passive. To hope something will happen still lies outside your control. I can hope someone rescues me and gives me all the things I need to live a successful life, but it's still passive. Believing is much stronger. You need hope to survive, but you need belief to thrive. Hoping is like wishing, hope is out of your control. As much as it's needed, hope won't help you improve your life. It's vital for survival, but hope alone won't get you there, because when you have hope, the change you are wishing for is not necessarily within your control. If you believe something can change, you are putting some power behind the idea. When you believe, you know it can happen. You have an expectation, conviction, and acceptance your life will change. You haven't done the work yet to create the change you want to see, but you know it's possible. You no longer hope it's possible, you know it's possible, because you believe it's possible. When you have awareness and expectation, then you can adopt your truths: that you can be free to live a life of freedom and choice instead of circumstance and consequence. When this happens, the transformation onto the 1st Journey can occur for you.

The Transformation: *"I have the power to choose to change my life."*

Only in seeking the truth and speaking our truth can we truly begin to gain back power and control over our lives. The transformation we want to see cannot happen without first, uncovering our truth, second, understanding our truth, third, telling our truth, and fourth, standing in our truth. Once we follow that process, we can begin to transform.

Thus, the 1st Journey in recovery is: The victim comes to believe they are not living a life of choice and freedom, but a life filled with internal traps and external trappings, but this can change. The goal of the 1st Journey is to realize you have lived your life by circumstance and consequence instead of freedom and choice. Therefore, in the 1st Journey, you make a commitment to no longer allow yourself to suffer the circumstance and consequence presented by the traps in life.

In coming to believe, you understand it's not just the experience of abuse, violence, and exploitation you need to heal from, it is the struggle of vulnerability. It's the expectation you want and can take control to live an emotionally healthy, safe, and prosocial life where you live by choice and not by consequence. As the saying goes, "the best day of your life is the one on which you decide your life is your own. No apologies or excuses." (Bob Moawad)

You have experienced the 1st Journey. If you believe in your heart that you have been trapped and your life can change, you are ready for the 2nd Journey. To maintain the 1st Journey, you must always remain aware and expect that your life can change. Also, no matter what happens, if you have hope and belief, you always have the power to change your life and mold it into the life you want. Even if you are in prison and have no control over your external self. Even if guards will tell you what to do, when to do it, and how to do it, you have the power to choose what you will feel, think, and how you will behave. Internally, you can always be free.

2

2nd Journey: *The victim answers the call and assembles the team.*

2nd Truth: *I can't live the life I want without help.*

2nd Transformation: *I work with others to regain my power, choice, and voice.*

Trigger or Validation:
Remember for some, the material in this Journey may be triggering.
If it triggers you, reach out to your support system including those
you trust and/or engage in some self-care activities. For others, this
information will be validating. In those cases, use the material to help
validate you and affirm what you are or have been experiencing is real.

CHAPTER 2: COURAGE AND CONNECTION

"Courage starts with showing up and letting ourselves be seen."
~ Brene Brown

T he second Journey focuses on understanding the truth where you can work to create the change you want to see in your life. The truth is, you can live a joyful and fulfilled life making your own choices, directing your own life, and living free of abuse, control, or violence. Your transformation is in making the decision your life can change for the better and then obtaining the proper help to do so.

Thank yourself for realizing you can gain true power and control over your own life! Because you can! Hopefully the 1st Journey wasn't too difficult, because it only required that you begin to believe in YOU! For some, the 1st Journey may have been incredibly hard. But if you're reading this chapter, then you must be ready to explore the 2nd Journey.

The 2nd Journey is all about gathering a team of targeted professionals who will help you change your life and live the life you truly want to live. Later in this Chapter, we will talk about who exactly you should get to be on your team helping you, but before assembling your team, you'll need to come prepared to take this Journey with two things: (1) enough genuine love for yourself and (2) enough internal strength to put your deeply held fears aside. Do you know what the key to being happy and fulfilled is? Happy and fulfilled people operate from a place of love. They conduct their life and make decisions rooted in love and not rooted in fear. It takes a great capacity to love yourself enough to push past fear to create the change you want to see in your life.

It has been argued there are only two emotions: love and fear[1]. Every other emotion falls under those two emotions. Behind anger, for instance, is always fear. Someone who acts out in anger is often afraid of losing something they don't want to lose or gaining something they don't want to manage. They may be in fear of losing something tangible, like their job, relationship, house, car, and more. They may be in fear of losing something they can't see, like their credibility, self-respect, or the love of someone else. Many people function out of a fear-based mentality. They are afraid of losing and feeling pain as a result. They may drastically attempt to control something or someone else out of fear. Look at all the emotions that are fear-based: anger, anxiety, guilt, shame, sadness, frustration, uneasiness, loneliness, worry, jealousy, emptiness, cautiousness, shyness, embarrassment, and panic, to name a few. Now look at some of the emotions that are love-based: love, like, happiness, hopefulness, confidence, pride, optimism, amazement, joy, desire, passion, courage, triumph, pleasure, and thrill.

People can live their entire lives rooted in fear. People leading a fear-based life often do so because they have been abused, neglected, assaulted and/or exploited. Some have been rejected, beaten down, and treated so horribly by others or themselves they are afraid to try to obtain the life, career, and lifestyle they really desire. What they don't understand is when they settle out of fear, the cost to them is enormous because they have to give up their true hopes, wishes, and dreams and pretend they are happy with what life has handed them or what they have orchestrated and manipulated to get. Being satisfied with life's scraps is not the way to live a happy life.

When you live a fear-based life you make a deal with the devil to decide your life is not worth it. If you believe the devil wears a red suit and has a fiery red tail, you have missed the massively important message of religion. Whenever you believe and treat yourself like you are worthless or valueless, you have given yourself over to the dark side and away from the divine light. The fear you live in helps you create a life

---

[1] *Love is Letting Go of Fear* by Gerald Jambolsky

of denial, pretending nothing is wrong. The parts of your life that are unhealthy and unsatisfactory to you are ok. In reality, you may not have the love you want and deserve. You may not have the peace you deserve. You've been willing to give-up those essential fruits of life because you live in fear. Love and peace are essential items for living. Without them you are surviving at best. Living in fear is crippling to the soul and spirit because it serves to bury the truth deep inside you. And the truth is, you are yearning to be free and not to be controlled by anyone or anything, including fear.

Yet you believe your sacrifice is ok because it only affects you. That's where you're wrong. Your self-sacrifice not only hurts you, but it also hurts others in your life right now. It hurts those who depend on you. It hurts those hoping to look up to you. It hurts the people who want to and are ready to come into your life you haven't met yet and will never meet if you continue to give into your current life of fear. It hurts your future friendships and relationships. It hurts your future dreams. You are giving up a lot to stay where you are in a miserable existence and the price you are paying is way too high.

Fear literally destroys lives. It destroys dreams. Fear leads to alcoholism and drug abuse as people try and cope with a life they no longer want. Your self-made prison asks you to give up your hopes and dreams, talents and gifts, happiness and rightful place in the world. In exchange you may have believed you would receive love and safety. This deal always goes bad because those out to do you harm will not only take your love and safety, but they will ultimately take your peace. There is no deal you can make with the devil where you will win in the end. It's a trick. It doesn't exist. The sooner you realize that the faster you'll muster up the courage to slay the fear and begin to take a chance on living the life you want to live. Make a decision to be courageous enough to live a love-based life whenever possible.

I had a friend who told me a story about her abusive husband. She said that all of the years she stayed and was tormented by him, she thought she was doing the right thing by her children. She described her time with him as someone living underground, buried in a cold, hard, dark ground where she was controlled so badly, she felt she could do nothing much more than breathe. But she was so afraid, so she stayed there for years. When she finally left him, she said it felt like she pushed her way above the ground to find out she was a flower among a field of beautiful flowers. The other flowers said they had been waiting for her to bloom and enjoy the sun with them. Don't let life pass you by. Make the decision to live the love-based life you deserve for yourself.

Even though living a love-based life is the goal, there are legitimate reasons to choose to be afraid. For example, if you are confronted with an angry dog, you should feel frightened. You might freeze up, or you might try to soothe the dog. However, a fear-based life is different; it means most of your responses in life are fear-based. Anything you dream of doing is therefore shot down by fear.

Fear also has biological roots. When someone is under threat, there is a physiological response from the body. When we are confronted, for example, by a large angry dog, the body tenses up, adrenaline starts flowing, and cortisol levels increase. When we are afraid, our bodies are preparing us to handle the threat in one of five ways: Fight, Flight, Freeze, Fawn, or Flow.

The fight response is commonly used by those in survival mode who have been scratching and clawing through most of their lives. Not only have they consistently been worried about meeting their basic external needs like food, clothing, and shelter, there has been scarcity when it comes to others meeting their internal needs for love, support, and compassion. Because they have been living in survival mode, they are likely to come out fighting when they feel threatened or fearful. For example, if a fight response is our common reaction to fear, then we tend to enter the search for professional help already with an attitude and are just waiting for it to be confirmed by someone on the other end of the phone. Once we hear someone with a negative attitude or we face the smallest of barriers, we get mad and quit. We use someone else as the reason for why we quit. It can appear to others like we are argumentative and difficult to deal with. In fact, we are experiencing a reaction to fear, and that reaction is to fight.

If this has been a normal response to fear for you, then it will happen as you begin to put your professional team together. It's ok. Recognize this is your reaction to fear. It's normal for you. Apologize to whoever you cursed out or told off in the process. Make amends and get back to your goal of putting your professional team together.

The flight response is another typical response to fear. When confronted with something that is fearful, our mind and body might choose the flight response. In a flight response we are trying to run away or get away from the threat. In doing so we feel anxiety, nervousness, and fear, and then we run away. For example, someone in a flight response to fear will begin their journey of change, then quit and run away from their recovery because they are afraid. This won't be obvious, not even to them. Instead of confronting the fear, they will create logical reasons why they quit and ran away. We have to remember it is always ok to feel like quitting or running if that has been a normal response for you. Just recognize as you work through the 2nd Journey, when you feel the anxiety, fear, and an overwhelming feeling of wanting to quit and run, recognize it, breathe, relax, and continue to move forward assembling your team of professional helpers.

The freeze response is exhibited by someone who in the face of danger or a threat will freeze. This response may show up as someone who becomes incapable of making a decision when faced with choices or can't make a critical move in life when they need to make a move. People who freeze feel like they are detached from the situation, in a dreamlike state, or disconnected from their surroundings. During the freeze response we might feel numb, stuck, and unable to move forward. It can appear to others like we are lazy, uninterested, or unmotivated, when in fact, we are frozen with fear. When seeking help, we just never follow through. We don't know what to say, what to ask, where to look, or what to do to create the change in our lives we say we want. Others frozen by fear will engage in a relentless search on the internet or checking every person out and selecting every box to make sure they have made the perfect choice. Our excuse is we are still preparing and getting ready to move our lives forward, but we never do because we are petrified. If you are the type who says they are "getting ready" or "waiting for" things to happen first, you are likely putting it off because you are frozen in fear. If this is your response, recognize it and use your courage to push past it. While you are "getting ready" or "waiting", make one call to someone that wants to help you and then another. Make one appointment, then another. Give yourself permission to feel afraid but move forward anyway.

Someone who exhibits the fawn response hides their genuine feelings of fear and will attempt to please the person or appease the situation threatening to them. The fawn response is chosen to avoid conflict. This is the response often chosen by those who have been abused early on. It's a preemptive response to please and avoid any potential threat causing the fear. We agree with anything the threatening person wants to hear and will ignore our own hesitation because we are afraid. The problem is we never really bought into what we agreed to do. This can show up in many different ways throughout our lives, and the result is we begin living a life not ours and not based on who we want to be with, what we want to spend our time doing, or how we want to live. When we are putting our professional team together to complete the 2nd Journey, we may be willing to just accept anyone on our team so we can say it's done and please the Survivor's Journey Facilitator. Someone who typically uses a fawn response in the face of fear will have to stop and take their time to carefully select their professional team members because they are a good fit and not just to please someone else.

Closely related to the fawn response is the <u>flow</u> response. This is known as the response of the manipulator. When facing fear, the person uses the flow response to convince someone they are indeed doing the very thing they are not doing. This may be the tactic of the con artist, the manipulator, the person who is so afraid they create a ruse for you to believe they are moving forward when in fact they are too afraid to create any meaningful change. If this is your response, it's likely you've been using this response for many years. You are too smart for your own good because flowing takes skill. It will be difficult but recognize when you are just flowing, because in truth, you are afraid. Once you understand it's just fear talking, stay afraid if you want to, but take the necessary action steps to reach out and assemble your professional team one by one.

When you haven't had many opportunities to live through love instead of fear, it can prevent you from even working through the Journeys toward your recovery. When you stop working on your recovery, you stay exactly where you are.

Truth: *"I can't live the life I want to live without help".*

The victim's call is all about the challenge in front of you. In order to do that, you have to make a decision to gain the support you need. Don't let fear block you. Do it. Keep moving forward. Be aware of your own response to this fearful situation.

Love yourself enough to want to live the life you've always wanted. It is entirely possible, but to do that you'll need to love yourself enough to push past the fear. Loving yourself isn't selfish. It's about finally prioritizing you. No one else knows your heart as well as you do. No one knows your great capacity to love more than you do. No one knows how much you've been hurt more than you do. No one knows how much you want to be loved and be happy more than you do. Loving yourself enough to take care of yourself and make your dreams a reality is not too much to ask. It's exactly what your creator wants for you. The 2nd Journey is all about pushing your fears aside and using your courage to put the people in your life you need and to make that happen. When you do that, true happiness and emotional freedom is right around the corner.

Tools: Courage and Connection Through the Bomb Squad
Instead of fear, let's love ourselves enough to start saying "yes" to our lives and ourselves and go on this Journey together. You will not be alone on your Journey. There are lots of people just like you taking this Journey. And there are a number of people we want you to take with you on your Journey to recovery. To begin making the decision to gain the sup-

port, you need to reclaim your power, choice, and voice, seeking out the formal support systems you need to fully recover. In the Survivor's Journey world it means finding key professionals who will help challenge you and help you recover. We call those key players in your life your Bomb Squad or your professional team. Here's who they should be and why.

Survivor's Journey Group Facilitator

Your Survivor's Journey group facilitator is a member of your Bomb Squad. They are there to support you and help you grow by processing through the 12 guided Journeys with you. Their job is to always support you, but not always agree with you. They challenge you to grow emotionally, mentally, socially, spiritually, and more. They become a person you can learn to trust because they have your back and want the best for you. However, your Survivor's Journey group facilitator is not your therapist. They serve as a facilitator, which means they help and coach you to interpret and live the Journeys. To give you an example, your therapist is like a surgeon. They are highly trained to examine, assess, and identify your issues, and then to provide targeted and skillful interventions to root out or minimize your problems. Depending on their level and skill, your Survivor's Journey group facilitator has critical first aid kits that complement what a therapist can provide.

Case Manager

There are various types of case managers. There are those who simply manage a case that involves you or resources you have or want to have. In the case of government benefits, you may have a case manager or case worker who sends you a notification asking for paperwork or for you to meet some criteria in order to get benefits. You may have more than one of those types of case managers in your life. Their purpose is to help you receive and maintain the services and/or resources you need. While they may serve an important purpose, this type of case manager is not an active part of the Bomb Squad.

The type of case manager that becomes a member of your Bomb Squad is known as an intensive case manager. They also go by other names, like direct service provider, advocate, care coordinator, peer advocate, case worker, or whole person advocate. This is someone who will help identify your needs and link you to the services you want based on the goals you identify. "Want" is the important word here. The case manager who is on your Bomb Squad team typically will not spend time trying to make you do something you don't want to do. If they are, then maybe they are not the case manager you want as a member of your Bomb Squad. Find one who will focus on helping you achieve the goals you have.

You can typically find them at substance abuse treatment programs, mental health programs, domestic violence programs, and anti-trafficking focused programs. They are also sometimes located within health care focused agencies, veteran's administrations, community-based programs and more. Your intensive case manager is like a professional friend and support system for you. They come into your life to identify your needs and then find the services you need. They can be great teachers, mediators, supporters, and very good advocates. If you need help to talk to another professional or to fight for your rights, they are there to help you do that. They also have the ability to speak up on your behalf or with you to help you handle your business. A good case manager is someone who should meet with you periodically and walk beside you so you are not battling alone.

Other than your Survivor's Journey facilitator, your case manager is likely the person you know the best on the Bomb Squad. Your case manager can help you find legal help, housing, mental health services, substance abuse treatment, health care providers, food, clothing, and a host of other essential services you might need. Here's what they won't do. A case manager will not get themselves involved in anything illegal or unethical. They will also never go along with any plan to hurt someone or for someone to hurt you, or if you or someone else says they will abuse or have abused children. In those instances, they will make a report to the authorities because in many cases they are mandated by law to do so. Also, your case manager is not your personal slave. They don't ask "how high" when you say jump. However, your case manager should be there for you. This is the person you may know the best and might be one you begin to trust and feel you can be yourself with. If this is not the case, you might have to switch case managers until you feel your case manager has your back. The important point is to find the case manager who supports you and your recovery.

Therapist and a Trauma Treatment Therapist

We recommend obtaining and actively seeing a therapist at least once per week before pursuing the 3rd Journey and continuing to see them throughout all of the Journeys. We recommend you see a therapist who is trained in trauma treatment, preferably one trained on a specific trauma treatment approach. A clinical therapist trained in trauma treatment is someone who has graduated with at least a master's degree in counseling or social work or someone who is a psychologist. A psychiatrist is acceptable as long as they are providing you with one hour per week of counseling. If you are under the care of a psychiatrist or any professional who is providing you with medication for your mental health, do not stop seeing them and do not stop taking your medication. The Survivor's Journeys should NOT be used in place of anything you may already be receiving. The Survivor's Journeys may be used in addition to what you are already doing.

Substance Abuse Treatment - Alcoholics Anonymous (AA)/Narcotics Anonymous (NA)Sponsor for Recovery

If we had to rank in order these people in your life, attending to a substance use disorder is first on the list. If you use drugs or drink alcohol and believe you have a problem, the first thing you should do is enter a substance abuse treatment program. When we are under the influence of drugs, we can't rely on our own thoughts and feelings. We have to give our life and ourselves over to allow someone who has our best interest in mind to get us through to sobriety. Our brain is fuzzy because of the months or years of abuse and our own thought patterns, feelings, and cravings will lead us back to drug and alcohol use. In AA and NA, they say drugs and alcohol are both powerful and baffling. They will lead us to "stinkin-thinkin" that will eventually lead us back to abuse. We give our lives over to the healing power of treatment and recovery because it works.

There are several types of treatment programs. A few-days long detox program will help you withdraw from the substance in a safe manner. Then there are inpatient treatment programs that may provide you with 30, 60, or 90-day inpatient treatment. There are a variety of intensive outpatient treatment programs (IOP) offering a variety of treatment options, from attending a daily treatment program for a half-day to a full-day, across several weeks. Once you complete a treatment program, it will be time to enter the recovery phase of your sobriety. Recovery will include attending AA or NA meetings from daily to a few times a week. There are also residential sober living homes and facilities for those who need to leave their environment or need long term residency.

It will be critical to participate in ongoing AA/NA meetings and obtain an AA or NA sponsor and meet with them regularly. Why is having an AA or NA sponsor critical? Because as they say in AA, you can't bullshit the bullshitter. They see you and know you because they were you. Your own personal Bomb Squad sponsor is who you need to stay in touch with during recovery and reality at the same time, because your sponsor will tell it to you straight and will keep you on track with working the 12 Steps of AA and NA recovery.

Getting a sponsor is also a critical part of sobriety. An AA or NA sponsor will help you navigate life, understand, and apply the AA or NA 12 steps to your daily life. This is someone who you can share confidential information with and receive wise advice. Once you obtain a sponsor, you should be meeting with them regularly.

Trauma Sensitive Yoga Instructor, Art Therapy, and Mindfulness
When it comes to recovery from any form of trauma, whether it be sexual exploitation, violence, abuse, assault and/or other sources of trauma, mind and body work is said to be just as important as talk therapy. The body holds the trauma, even when the mind has blocked or suppressed the memory.

According to several researchers and medical experts, trauma can get blocked in the body and can take a toll on your health, creating poorer health outcomes such as heart disease, obesity, diabetes, and cancer to name a few. Yoga helps to unblock trauma and promote health.

Trauma-body work helps the body move those associated toxins related to stress through the body and be released. Trauma-body work helps calm your mind and helps you bring your body back to a relaxed state. Repeated exposure to yoga is a wonderful way to heal the body and relax the mind. Trauma sensitive yoga involves poses, breathing, and has positive effects on the nervous system. Restorative yoga may also help improve your mood and sleep, reduce chronic pain, soothe your nervous system, and relax your mind and body.

There is a great book we recommend called, *The Body Keeps the Score: Brain, Mind, and Body in the Healing of Trauma* by Bessel van der Kolk, M.D., who talks more in depth about trauma and recovery and trauma's effect on the body.

Some of the experiences of trauma we had were so disturbing we didn't have words to describe and do justice to what happened to us. For some of us, we didn't have words to describe our trauma because we were too young. When trauma can't accurately be described by words, it's therapeutic to describe it in other ways. Art therapy is a great way to express yourself nonverbally. Art therapy is also one way of promoting good health and relieving stress by being able to express oneself artistically. There are various types of art therapies available, including painting, sculpture, and other forms of expressive art.

Mindfulness is a form of meditation involving breathing methods, guided imagery, and other practices helping to relax the body and mind. Some of the benefits of mindfulness is, when practiced, may lower blood pressure, reduce chronic pain, improve sleep, keep you from ruminating over the same experience, decrease stress, and promote relaxation.

Why Do You Need Your Bomb Squad?
Why do we call these professionals YOUR team? Because you need to begin thinking of them as your personal support team. Too often when

we think of and engage with professionals, they enter our lives and take over, telling us what to do, when to do it, and how to do it, without much consideration for what WE want to do. If we don't do what they say, they cut off their support, turn off our lights, take us to jail, or remove our children. We often engage them out of fear. So we don't suffer the consequences, we give over our power and do whatever they say. Secretly we wish they would just leave our lives and leave us alone! We are tired of people stepping into our lives and taking away power and control.

This specific team of supporters you choose will be there to help you live the life you want to live as directed by YOU. Flip the way you think about your team. Instead of those who are there to control and tell you how to run your life, how about thinking of them as a whole team of people who are there to help support you? Most people would love it if they opened their door and there were a team of people standing there saying, "We'd love to help you live the life you want. How can we help you do that?"

Remember, your Bomb Squad is not the people who have the power to cut off your monthly check if you don't do something they demand. They are not the court system demanding you do or do not engage in certain behaviors. And they are not the child welfare department making sure you care for your kids in a way suitable and appropriate. Your Bomb Squad is a group of people who are there for YOU in a way you need them to be.

However, it is important to note you can't treat your Bomb Squad like they owe you something, because they certainly do not. Treat your Bomb Squad as you would want to be treated. Occasionally, give them grace even from time-to-time when they don't deserve it. In other words, forgive them when they mess up - like you would like to be forgiven when you mess up. Also, when there are people often in your life who are there to truly help you, they tend to speak the truth to you. Your Bomb Squad will challenge you and help you grow in ways they know you need to grow. Therefore, they will not always be pleasing to you. You always have the power to quit or fire a member of your Bomb Squad, but think twice before doing so. They may be providing you with the push and challenge you need to get through an emotional or psy-chological barrier, face something you need to face, or be confronted about thoughts, behaviors, and feelings that aren't helpful, accurate, or healthy for you to hold on to. Love and appreciate your Bomb Squad and have a healthy respect for what they bring to you. Truth and transfor-mation are genuinely not possible without them.

Asking for help from professionals is hard. It takes courage to ask for help. Maybe we've tried to ask for help before and it didn't work out. Or maybe the professionals in our life were downright mean and it was almost like pulling teeth to get them to help us and we never want to go through a similar experience again. But to take this Journey to recovery, it takes a village. And not just any village, but specific professionals who can walk beside you on your Journey.

Even though we are afraid, and even though our past experiences with professionals may not have been the best, we have to try and try again. Why? Because you are worth it. Your recovery is worth it. Your dreams are worth it. Your future is worth it!

Give them another chance. Show them grace. Do you know what grace is? Grace is what the divine shows you every day. Grace is honor, credit, and forgiveness given to someone who likely doesn't deserve it, but we give it to them anyway. Practice grace and reach out. What will ultimately happen is you will eventually find a good fit between what you need and the professional equipped to provide it.

Mind-fields: Complacence and Collusion

"Life's too short to spend another day at war with yourself."
~ Ritu Ghatourey

When you don't make a decision to gain the support you need to reclaim your power, choice, and voice, you become complacent with your cur-rent life situation and are willing to accept whatever scraps life throws you. You are rooted in fear instead of love. You'll blame your frustra-tions on everybody and everything else except your fear. Or you'll just consider yourself unlucky. In reality, it's not about who to blame or that you're unlucky. You chose to be complacent with what is. This is a mind-field that will cost you your dreams.

Another mind-field is collusion. Collusion comes from not loving ourselves enough. Someone who will collude and conspire with the enemy against themself is someone who will lose 100% of the time. You will not only go along with what isn't in your own best interest, you'll create situations that will keep you down. If you can't afford another baby, you'll have one. If it's in your best interest NOT to date this person, you'll date them. You'll willingly accept people and situations in your life without forethought and you'll suffer the consequences every single time. Old people say, "a hard head makes a soft ass." You'll go through life fighting, struggling, and be unhappy. Being "hardheaded" is not taking time to listen and look over your choices in life and choosing differently. Being hardheaded causes life to beat your ass over and over again, like kneading dough, your ass becomes very soft; thus, a hard head makes a soft ass. You'll chalk it up to having a hard life, when it was a life you kept choosing. Love yourself more.

Finding Each Bomb Squad Member

The 2nd Journey is all about gaining the support you need to be successful at achieving full freedom and living the life you want to live. Just because you find someone to be on your Bomb Squad, doesn't mean there is a good fit between you and them. Most people who have a case manager or a therapist believe they have to take the one offered to them. They don't realize in gaining back their own power, choice, and voice they should make decisions about who will be involved in their life. When you choose a therapist, a case manager, or an AA or NA sponsor for example, it is your responsibility to find the one that best fits your needs and who you have faith will help you the most. Sometimes this requires looking around, trying professionals out, interviewing them, and choosing the one who best meets your needs. Remember this is a person or set of persons who will know the most about you. These will be people who you will be relearning to trust. Choosing your Bomb Squad members should be a serious process and you should invest time to make sure you have chosen professionals whom you can trust and you believe can truly help you.

How do you know if they can truly help you? Do some digging. Look them up online. Do they have any reviews you can look at? Find out what type of degrees they have, where they went to school, and what type of licenses they have. If they are a therapist, ask them what type of modality, theories, or therapies they use or are considering using with you and why? Have them explain it to you in plain English. If you don't understand, don't be ashamed to ask them to explain it in clear, simple words. Their rationale should make sense to you. Also, google the theory, therapy, or modality. Once you read about it, see if it makes sense to you and if you think it suits your needs. Ask your case manager how many people they have on their caseload right now, how often you both will be meeting, and what you will be doing together. Ask for a copy of your case plan or treatment plan so you are fully aware of what your work together will involve. If there is no case plan or the case plan includes goals you didn't help create, this person may be in your life if you want them to be, but they are not a member of your Bomb Squad. They are not on your Bomb Squad until they are following a plan you helped develop including goals you both agree.

Ask anyone you are considering including on your Bomb Squad if they deal with diverse clients and if they have experience working with someone like you? Ask how many clients they have had who represent the diversity you bring to the situation. Have they had diversity training or cultural competency training giving them specific knowledge about the population you represent? Ask if they have worked with survivors of sexual abuse, assault, or exploitation. Take all their responses and your research into consideration when choosing your Bomb Squad. It is your responsibility to make sure you place yourself in the hands of someone caring, compassionate, and competent.

The Transformation: *"I work with others to regain my power, choice, and voice".*

This Journey is all about setting up your team to help you gain the freedom you need to live the life you truly want to live. When you have suffered any form of abuse, been a victim of emotional and/or physical violence, been stigmatized or overlooked, or the violations committed against your heart and body have been minimized or dismissed; your spirit is not settled, and your soul is not ok with what happened to you.

If you just sit for a minute and think about your life, you will realize how strong you really are and how much courage it has taken for you to get to this point in your life in one piece. Before you take this Journey, take a moment to say thank you to yourself for your own personal strength and for getting yourself this far.

But you shouldn't have to go through life white knuckling it just to survive. Life should not be this hard for you or for anybody. There are lessons in life to learn, but it should not be the struggle you had to endure. A lot of life is meant to be enjoyed and the majority of your life should be happy and fulfilling.

Call in your Bomb Squad. Look up trauma treatment therapists in your community. Find that trauma-focused yoga instructor. Find the AA or NA sponsor. Make it your personal mission to ask someone at every single AA or NA meeting you attend if they will be your sponsor. Complete the paperwork to get the case manager you need, and so forth. It's not a good idea to move into the 3rd Journey without at least working with a trauma treatment therapist. And if you have basic needs you struggle to maintain, obtain the services of a case manager who can help you get housing, food, clothing, legal services, health care services, and more. You'll need to start becoming the best and strongest version of yourself.

What your Bomb Squad will do for you:

a. They will help you meet your daily needs and provide you with a solid foundation so you can grow your dreams.
b. They will help you secure food, clothing, safe housing, legal assistance, sobriety, education, benefits, life-skills, health care, and more.

c. They will help you work through your past trauma and maintain healthy mental health.

d. They will help challenge your fears and help you to be empowered.

To prepare for the 3rd Journey, you'll need to be strong. To successfully take the 3rd Journey, you'll need to bring your courage, your strengths, and your endurance. These are the three skills you used over and over to survive, and these are the three skills that will take you to where you want to go physically, emotionally, mentally, socially, and spiritually.

Those elements are needed so that you are equipped to establish your goals and go after your dreams. When you're ready, let's get busy and move into the 3rd Journey.

3.

3rd Journey: *The victim works through their trauma and consistently combats their triggers.*

3rd Truth: *Trauma is the source of my pain.*

3rd Transformation: *I can consistently combat my triggers and heal from trauma.*

Trigger or Validation:

Remember for some, the material in this Journey may be triggering. If it triggers you, reach out to your support system including those you trust and appropriate members of your Bomb Squad and/or engage in some self-care activities. For others, this information will be validating. In those cases, use the material to help validate you and affirm what you are or have been experiencing is real.

CHAPTER 3: SELF-DISCOVERY

Working on your trauma is critical to your recovery, however, before going on the 3rd Journey talk to your trauma treatment therapist. Your therapist may recommend that you NOT engage in a deep dive of your past in detail and write it in your workbook. You, along with your therapist's recommendation, will be in the best position to decide if taking the entire 3rd Journey in the manner in which we laid it out is in your best interest. Some therapists prefer to move you along your Journeys using the sessions you have with them. Remember the Guided Survivor's Journeys are all about you reclaiming your own power, choice, and voice, so the decision is ultimately yours. Listen to the wise counsel of your therapist and make your decision accordingly.

"The journey into self-love and self-acceptance must begin with self-examination... until you take the journey of self-reflection, it is almost impossible to grow or learn in life." ~ Iyanla Vanzant

In this Journey, we take a look at your traumas, including what occurred, when, where, by whom, and for how long. To take the victim's path toward recovery you'll write about how you felt about it, thought about it, did or didn't do related to it. We will examine if you told anyone or didn't tell what they did or didn't do and what happened. Refer to your workbook after reading about this Journey to write about and examine your experiences.

Trauma is psychological wounding that comes from physical, sexual, and institutional abuse, neglect, intergenerational trauma, and disasters that induce powerlessness, fear, recurrent hopelessness, and a constant state of alert (National Center on Trauma-Informed Care, 2014). Trauma happens when one suffers abuse, loss, or chronic stress.

If this is your first time through this next Journey, it's important you have your Bomb Squad in place. In particular, it's important to make sure you are working with a trauma-treatment therapist who can help you process your thoughts, feelings, and experiences.

Some of our past experiences may have involved childhood sexual abuse. Sexual abuse is a critical violation in that it damages so many vital qualities we need in life such as our core self-esteem and our trust and belief in others. The secret, who we told, and their reaction is so important to the way we began to view ourselves. Because we were violated, we may have felt worthless and blamed ourselves. What we have to learn is it was not your fault, even if your body biologically responded or if we became emotionally confused or even loved our abuser. We may still have some mixed emotions with many of us hating our abuser. To this day we may feel uncomfortable talking and thinking about it. We have unresolved feelings about it.

For some of us, our past includes physical abuse. Someone hurt us. Not only were we physically hurt, but the damage they did went deeper than just the physical pain, and we suffered extreme emotional pain. Some of us were neglected. No one cared or had the capacity to take proper care of us and we suffered. For some, we didn't have enough of what we needed like food, proper clothing, a safe and warm home, the love and concern of others, the healthy attention of others, and a healthy village of family members to shepherd us through life. In some of our households, there was violence, and we were afraid. As a result of these experiences, we got lost. We didn't develop in a way that made us feel safe and secure. We didn't learn about healthy, safe, supportive love from family. We didn't learn to trust those who are trustworthy. We didn't skip off to school, happy to learn and play with our friends. We had heavy thoughts and seemingly the weight of the world on our shoulders. We weren't like other kids. When we laid down to sleep, we weren't always feeling content about the day or feeling safe. We sometimes felt alone, rejected, invisible, and scared.

Some of us have experienced sexual assault or have been raped when we got older and have not worked through the emotional and psychological pain, anger, fear, and grief that is still embedded within us. Some of us got involved in psychologically abusive and physically violent relationships.

The Truth: *"Trauma is the source of my pain".*

No matter which type or form of abuse or neglect you experienced, it did not go away. Even if it was a long time ago, if you haven't resolved it and worked through it, the trauma connected to it is still with you. Even if you ignore it or try to forget it, it is hidden deep within both your body and mind, and it may show up in your life in ways that are destructive and damaging to your physical, mental, spiritual, and emotional health. Unresolved trauma can ruin lives and derail us from living the happy and joyful life we were intended to live. We developed and learned not to trust. We learned that genuine love may be rare. We learned dysfunctional ways to relate, and we got into dysfunctional relationships. We internalized much of the dysfunction and blamed ourselves for what happened and why it happened, and took this way of being into our relationships, our parenting, and our friendships.

What you have experienced is trauma. What we know about trauma is it can affect every aspect of your life, from your ability to be happy and at peace with yourself, to your ability to have healthy and prosocial friends and a successful intimate relationship. Trauma can deny you a restful sleep and it can negatively affect your ability and motivation to get and keep a job. It can affect your relationship with family members and even your ability to keep a safe and proper roof over your head.

Because you suffered trauma and it has been such a driving force in your life, it's important you educate yourself on the various types of trauma that exist, and what you can do to resolve your trauma.

There is the trauma you experience when you stub your toe. You feel pain right away, or what we call "acute pain." Then, depending on how hard you stubbed it, the acute pain eventually turns into a throbbing pain. The throbbing pain may subside enough that you can continue with your day. A day or two later you develop a bruise that lasts for a while. What you don't know is you also developed a hairline fracture in your foot which stays with you, causing you some pain when you walk. No one can see the fracture and it's hard to even detect on an Xray when you visit your doctor, but it's there and it continues to hurt and ache when you walk. You now feel most comfortable walking in your bare feet. You also start to favor the good foot while you walk. While outside you step on a piece of glass and your good foot starts to bleed. You put a band-aid on it. You didn't realize you hadn't cleaned it properly and there is an infection starting. Now each time you walk, you feel a level of pain in each foot. You compensate by walking the best way you can, but it hurts to walk. Over time you lose your ambition for walking. You really prefer to sit. You haven't visited a doctor about it because the first doctor didn't even find out what was wrong, so why go to another one?

Instead of working diligently to heal yourself from the pain caused from the traumas you suffered, you decided instead to alter your existence and limp around making the best of life following your trauma. You are now vulnerable to falling down and causing additional trauma. If you cause trauma to something else like your arm, you may be walking around holding that together. You can see how over time, not attending to your trauma can cause more problems. Over time these traumas continue to cripple you and damage your ability to live a full, free life.

You notice in the story how the "acute" trauma of initially hurting the foot caused chronic trauma because it kept getting reinjured every time you walked on it.

Acute trauma can happen when a sudden event occurs and is deeply disturbing to an individual. For example, this may occur because of involvement in, or being a witness to, a car accident or violent event, being a victim of a violent crime, or a natural disaster. In our case, it might occur as the result of being hit, slapped, beaten, robbed, sexually abused, being a victim of intimate partner violence, emotional abuse, child abuse or neglect, or witnessing violence.

Chronic trauma is experiencing repeated or prolonged abuse or prolonged exposure to trauma. In our example of our foot, each time we step on the fracture we re-traumatize our foot. This may be repeated exposure to our abuser, repeated rapes, repeated intimidation, ongoing threats, prolonged neglect, and continual emotional violence.

Complex trauma is the exposure to varied (different types) and multiple traumatic events often interpersonal in nature. It may include dating violence or intimate partner violence; family violence; commercial sexual exploitation; labor trafficking; childhood sexual, physical, or emotional abuse or neglect; and various forms of acute trauma. It often begins in childhood, but does not always have to have involved childhood trauma. In our example of initially hurting our foot, we hurt our other foot causing two different types of trauma. That is an example of complex trauma.

Thus, an acute trauma can happen and if prolonged may become a chronic trauma. If other traumas also occur, the victim suffers from complex trauma. For example, if you suffered the trauma of childhood abuse or neglect and then grew up to be victimized, you may be suffering from complex trauma. Or if you were raped and have also been a victim of domestic violence at one time in your life, you likely have complex trauma. In addition to various traumas, on a daily basis, survivors of abuse and exploitation, may also suffer from one or more of the following stressors.

Daily hassles are stressors that occur over time. Individuals who experience repeated stress can experience trauma. Daily hassles are typically minor irritations that occur as we go about our daily life. Stressors cause the individual to be in a state of emotional strain or tension. There are obvious and less obvious types of stressors. Obvious stressors are experiences like getting stuck in traffic, losing your keys, arguments with friends, or driving in bad weather. Other less obvious stressors include not having enough money to pay the bills, not being able to move to a safer location, or not having enough time in the day to get things done. Additional stressors may come from certain societal pressures, such as not living up to society's ideal body weight, not reaching a desired level of success in life, or perceived quality of one's intimate relationship, and more.

Microaggressions are indirect, subtle actions, statements, or inactions that are prejudicial in nature against a member of a stigmatized group because of their national origin, ethnicity, gender identity, sexual orientation, age, disability, religion, or difference. Because microaggressions are subtle and often indirect, many people experience them, but don't address them. In other words, the victim of a microaggression is wounded, but often doesn't defend themselves. Over time, this periodic and frequent wounding is like death by a thousand cuts. It hurts and damages self-esteem. An example of a microaggression might be when a black person is followed around a department store, signaling to them that the clerk believes they have the character of a thief. A microaggression occurs when a businessman explains what a woman needs to know by talking slowly as if she is obviously not educated enough to understand. A microaggression occurs when it is assumed one of the people in a lesbian relationship acts as the man. It shows up whenever anyone looks you up and down as if you should not be here or even on the planet. Your kind should not exist.

Both stress and microaggressions cause a wounding to one's self-esteem. Because they are frequent, pervasive, and difficult to address, many people discount them, but added together they can be just as damaging and wounding to you as a major trauma. Trauma, stress, and microaggressions serve to hold you back from the happiness you so much deserve.

PTSD can result from exposure to trauma. It is common to suffer acute stress after a traumatic experience, however, Post-Traumatic-Stress-Disorder can be long term. It is an anxiety disorder where the victim continues to re-experience the trauma and its symptoms for more than a month. PTSD can last months or even years after an experienced trauma.

According to SAMHSA (1994), there are numerous symptoms, all connected to the trauma you experienced. If you don't think your past trauma has anything to do with what is happening with you now, just look over the 80+ ways trauma may affect someone.

Immediate Emotional Reactions

Numbness and detachment

Anxiety or severe fear

Guilt (including survivor guilt)

Exhilaration as a result of surviving

Anger

Sadness

Helplessness

Feeling unreal; depersonalization (e.g., feeling as if you are watching yourself)

Disorientation

Feeling out of control

Denial

Constriction of feelings

Feeling overwhelmedDelayed Emotional Reactions

Irritability and/or hostility

Depression

Mood swings, instability

Anxiety (e.g., phobia, generalized anxiety)

Fear of trauma recurrence

Grief reactions

Shame

Feelings of fragility and/or vulnerability

Emotional detachment from anything that requires emotional reactions (e.g., significant and/or family relationships, conversations about self, discussion of traumatic events or reactions to them)

Immediate Physical Reactions

 Nausea and/or gastrointestinal distress

 Sweating or shivering

 Faintness

 Muscle tremors or uncontrollable shaking

 Elevated heartbeat, respiration, and blood pressure

 Extreme fatigue or exhaustion

 Greater startle responses

 Depersonalization

Delayed Physical Reactions

 Sleep disturbances, nightmares

 Somatization (e.g., increased focus on and worry about body aches and pains)

 Appetite and digestive changes

 Lowered resistance to colds and infection

 Persistent fatigue

 Elevated cortisol levels

 Hyperarousal

 Long-term health effects including heart, liver, autoimmune, and chronic obstructive pulmonary disease

Immediate Cognitive Reactions

 Difficulty concentrating

 Rumination or racing thoughts (e.g., replaying the traumatic event over and over again)

 Distortion of time and space (e.g., traumatic event may be perceived as if it was happening in slow motion, or a few seconds can be perceived as minutes)

 Memory problems (e.g., not being able to recall important aspects of the trauma)

 Strong identification with victims

Delayed Cognitive Reactions

Intrusive memories or flashbacks

Reactivation of previous traumatic events

Self-blame

Preoccupation with event

Difficulty making decisions

Magical thinking: belief that certain behaviors, including avoidant behavior, will protect against future trauma

Belief that feelings or memories are dangerous

Generalization of triggers (e.g., a person who experiences a home invasion during the daytime may avoid being alone during the day)

Immediate Behavioral Reactions

Startled reaction

Restlessness

Sleep and appetite disturbances

Difficulty expressing oneself

Argumentative behavior

Increased use of alcohol, drugs, and tobacco

Withdrawal and apathy

Avoidant behaviors

Delayed Behavioral Reactions

Avoidance of event reminders

Social relationship disturbances

Decreased activity level

Engagement in high-risk behaviors

Increased use of alcohol and drugs

Withdrawal

Immediate Existential Reactions

Intense use of prayer

Restoration of faith in the goodness of others (e.g., receiving help from others)

Loss of self-efficacy

Despair about humanity, particularly if the event was intentional

Immediate disruption of life assumptions (e.g., fairness, safety, goodness, predictability of life)

Delayed Existential Reactions

Questioning (e.g., "Why me?")

Increased cynicism, disillusionment

Increased self-confidence (e.g., "If I can survive this, I can survive anything")

Loss of purpose

Renewed faith

Hopelessness

Reestablishing priorities

Redefining meaning and importance of life

Reworking life's assumptions to accommodate the trauma (e.g., taking a self-defense class to reestablish a sense of safety)

In general, trauma is like a bomb that goes off inside of a person. Fragments of the bomb can go anywhere, negatively affecting the person's health and well-being. Not only does trauma affect your thinking, feeling, and behavior as demonstrated above, there is new evidence if left untreated, it can negatively affect your physical health.

The body reacts physiologically to trauma. One way is through the nervous system. Being exposed to trauma can affect a person biologically. Research has proven when the body experiences trauma it goes into high alert, becomes stressed, and produces cortisol. Cortisol is used in the body's fight, flight, or freeze response and is a natural, normal response. If we are confronted by a bear in the woods, we want our body to release cortisol and become hyper-focused in order to survive. However, some people who have experienced trauma don't just remember it, they relive it over and over in their minds and their bodies, suffering chronic stress. Some don't ever really feel safe and as a result cortisol remains higher than usual in our bodies. When the stress related to earlier trauma stays high or is unresolved, cortisol remains higher than usual and is aroused more quickly. It becomes more difficult for the body to return to its calm biological state. Cortisol breaks down some tissues in our bodies and can suppress the immune system, thus our bodies can function at a weaker state. This increases the opportunity for infection or disease to enter. This stressed state can also affect our digestive system and cause us to hold weight. Finally, trauma victims may complain of chronic pain longer than other patients who have suffered an injury or illness. Overall, trauma can keep you sick emotionally, mentally, and physically.

Lots of us are walking around today disabled by our trauma, pretending it is something else. Some of us are confused about why we don't have the life we want to live. Some of us blame everyone else and have logical and rational reasons why our limitations and unhappiness are someone else's fault. When we deal with our trauma, we can begin to live a full, rich life. We can run toward our dreams because we are not having to limp and protect our limitations. We begin to be free to live the life we want. We begin to live by choice and not by circumstance.

Psychologically, trauma can keep you stuck. It's like plumbing in a house. If there is a blockage in a pipe, nothing can get through. It is blocked. Continuing to not process your trauma makes things worse. Each problem you have builds on top of the blockage. It's dysfunctional and toxic to the mind and body and the person's interactions with others. It can alter and limit your life in a negative way. When the traumatized person begins to work on their trauma with their therapist, they begin to move the blockage. They begin to flush the trauma through the system (K. Gumus, personal communication, 2021). It can come out in ways that just plain stink at first. When they begin to address the blockage, some survivors initially experience more emotional symptoms and sleep disturbances and even physical symptoms. For this reason, survivors should be working with a trained trauma therapist and meet with them weekly.

Not all trauma therapies are effective for all types of people. Be empowered to let your trauma therapist know if what you are instructed to do is working, not working, had been working for a while and is no longer working, or if you have hit a plateau and are no longer making progress. Most certainly let them know if the therapy is NOT working and making your symptoms WORSE. If so, don't give up. You may need to try a different type of trauma treatment.

What is dangerous about trauma, is it makes us vulnerable. Because even when we don't see the vulnerabilities caused by our trauma, others may see it. Your trauma makes you vulnerable for others to take advantage of. Some previous victims of abuse, assault, or exploitation will get away from one abuser only to meet and get into a relationship with another one. They wonder why they continue to do this. Survivor Lydia asked herself this over and over again.

"I ask myself, what is this mark I have on my forehead that attracts...abusive men who want to hurt me and use me or abuse my children. A lot of us survivors ask ourselves this."

You fight so hard to get out of an abusive relationship only to meet the same person with a different face. You meet your next abuser who may beat you, sell you, emotionally abuse you, or all the above. You may have met a man who sexually abused your children. You promised yourself you would do everything possible to protect your children. As a mom, you will stand in front of an oncoming train to protect your children, yet you opened the door and allowed the predator in. Why? How could this happen?

I answer Lydia: "Secretly, I know what the mark is. It's the mark of vulnerability. He sees it. He sees the real me. He sees past my bravado, my fakeness, and the image I portray. He sees the child inside, the one he's attracted to in the first place. He knows what she thinks, what she feels, and who she is. He's seen her many times in other people. He knows her. He connects with her. Just like child molesters are attracted to children, he is attracted to wounded children living inside adult bodies. He connects, not with the adult me, but with the one he is seeking; the one buried deep inside me. He knows how to attract her to him. Just like candy in a child molester's hand, he knows what she likes. He knows how to blind her with smiles and promises of love and when he gets her right where he wants her to be – blinded by love – he takes what he wants, which might include abusing the child inside again or take advantage of the wounded adult. It's because he's also wounded."

"Because of his past experiences, he only knows two ways of being: the victimizer or the victim. He chose the victimizer. He is an opportunist, looking for opportunities to abuse. 'He wants me' I say to myself. But I find out he doesn't want me, not the adult me, not the powerful, beautiful, smart woman I could be. He wants the wounded child, the one who would make him feel powerful. The one who would fulfill his weak ego. He wants to love the one who is needy, dependent, and controlled by him. He is threatened by the woman, but powerful over the child. I connect with him because I'm looking for someone to heal the child. I want a father figure, one who will take care of me and let me know everything is alright. I want the one who will protect me and protect my heart. I confused love with healing. Healing is different. Healing is what I can do for myself with a strong and skilled professional. Healing is what protects my heart. Through healing I am the one, and the only one, who can protect the wounded child. Healing is what allows me to grow the child and become one with myself. I am the person I've been looking for. When I love and protect my own child within, I will find the love I want because I'm operating out of a healthy and fulfilled mindset and not a deficit mindset."

Spoiler Alert: You have connected on a unconscious level with this victimizer. He is looking for adults with a previously wounded child within. You are looking to heal your past and connect with what is familiar on an unconscious level. When you become healthy and process your past traumas, you will be ready to move on and connect with life partners who are interested in loving you, caring for you, and making you feel safe, secure, and wanted as a healed and strong adult.

Tools and Transformation: Self-Discovery through Trauma Work

"I consistently combat my triggers and heal from trauma".

As you can see, it is very important to work on and through your trauma, as well as those situations and experiences triggering your trauma. If there is anything you take away from your Survivor's Journey work, it is this: *Your trauma is real and it has real consequences for your life. See a trauma treatment therapist regularly to treat your trauma.* Doing this will improve the quality of your life.

Oftentimes, those suffering from the symptoms related to past trauma don't know what type of treatments are available. Some people believe all therapists are alike. This is so not true!

Some people think this about lawyers. The average person thinks you go to a lawyer when you need legal advice or legal representation. Most people have no idea they need to go to a specific lawyer based on their type of problem. If you invent something, for example, you need to go to a patent attorney. If you want to secure a Will, you might hire a probate or estate planning attorney. If you get into trouble, you'll hire a criminal defense attorney. Just like attorneys, there are different types of therapists based on their training and expertise. There are social workers, clinical mental health counselors, psychologists, and psychiatrists. These professionals use different types of therapeutic modalities or tools based on their training. To address your trauma, you are looking for a therapist who has expertise and experience in trauma treatment. If they are not trauma trained to use a specific trauma treatment therapy, avoid them.

Knowledge is power. In order to empower you to think about the type of trauma treatment therapy which might be helpful for you, we provided a few suggestions below. Your therapist will also have suggestions based on your past trauma and current symptoms. Be empowered to ask your therapist questions about the treatment model they use, why they prefer it over others, how long they have been practicing it, where they were trained, if they are certified in this trauma specific therapy, and the number of people they've treated using this therapy. If the answers sound acceptable to you, hire them. If not, keep looking.

TRI-Phasic Model for Trauma Treatment

In using the TRI-Phasic Model, the therapist will take you through three phases. The first phase is called "Safety and Stabilization". During this phase the therapist will help you stabilize and become somewhat calm and safe before moving into any discussions or trauma work. The second phase is called "Trauma Memory Processing", where you work with a therapist on your trauma, including your memories and experiences, in a safe manner. The third phase is called "Reconnection". This is where the therapist helps you gain closure and redefine yourself.

Eye Movement Desensitization and Reprocessing (EDMR) for Trauma Treatment

This is a therapy in which the therapist guides you through a traumatic memory while you are creating consistent movement. The therapist will work with you to establish a relationship and provide you with some skills to cope with uncomfortable feelings. The therapist will then have you identify a traumatic memory which causes you distress and possibly even PTSD symptoms. You'll work together to reprocess the memory. The therapist will ask you to focus on your thoughts, feelings, and sensations as you are remembering the situation. You'll be asked to move your eyes back and forth like you do when you are in REM sleep. The therapist will stop you occasionally to help you process your emotions and perceptions. Over time, the intensity of the emotion is lowered and so is the pain associated with that memory. When it's time, the therapist helps you replace the negative emotions and thoughts with more appropriate ones. For example, the therapist might help you replace a feeling of shame and powerlessness with a feeling of strength and empowerment. There is some strong evidence about the effects of EMDR. For example, it is endorsed by the American Psychiatric Association and the International Society for Traumatic Stress Studies.

Cognitive Processing Therapy (CPT) for Trauma Treatment

Cognitive Processing Therapy is a 12-session therapy which helps you process your thoughts related to your trauma. By changing your thoughts, the goal of CPT is to also have your feelings change. CPT helps you handle distressing and intrusive thoughts. You learn more helpful ways to think and process your trauma. The goal is to reduce symptoms related to PTSD and to get you unstuck. This type of therapy is also endorsed by the U.S. Departments of Veterans Affairs and Defense, as well as the International Society of Traumatic Stress Studies.

Prolonged Exposure (PE) Therapy for Trauma Treatment

This type of therapy is for those who have largely avoided processing their trauma. Prolonged Exposure Therapy or PE, is typically done over the course of 8 to 15 weekly 90-minute sessions with a PE trained therapist. The therapist will teach you some breathing exercises to manage your anxiety. When you feel safe enough, they will begin exposure. Two types of exposure take place, imaginal exposure, and in vivo exposure. In imaginal exposure, the client describes their experience in the present tense. The therapist helps the client process the experience. The client's description of the event is recorded so the client can take it, listen to it, process their emotions, and practice breathing exercises. In vivo exposure homework is given to the client. During the week, the client begins to slowly expose themselves to a feared stimuli, such as people or places. This is only done after the client and therapist agree on the homework. The client gradually challenges themselves, experiencing success along the way.

Stress Inoculation Therapy (SIT) for Trauma Treatment

Stress Inoculation Therapy teaches you coping skills to manage your stress and anxiety. There are lots of techniques associated with SIT, including, but not limited to, role playing, deep muscle relaxation, assertiveness skills, thought stopping, guided self-dialogue, and breathing exercises.

Trauma-Focused Cognitive Behavioral Therapy- (TF-CBT)
TF-CBT addresses a broad array of emotional and behavioral issues associated with single, chronic, or complex trauma. Clinicians are trained and certified in using this treatment.

Medications for Trauma Treatment
There are several medications which can be taken in conjunction with therapy to help you manage PTSD related symptoms. For example, some medications help with anxiety and depression associated with trauma. Medications alone will not likely make the symptoms connected to your trauma go away, but it can help you better manage your symptoms.

Trauma-Informed Approach for Agencies
Social service and health care focused agencies are learning more about trauma and are working to change their policies and practices so they are more trauma-informed. When agencies are trauma-informed, it means they understand the impact trauma has on people and this understanding helps guide the way these professionals engage and treat the people they serve.

Before you decide to work with an agency, empower yourself enough to ask if they have received trauma informed training and if they have implemented practices which are trauma informed. Social service and health care focused agencies who are sensitive to trauma try to provide their clients with a trauma informed care focused response. They may practice what is called the 4 R's of a trauma informed response. The first R is the *realization* that a traumatized person is affected in profound and significant ways. The agency then works to *recognize* trauma, *respond* to the trauma, and *resist* retraumatizing a client. Thus, when you engage social service or health care focused agencies, the language they use, their policies, and their approaches should be trauma informed so they avoid retraumatizing you.

In addition, empower yourself enough to find out the agency's mission statement. It should be proudly displayed when you walk into their agency. An agency's mission statement cuts to the core of who they are and what they do. One hundred percent of the time they should be serving their mission statement. If someone does something which re-traumatizes you or does not serve their mission, call them out on it. Give them a chance to correct it, but it is within your rights to address it with them. This could be a simple conversation with them, or depending on the severity of the complaint, you may ask if they have a mechanism for you to file a formal grievance or issue a formal complaint. You may also be within your rights to contact an ombudsman. If one exists, an ombudsman is a person whose responsibility it is to investigate complaints brought by private citizens against businesses, universities, financial institutions, and government departments.

Mind-fields: Clenching and Clawing

Many who have experienced trauma suffer from various symptoms, from minor and bothersome symptoms to debilitating symptoms. As you are working with your trauma treatment therapist, talk about your symptoms. This is the time to practice trust and truth telling. Let them know what you feel and think, and what is happening to your body and behavior as a result. Tell them about your thoughts and feelings. Inform them of your eating habits, any drug or alcohol use, and your sleep patterns. If things are getting worse or better, let them know. Lay it all out for them. Attend your sessions regularly and soak up whatever it is they have to give you. The more you work on your trauma, the better you will sleep and feel, and you will become more empowered and increase the quality of your life.

Trauma may be the root of a substance abuse problem, mental illness, or chronic disease. There is a well-known study called the Adverse Childhood Effects or the ACE study. This study found trauma was the root cause of many of the social problems people experience including obesity, smoking, abuse, violence, addiction, and more[1]. There is also a biological connection among trauma, brain development, and the development of chronic diseases including physical diseases, mental illnesses, addictions, and other life impairments. The results of the ACE Study were used to create a 10-question survey on trauma called the ACE Quiz. When completed, the results provide individuals with an ACE Score of 0 to 10. Since the ACE study was developed, several additional studies have taken place connecting a person's ACE Score with their quality of life.[2] For instance, a person with an ACE Score of 4 is two times more likely to smoke, 7 times more likely to become an alcoholic, 4 times more likely to suffer depression, and 12 times more likely to be at risk for suicide (Centers for Disease Control, 2019)[3]. The higher the ACE Score, the more severe the toll on the person's health and the more likely they are to engage in behaviors negatively affecting their health. It may be the higher your ACE score, the more intense and serious you should consider your recovery to be. Treating the root of your problems, aka trauma, will support your recovery.[4]

We invite you to take the ACE Quiz for yourself. You can find it by googling it. Once you know your score, empower yourself by reading more about your score and thereby learn more about yourself, your needs, and what might work best in helping you resolve any of the trauma you have.

---

[1] Adverse Childhood Experiences (2020). Center for Disease Control https://www.cdc.gov/violenceprevention/aces/index.html

[2] National Center on Trauma-Informed Care, (2014) Trauma informed care in behavioral health services. https://www.ncbi.nlm.nih.gov/books/NBK207201/ Rockville (MD): Substance Abuse and Mental Health

[3] National Center on Trauma-Informed Care, (2014) Trauma informed care in behavioral health services. https://www.ncbi.nlm.nih.gov/books/NBK207201/ Rockville (MD): Substance Abuse and Mental Health Services Administration (SAMHSA)

[4] Centers for Disease Control (2019) Adverse childhood experiences.: Preventing early trauma to improve adult health. https://www.cdc.gov/vitalsigns/aces/index.html

Trauma keeps you vulnerable because it can distort your worldview and keep you in a hypervigilant and protective mode, inhibiting your ability to live your life in a joyful way. It can affect the quality of your social, cognitive, environmental, emotional, physical, economic, and interpersonal life.

Without doing your trauma work, you will go through life clenching your jaw and clawing your way through. You will continue to see the world as a scary place where you always have to defend yourself because someone may be out to take advantage of you. It's hard to relax and enjoy your life if you're always on guard. Life is beautiful. There are many ways to enjoy it. Going through life always on guard is not the way to do it. Going through life with a stubbed toe, hairline fractures, and cut feet, like the example provided earlier, just makes you hobble through life in pain. Life is not meant to be lived like that. Throughout your life, there are lessons you are meant to learn. You can't partake of the lessons and learn from them when you are preoccupied with not getting hurt again. There are also opportunities in life that will be presented to you. Every new opportunity will seem too scary and overwhelming. That's no way to live.

In Alcoholics Anonymous they call it "white knuckling" through life or "being a dry drunk". You haven't learned the lessons. You haven't recovered. You just stopped drinking. The same applies here. Perhaps you are no longer being victimized, but you haven't started to truly recover and live until you address and resolve your trauma.

4

The 4th Journey: *The Survivor wins the internal battle to gain an inner voice that supports them.*

The 4th Truth: *I have the power to control and change my internal thoughts and feelings about myself.*

The 4th Transformation: *My inner voice loves, embraces, and supports me.*

Trigger or Validation:

Remember for some, the material in this Journey may be triggering. If it triggers you, reach out to your support system including those you trust and appropriate members of your Bomb Squad and/or engage in some self-care activities. For others, this information will be validating. In those cases, use the material to help validate you and affirm what you are or have been experiencing is real.

CHAPTER 4: INTERNAL SAFETY

"If there is no enemy within, the enemy without can do me no harm."
~ African Proverb

Y ou are now no longer a victim of your circumstance. You are a survivor because you have moved beyond victimhood and are traveling a path which is helping you grow and become the person you were always meant to be. Let's just take a moment to consider all you have done. Congratulations on your hard work!

According to the National Science Foundation 80% of our internal self-talk is negative. Thus, the 4th Journey involves the internal battle within ourselves. Working to establish a positive inner voice is important to our recovery. It's true, if there is no enemy within, it is difficult for all enemies outside of us to do any lasting damage. This journey is about interrupting our negative self-talk and replacing it with positive self-talk. It sounds easy, but on some days, it will seem like you are doing that most of the day. But the journey is well worth it. If we told you to work the 4th Journey every day for one month and we would give you a thousand dollars, you might invest the time to do it. Well, we don't have a thousand dollars to give you, but we do have something else even more valuable. If you work this journey your self-worth will begin to rise up and over time you will feel a thousand times better about yourself. And that is worth more than a thousand dollars, right! Exactly what type of price tag would you put on increased peace of mind and feeling better about yourself? Maybe a million dollars?

Truth: *"I have the power to control and change my internal thoughts and feelings about myself".*

The development of our self-talk began in our earlier years. What we were told and how we were treated helped to imprint who we are. Those childhood years were critical in helping us determine our value in the world. If someone told us or showed us we weren't worth much, we began to believe them. What was said and done to us stayed with us. It is embedded in us. In turn, what was not done is also imprinted on us. When and if we needed love, support, and a sense of safety, and those were withheld or nonexistent, that also helped shape us. We would think if we were loved most of the time then we should *mostly* be ok. In reality, therapists say it takes about a thousand "attaboys" to counter one negative and significant experience said or done to a child. In other words, one negative experience can outweigh a thousand great experiences. By far, the worst thing you can impress upon a child is "I don't love you," "you are a mistake," "you are stupid," "you are unsafe," or "you are not valued". These comments and impressions, expressed in various ways, damage a child's core self-esteem.

A parent or loved one who withholds affection, remains distant, is absent from the home, is neglectful, misuses drugs or alcohol, or is otherwise emotionally distant or unavailable communicates to a child they are not esteemed or valued.

Our little minds and hearts received those messages said and shown, or not said or shown, and those messages helped to develop our core self-esteem. Core self-esteem is the sum of our self-worth, self-value, and self-evaluation. It is what we feel and believe about ourselves and our value in the world. If the message we received is our loved ones didn't care much for us, we took those messages to heart, and those messages became our messages to ourselves about ourselves.

Today you may have areas where you feel good about yourself or have high self-esteem because you believe you are good at some things. Perhaps you think the way you dress is a great look for you, or you have certain skills and talents you are proud of. Maybe you know you are smart, kind, and generous. You take pride in these qualities and skills. However, when your core self-esteem has been damaged you can believe you are good at some things and still have a damaged core self-esteem. If you have a damaged core self-esteem, you will need to consciously and consistently be aware of how and what you say to yourself and how you treat yourself. Just like someone with diabetes has to watch what they eat and check their blood sugar to make sure they are healthy, you may always have to watch what you say to yourself and periodically check in to make sure you are healthy inside.

If you believe what you think about yourself isn't really influencing your feelings and actions, just listen to your self-talk. Listen intently. Some of us have largely tuned it out over the years and can barely hear our thoughts about ourselves anymore. Turn up the volume on it. If it is positive, make note of those areas where you have positive self-talk. Positive self-talk results in improved well-being; increased self-esteem, appreciation, hopefulness, confidence, pride, optimism, joy, recognition of strengths, and pleasure; and decreased anger, sadness, nervousness, and guilt. If it is negative, think about it. Negative self-talk can result in low self-worth, feelings of inadequacy, worry, stress, jealousy, and anger to name a few.

But even deeper than your self-talk, there are core beliefs you carry around with you. While you can sometimes hear your negative self-talk, you don't necessarily hear your core beliefs because they are buried deep inside. There are numerous core beliefs, some positive and some negative. An example of some negative core beliefs might be "I'm no good," "I'm worthless," "I'm ugly," "I'm ashamed," "my life is meaningless," "I'm used goods, no one of value will want me," "I'm bad," "I'm a failure," "I'm unlovable," and so on. These core beliefs are where those constant, yet quiet, messages you receive all day are coming from. When you have negative core beliefs, they can lead you to engage in self-destructive patterns of behavior and can keep you away from positive patterns, such as working on and achieving your goals and fulfilling your dreams. As the name implies, core beliefs are at the core of what you believe about yourself. You weren't born with core beliefs. Someone conveyed them to you, and you adopted them, took them straight to your heart, and believed them. Negative self-talk comes from core beliefs. They work together to make you believe they are true. These are lies. They are the lies that bind you and keep you from the freedom you so desperately deserve.

The Survivor's Journey way is to get to the core of these lies and change them. You would think all we have to do is change our negative self-talk and that would eventually begin to change our core beliefs. That might eventually work, except what we call "schemas" are also happening in our lives. The word "schemas" sounds a little confusing, but follow us and it will all make sense soon.

Schemas are the way we see the world and how we interpret what is happening to us and around us. They are our worldview or our perspective about our experiences and interactions with the world. Schemas are kind of like sunglasses we put on. When we put these sunglasses on, the world looks a little different to us. We see our experiences through the sunglasses we wear. As we wear the sunglasses, we can even start to explain our negative experiences in a certain way as to assign them to a particular schema we have. Our schema (or the way we see the world and describe our experiences) continues to fuel our core beliefs. For instance, if we saw ripe bananas hanging from a tree, but were wearing blue tinted sunglasses, we would say the ripe yellow bananas are green. It is the truth from our perspective. But if we were to take the blue sunglasses (schemas) off, we would see the bananas are indeed yellow. The blue sunglasses (schemas) are the lies. They are simply lies, and when we learn to take the glasses off, we see the truth.

What happened in your life is that you received and understood the lies you were told and adopted them. Then you looked around for people and experiences in your life who would continue to reaffirm the lies over the years so you could continue to believe them.

Below are 18 schemas (sunglasses), or beliefs, about ourselves which we may have taken to heart. You might see yourself in one or many of them. What we want you to do is identify your top one to three schemas from the 18 schemas below which you think best represent you.

1. *Emotional Deprivation:* The belief and expectation your primary needs will never be met. The sense no one will nurture, care for, guide, protect or empathize with you.
2. *Abandonment:* The belief and expectation others will leave, others are unreliable, relationships are fragile, loss is inevitable, and you will ultimately wind up alone.
3. *Mistrust/Abuse:* The belief others are abusive, manipulative, selfish, or looking to hurt or use you. Others are not to be trusted.
4. *Defectiveness:* The belief you are flawed, damaged or unlovable, and you will thereby be rejected.
5. *Social Isolation:* The pervasive sense of aloneness, coupled with a feeling of alienation.
6. *Vulnerability:* The sense that the world is a dangerous place, disaster can happen at any time, and you will be overwhelmed by the challenges that lie ahead.
7. *Dependence/Incompetence:* The belief you are unable to effectively make your own decisions, your judgment is questionable, and you need to rely on others to help get you through day-to-day responsibilities.
8. *Enmeshment/Undeveloped Self:* The sense you do not have an identity or "individuated self" separate from one or more significant others.
9. *Failure:* The expectation you will fail, or belief that you cannot perform well enough.
10. *Subjugation:* The belief you must submit to the control of others, or else punishment or rejection will be forthcoming.
11. *Self-Sacrifice:* The belief you should voluntarily give up your own needs for the sake of others, usually to a point which is excessive.
12. *Approval-Seeking/Recognition-Seeking:* The sense of approval, attention, and recognition are far more important than genuine self-expression and being true to oneself.
13. *Emotional Inhibition:* The belief you must control your self-expression or others will reject or criticize you.

14. *Negativity/Pessimism:* The pervasive belief that the negative aspects of life outweigh the positive, along with negative expectations for the future.

15. *Unrelenting Standards:* The belief you need to be the best, always striving for perfection or to avoid mistakes.

16. *Punitiveness:* ld be harshly punished for their mistakes or shortcomings.

17. *Entitlement/Grandiosity:* The sense that you are special or more important than others, and you do not have to follow the rules like other people even though it may have a negative effect on others. Also, can manifest in an exaggerated focus on superiority for the purpose of having power or control.

18. *Insufficient Self-Control/Self-Discipline:* The sense you cannot accomplish your goals, especially if the process contains boring, repetitive, or frustrating aspects. Also, you cannot resist acting upon impulses which lead to detrimental results.

Bricker, D.C., Young, J.E., (1993). "A Client's Guide to Schema-Focused Cognitive Therapy. Cognitive Therapy Center of New York.

To put this all into practice, let us give you an example of how negative self-talk comes from negative core beliefs maintained by our schemas (sunglasses).

Let's say when you were younger you were told or shown you were unlovable. You adopted this as your core belief. Your negative self-talk then might include saying things to yourself like "I am ugly," "I am too fat," "I am not smart enough," "I'm not funny enough," "I'm stupid," etc. You adopt a "Failure" schema, believing *you will fail, or you cannot perform well enough.* Each time you try something and fail, you say to yourself "See I failed, because I am a failure. I should stop trying."

With a "Failure" schema, everything you try, you see failure because you are wearing the "failure" sunglasses which enable you to see failure. You assign your attempts and tries as you being a failure. You believe there is something unique about you making you fail at everything while other people succeed. You would be correct, there is something unique about you. You are wearing your schema glasses causing you to see everything you do as a failure. If you were to take your schema glasses off, you would find many people fail the first and second time and even many more times before they succeed at something. For instance, four out of ten people fail their driver's test the first time. Because they failed a test, they didn't define themselves as failures. Failing at something and adopting the belief you are a failure are two different things. It's ok to fail, and in some cases it's good practice because in failing you learn how to perform better in your next try. Many successful business owners failed over and over and kept trying until they succeeded. Major athletes come up short many, many times before they succeed. Most successful people succeed because they change their self-talk to get over the self-doubt.

Let's use the same example, but with someone adopting a different schema.

When you were younger you may have been told or shown you were unlovable. You adopted this as your core belief. Your negative self-talk might include saying things to yourself like "I am ugly," "I am too fat," "I am not smart enough," "I'm not funny enough," "I'm stupid," etc. Instead of adopting a "Failure" schema you adopt a "Dependence/Incompetence" schema, believing you are *unable to effectively make your own decisions, your judgment is questionable, and you need to rely on others to help get you through your day-to-day responsibilities.* Your self-talk is then about not being able to make decisions, being incompetent, and making the wrong choices. Because you believe you are incompetent, you subconsciously look for intimate partners who make all the decisions and control your behavior, your thoughts, and your feelings. As you begin to change your self-talk, your core beliefs, and your schemas, you will start to feel more competent and will be less interested in being controlled. You'll begin to believe you deserve the freedom to think, feel, and be exactly who you want to be.

Here is another example:

If you had a learning disability and you didn't do well in school, you may have received messages from your teachers and others that you are not as smart as you should be. Perhaps you tried and tried and tried, and without the help you needed you felt frustrated and unsuccessful. In turn, you might have told yourself you were incompetent, stupid, and can't make a decision because you are always wrong. You might further believe no one would truly love such an incompetent and stupid person. You may then adopt a "Dependence/Incompetence" schema. Because of this schema, you might look for partners who have to take care of you. You are not comfortable making decisions, surviving on your own, and standing in your own right. Because you feel incompetent, you go along with relationships where others are in control. Because you are not healthy, you tend to connect with unhealthy people. These relationships may be abusive or controlling. What you need to know is if you want a healthy and loving relationship, you need to learn to stand in your own right, make decisions, and be more confident in yourself. If you do, then you will have loving and healthy relationships with your friends and/or a potential life partner.

Often people who have negative core beliefs and negative schemas can be vulnerable to abuse, violence, and the control of others over them. True freedom lies in what we tell ourselves because what we tell ourselves is what we think of ourselves. If we change the way we think of ourselves, we will change the way we feel about ourselves. And if we change the way we feel about ourselves, we will experience improved self-worth and will be able to begin to live the lives we want, which is increased happiness and improved internal peace within ourselves. This poem describes our 4th Journey struggle:

> *"If you always <u>think</u> what you've always <u>thought</u>*
> *Then you will always <u>feel</u> what you've always <u>felt</u>.*
> *If you always <u>feel</u> what you've always <u>felt</u>*
> *Then you will always <u>do</u> what you've always <u>done</u>.*
> *If you always <u>do</u> what you've always <u>done</u>*

Then you will always <u>get</u> what you've always <u>gotten</u>.
If you always <u>get</u> what you've always <u>gotten</u>
Then you will always <u>think</u> what you've always <u>thought</u>."
~ Author Unknown

Tools: Internal Safety

"Change is not a bolt of lightning that arrives with a zap. It's a bridge built brick by brick, every day with sweat and humility and slips. It's hard work but it can be thrilling to watch it take shape." ~ Sarah Hepola

Once you've identified one to three schemas you would like to work on, read more about them. We recommend the book *Reinventing Your Life* by Jeffrey Young and Janet Klosko. Learn more about your schemas. Watch YouTube videos about them. Attend webinars and become as educated as possible about YOU. Work on the exercises in your workbook. There you will find tools and suggestions for engaging in a deeper dive to change your self-talk, core beliefs, and address your schemas. Be careful not to choose more than three to work on because you will become overwhelmed and the self-talk work you will do for the 4th Journey will become diluted and lose its meaning.

We have to practice thinking about and remembering our good qualities. These are our strengths. Many of us are good, kind, helpful, understanding, and loving. In fact, it was some of our good qualities that others tried to manipulate and use to abuse and exploit us. But now that we are stronger, we can once again call forth all our positive qualities, because these are a source of strength for us. When we realize these truths, it becomes easier to take off our sunglasses (schemas) and put on our prescription glasses allowing us to see the world and our experiences in clearer and healthier ways. We will find out we have been using our positive qualities and strengths all along to survive. Now we need to use them to thrive.

The life you want is entirely possible. We first go about helping ourselves by not working against ourselves. We do this by improving our self-talk. Next, we work to identify and own our true value. The 4th Journey is where we first begin to outline a path toward the lives we want. We have lots of work to do to get there, but with your hard work, the support of your Bomb Squad, and your fellow Journey members, you can get there. If you doubt it, re-read the Survivor's Journey Chain Reaction, which are your promises.

Remember, throughout your life you will need to be aware of your self-talk, recognize your negative self-talk, and change it to positive self-talk. When you are not believing your own self-talk, go deeper to work on your core beliefs.

Your book and workbook, supported by the Survivor's Journey group meetings, will help you identify your schema, your core beliefs, and your negative self-talk, and will help you change those to healthier, life fulfilling ones. However, the absence of negative schemas, beliefs, and self-talk is not enough; we must work to insert positive, healthier beliefs and self-talk. In doing that, we are continuing on the path to loving ourselves in the way we should.

Transformation: *"My inner voice loves, embraces, and supports me".*

Negative self-talk, negative core beliefs, and negative schemas can be chronic and life altering when they are not properly addressed. But when they are recognized and addressed, you can live a long, happy, and healthy life. Remember the diabetes example? Having diabetes requires you to eat well, exercise, and pay attention to the signs your blood sugar is not at a healthy level. Not doing these things will alter the quality of your life. Identifying and changing any negative self-talk, core beliefs, and schemas you might have means you will always be on the lookout, swapping out negative self-talk for more positive self-talk, and chipping away at negative core beliefs. You'll recognize the negative schema at play, and you'll address it right away. You'll regulate your thoughts just like someone regulates their blood sugar. In doing so, you'll live a healthy, more satisfying life.

To be successful, we must reach an internal agreement between our feelings, thoughts, and behaviors. They have to get behind us and support us. We have to address our schemas each and every time they pop up to sabotage the work we put in. In the 4th Journey, and throughout our lives, we have to have self-compassion, be kind, loving, and patient with ourselves. Think about it, if you were friends with yourself, would you like someone who talked to you the way that you talk to yourself?

A house divided cannot stand. We have to be our own ally. Even if no one in the world loves us at this moment, we have to love ourselves enough so we are willing to fight for ourselves and fight for the lives we want to live. We can't move forward through the Journeys if we are against our own selves. Our internal self must be in agreement that we will love ourselves and in doing so, we will fight for our peace, happiness, and the achievement of our dreams.

Read these life transformation stories below:

Story: Keisha's core belief was that no one wanted her because she was no good. This core belief developed when she was a child and was in foster care. Keisha believed her mother, who was on drugs at the time, didn't love her enough and chose drugs over her. Deep down Keisha felt worthless and unlovable. Keisha's outer appearance always looked good with her hair and nails always done right. She cleaned her house and always had a nice-looking boyfriend. Both loved to wear designer clothes when they could afford it. But if Keisha didn't work and give her man the money or buy him the things he needed to look good, he was violent. Keisha learned through the journey groups that her schema was "self-sacrifice," or the belief she should voluntarily give up her own needs for the sake of others. Keisha gave and gave and gave. With support, Keisha learned she didn't need to sacrifice everything in order to be loved, wanted, and happy. She consistently worked on changing her self-talk and her core beliefs, and she consistently challenged herself to take her schema glasses off and to see the real world and her life in it.

Story: James was 12 years old when he was sexually abused and asked by his uncle to keep the secret. From that day on, James felt scared and anxious. He was no longer as happy and carefree as he used to be. He didn't trust anyone. He had a hard time sleeping comfortably. He couldn't focus on his schoolwork as well as he used to. He couldn't really describe all the feelings he had at the time, but he was depressed a lot of the time. He didn't make friends like he did before. He never told anybody. He grew up to vacillate between anger and depression. He kept to himself most of the time and rarely dated. He adopted a schema of defectiveness believing he was flawed, damaged and unlovable, and would thereby be rejected by anyone he might be interested in.

Story: Lori was always told her purpose in life was to find a man to take care of her. Going to college wasn't as important. The reason to go to college was to find a man with a college degree so he would take care of her. The reason to dress up, put on make-up, attend parties, and go to events was to find a man. In fact, the reason for everything Lori did and her mom did for her was so she could find a man and be taken care of for life. She tried to be happy with just the beautiful things she received from men, but deep down she was unhappy. The messages Lori received was she wasn't good enough, smart enough, determined enough, or goal oriented enough to do it herself. Lori developed a schema of approval seeking. She needed the attention of men. Without it, she felt depressed. Her core belief was she was nothing and her existence was meaningless if she didn't have a man who chased after her. Her self-talk was she was only beautiful when someone else thought she was beautiful. She was only smart when a man acknowledged she was smart. She was only as popular as the men who desired her. But because Lori didn't much love herself, she always found men who were unavailable because they were married, they were tricks, they were addicted to drugs, or they were sugar daddies. Lori worked to identify her schema, challenged her core beliefs, and changed her self-talk so she could learn to love herself. Once she learned to genuinely love herself, she found someone who also genuinely loved her.

Story: Kyle knew he was different from a young age. His parents believed it was an abomination that he was gay. Kyle began to feel shame about who he was. For a while, he acted as if he liked girls, but secretly he had a crush on his best friend, Jim. After numerous fights with his family, Kyle ran away from home. He hung out around a gay bar and would go home with various men. At age 15 Kyle started trading sex with adult men who took care of him. For years Kyle wasn't happy. His core beliefs and self-talk were negative. To numb these, Kyle started using drugs. Kyle's schema became "Punitiveness" or the belief people should be harshly punished for their mistakes or shortcomings. Kyle was punishing himself for being gay by drinking and using drugs, by having sex with anyone in exchange for a place to stay, and not caring enough about himself or his health. Once Kyle learned about his schema and learned about his core beliefs and negative self-talk, he worked on learning to identify those instances when his thinking, feeling, or behaving were out-of-line with who he is becoming, which is a gay man who loves himself.

There are some committed Survivor's Journey members who will try and try and try to successfully take the 4th Journey, but will continue to have overwhelming negative self-talk and core beliefs. Your therapist may assess you and recommend a particular therapy or medication. Be open to learning more about any mental health diagnosis you receive. Research it. Read about it. Find out if this diagnosis seems accurate to you. If not, ask if a second opinion is possible. If it seems accurate, listen to the recommendations and plan for improved mental health. Medication may be helpful in that it may provide enough support for you to do the work, but medication is not a cure. You will still have to do the work. In working through the Survivor's Journeys, see your therapist regularly.

Where do you start to tackle the 4th Journey? The best way to take-on the 4th Journey is to work through your workbook and do the suggested exercises. Come to Survivor's Journey group meetings as often as you can. Make it a priority. The book, workbook, and group meetings will help you process through your core beliefs and change your thoughts, feelings, and behaviors. Feel free to go beyond what's provided in the workbook and seek out ways you believe will help you think more highly of yourself, feel better about yourself, and help you get involved in positive self-esteem building activities. Also process this Journey with your therapist.

Mind-Fields: Catering and Clashing

If you don't focus on and change your self-talk, you will cater to it and feed into it. Negative self-talk is like a toxin invading your body. It is a cancer. The more you allow this cancer to fester in your body, the more you poison your thoughts. Your thoughts become your feelings. Once your thoughts and feelings are negative, your behavior will fall in line with your thoughts and feelings. Negative thoughts and feelings kill your dreams, your hopes, and your motivation. You will not pursue the life you really want because you believe you don't deserve that life. You will spend your time continuing to wear your schema glasses seeing and interacting with the world as if your schema were reality. Without work, you will continue to self-sabotage so the world lives up to the expectations associated with your schema. You will continue to clash with reality, self-sabotaging your life so it lives up to the schema you believe. Without working through this Journey, you will continue to carry negative messages in your thoughts, feelings, and behaviors that are self-destructive.

5

5th Journey: *The survivor recognizes and minimizes external threats and increases external safety.*

5th Truth: *I know having unhealthy boundaries increases my vulnerability and decreases my safety.*

5th Transformation: *I maintain emotional and physical boundaries and am safer.*

Trigger or Validation:

Remember for some, the material in this Journey may be triggering. If it triggers you, reach out to your support system including those you trust and appropriate members of your Bomb Squad and/or engage in some self-care activities. For others, this information will be validating. In those cases, use the material to help validate you and affirm what you are or have been experiencing is real.

CHAPTER 5: EXTERNAL SAFETY

"We are the average of the five people we spend the most time with."
~ Jim Rohn

Ｎone of the abuse, assault, or victimization you suffered is your fault. That's an important statement because it's true. Survivors of abuse, exploitation, and violence need to know that. Someone mistook your kindness for weakness. They capitalized upon your vulnerabilities and used them against you.

Vulnerabilities are areas in which you are open to physical or emotional harm. Vulnerabilities aren't all bad. They are just another word for "needs." A child needs to be loved and cared for appropriately. When they are loved and cared for, their needs are met. As long as their needs are met, they are no longer vulnerable. Adults also have needs. Being in healthy relationships or friendships with loved ones allows you to meet your need to belong and be loved. Loved ones who can be vulnerable with each other have the love and trust we all want in a family member, friend, or intimate partner. However, when your vulnerabilities are exposed to people who are out to do you harm, you are defenseless and susceptible to being abused by them. Being vulnerable should be a choice you make with someone you trust.

The 5th Journey focuses on your need to minimize or eliminate threats to your safety. You do this by establishing and maintaining strong and healthy boundaries, and learning to control and self-regulate your emotions. Your transformation comes when you are able to stand in your truth and exercise control over who is in your life, how they are in your life, and how they behave toward you while being allowed to be in your life. In turn, this journey is also about controlling how to react and not react to others in your life. Let us first discuss boundaries.

Truth: *"I know having unhealthy boundaries increases my vulnerability and decreases my safety."*

What are boundaries? A boundary is a physical or emotional limit, rule, space, line, or guideline you establish where someone does not cross. It is a physical line or an emotional line where they end and you begin, or where you end, and they begin. Boundaries can be strict, loose, in between, or non-existent. When your boundaries are too loose or non-existent, you feel run-over, put upon, and not in control of your own feelings, thoughts, and behavior. It's like leaving your house unlocked allowing anyone to come at any time to do whatever they want. When you have loose or no boundaries, you sit in anger and resentment because people ask too much of you and you oblige them by doing or giving more than you're comfortable doing or giving. Instead of standing up for yourself, you go along. Instead of having healthy boundaries and saying "no," you do it, give it over, or keep doing it. This is unhealthy and dysfunctional and keeps other people confused as to who you really are -and- what you will and will not put up with. Sometimes having loose boundaries is a way for us to attract attention to ourselves. Think about it. If no one knows where your boundaries are, you can't stay offended when they keep crossing them.

In some cases, our boundaries have been so over-run we aren't sure where our boundary lines are or how to establish or reestablish them. Establishing or reestablishing healthy boundaries may be different, depending on the what, where, and with whom. For example, boundaries at work with a boss may look very different than boundaries established with children, with friends or with intimate relationships.

When you're not sure how to reestablish healthy boundaries, think of someone whom you look up to or whom you think is a fairly healthy person. Consider placing them in your shoes to determine what you think they would do. Would the treatment you experience be alright with them? If it would not, then that might be a place to focus on creating a boundary. For instance, would it be alright during a disagreement for this person to be called derogatory names by their intimate partner? Would it be alright to be embarrassed or disrespected in front of others? Would it be alright for a friend to slap them? Steal from them? Not be somewhere when they said they would? Identify with them. If it would not be alright with them, then that might be a place to establish your boundary line.

When your boundaries are too strict, you block everyone or anyone from gaining access to the real you. You store yourself away and no one can get to you or know the real you. You are isolated and often locked in your own private hell. You experience a stressful bind. You desperately want someone to know the real you and simultaneously block them from getting close to the real you.

When you have good healthy boundaries, you are happier, you have better emotional and mental health, and you have more autonomy and independence. You can engage in better self-care. Indeed, boundaries are critical to happiness and to living the life you want. Establishing boundaries means you are teaching people how to treat you.

In order to establish boundaries, you must:

1. Tap into your feelings and identify where and when uncomfortable boundaries are being crossed.
2. Identify the boundary you desire. Communicate your desires by saying what you need. Some good examples might be, "please don't read my Survivor's Journey Workbook because that is private," or "when we are with our friends, please don't talk about... because I would like that to stay between us," or "would you please back up, you are invading my space," or "No, don't touch me like that. I don't like it."

When establishing boundaries, describe what you want politely and calmly. It's not required, but if you feel the need to explain, keep your explanation simple. Don't overcomplicate it, don't over explain, and don't bring an over-abundance of emotional energy to it. Simply explain. Say why it's important to you and set consequences if your boundaries aren't respected. The most important thing is to say what you mean and mean what you say. If you establish a consequence, follow through on it. The consequence doesn't have to be life changing, but should be relative to the boundary violation. For instance, if you agreed to pick someone up after work each day, but they frequently stay inside talking to friends and they regularly get into your car 15 minutes later, they are wasting your time. They have committed larceny by stealing your time. Communicate your boundary very simply so they understand. You may decide the first time you do not need to impose any consequences because you have communicated your boundary and they have agreed to accommodate your boundary. The next time they violate your boundary you may kindly let them know the consequences for violating your boundary. You may say something like, "I know you may have had something going on which made you late, but if you are not in my car by 5:05 I will leave," or if it's possible you may decide to begin picking them up at 5:15 pm every day so they have time to chat after work. Whatever the resolution may be, the resolution won't be to waste your time. However, it would be an overreach the first time they violate this boundary to say you will never pick them up again in life. In other words, the consequence should be relative to the violation.

When you establish and maintain healthy boundaries you are practicing good self-care. When someone violates your boundaries, it may cause you stress, emotional pain, depression, or anxiety, among other negative consequences. On the other hand, when you maintain good boundaries, life becomes more predictable. You feel safer, happier, and emotionally healthier.

Physical Safety

Physical safety is critical to your recovery and in fact, is the cornerstone of your recovery. If you aren't physically safe, you can't move forward in your recovery because most of your emotional energy, spiritual energy, and daily motivation will focus on ways to be safe.

A theorist named Abraham Maslow developed a pyramid called, "Maslow's Hierarchy of Needs." In essence, Maslow said when you are attempting to grow as a person you have certain needs. Your first need is fundamental. You will work to first meet your physical needs such as food, water, shelter, and warmth. If you don't have those needs met, you will only be motivated to work on achieving those very basic needs. Once you have those, you will be motivated to search and secure your need for safety. Once safety is achieved you move on to meet your need to belong and be loved. You will then serve your need to achieve and have self-esteem. Finally, you'll work at your full potential and become "self-actualized," which is your ability to creatively express yourself and achieve your full potential.

Maslow's Hierarchy of Needs:

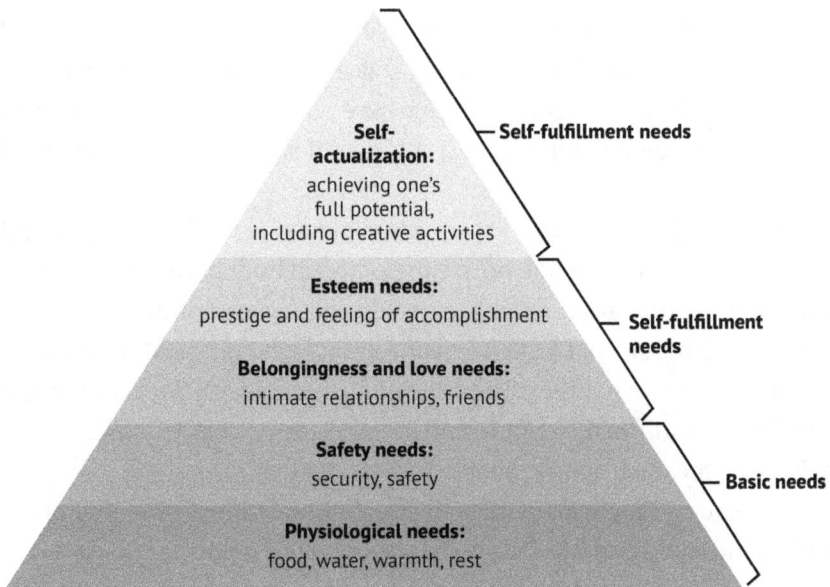

Self-fulfillment needs

Self-
actualization:
achieving one's
full potential,
including creative activities

Esteem needs:
prestige and feeling of accomplishment

Self-fulfillment needs

Belongingness and love needs:
intimate relationships, friends

Safety needs:
security, safety

Basic needs

Physiological needs:
food, water, warmth, rest

Simply Psychology

Without physical safety, you will not feel emotionally, socially, or internally safe, thus your first priority is your physical safety. Look around at where you live and who you spend your time with. Is your physical environment safe? Are the people you hang around safe? If they are not, then your first priority is to move yourself to a physically safe space to live and to begin to distance yourself from people who are not physically safe for you. This may sound drastic and harsh, but this is a high priority for you. If the place you live is not physically safe, make plans and leave for a safer place. Move to a temporary shelter, transitional housing, battered women's shelter, with a friend, or back with your family; do whatever you can to establish housing in a safe place. Every moment you spend feeling unsafe is a moment you risk your life, your sanity, and your recovery. If you're not physically safe right now, work on that FIRST. Get with your Bomb Squad, preferably your case manager, to help you create a solid safety plan to obtain safe and affordable housing.

In essence, your home should be warm, loving, and welcoming to you. This is a space where you should be able to be kind to yourself and where others are kind to you. It is a space where you can relax and be your full 100% self. This is a space where you can close your eyes and sleep without being afraid. This is a peaceful space totally accepting of you.

Establishing physical safety also means establishing physical boundaries. No one should violate the physical boundaries you have es-tablished. No one has the right to invade your space or touch you with-out your permission - EVER. In maintaining good physical boundaries, you communicate to others in both verbal and nonverbal ways *what* and *how* they are allowed to approach you and touch you. In other words, being safe means teaching people how to treat you.

If you don't have many people in your life who have healthy phys-ical boundaries, find physically safe people and begin to slowly bring them into your life, while at the same time working to slowly distance the others. Take this bit of advice to heart. These toxic, boundary-less people will have to learn to live without you in their life. They were in-appropriate and sick when you found them, and they may be that way when you leave them. And we know, some of these boundary violating people are in your family. That's ok. You can also learn to slowly distance yourself from toxic family members. We have the power to choose who we consider family. Those we call family members are loving, caring, and supportive people. Some of the family members you've been dealing with may not match that definition. If they aren't loving, caring, and supportive, distance them. From this point forward, you get to choose who your real family members are and are not. Family is who you determine them to be. Those who are not loving, caring, and supportive are just people you've previously had the unfortunate opportunity to spend time with, marry into, or share DNA with.

Emotional safety

"If they are serving disrespect for dinner, leave the table." ~ Unknown

Having emotional safety means you feel safe communicating your thoughts and feelings in an authentic way. It means you feel emotionally safe around those you spend time with. They don't force you to talk about what you're not ready to talk about and they don't push you to do something you're not ready to do. When you are vulnerable with them, they are good listeners for you, and they take good care of your heart and your feelings.

Someone who is emotionally safe will be transparent with you. They will give you the benefit of the doubt. They will show you they can be trusted because they are responsible and accountable, not so you can control them, it's so they can help you feel emotionally safe. They know how to practice empathy and have been empathetic with you.

In turn, being an emotionally safe person means you also demonstrate the above. You allow others to communicate their thoughts and feelings in an authentic way with you. You don't force the people around you to talk about what they are not ready to talk about and you don't push them to do something they are not ready to do. You are a good listener for the people you care about. You are transparent with those you trust. You give your friends and your partner the benefit of the doubt because you have good reason to trust them. You, in turn, are trustworthy. You say what you mean and mean what you say. You are empathetic and show it.

People who are not emotionally healthy are not emotionally safe for you. They will place demands on you. You will not feel emotionally safe around them. You will act in a way that is emotionally guarded and will even be a little more tense around them. This emotionally unsafe person may ridicule you, make fun of you, and not be sensitive to your feelings.

Sometimes you can be confused because some people in your life will never be physically violent with you but will act in emotionally violent ways toward you. Emotional violence is just as destructive and damaging as physical violence. The emotional violence they inflict on you is harmful. It cuts like a knife. Do not dismiss the harmful effects of emotional violence on you and on your self-worth.

To determine whether you have the proper emotional boundaries in place, once again picture the person you respect who has good boundaries. Instead of yourself, pretend they just heard a degrading comment made by someone who claims to care about them. What would they do if they heard such a comment? What would they do if someone attempted to make them feel bad about themselves? How long would they continue to stay and take that type of abuse and be subject to that type of violence inflicted upon them? Just because someone isn't punching you in the face, doesn't mean their words and thoughts don't hurt and do damage. They certainly do.

Other emotional boundary violations include making unreasonable demands of your time, undermining your thoughts or feelings, making you feel unworthy, encouraging you to give up on your dreams, using your past to hold you down, and ridiculing or disrespecting you, among others.

Addiction and Safety

It is important to mention that addiction often erodes safety. Someone in active addiction is vulnerable. They may have convinced themselves they are safe when they are not. Some may even know they are not safe but remain in active addiction and continue to choose their addiction over their safety. They dismiss their need for safety to focus whole-heartedly on their drug of choice. This is indeed very dangerous. Their judgement is clouded by their addiction. Some of us who are not in active addiction have invested our time and our heart into someone else in active addiction. We dismiss their manipulative behavior and excuse their volatility having convinced ourselves that we are safe with them. This is also a dangerous gamble. We are never safe with someone who would choose their addiction over us and our safety.

Tools: Increasing External Safety

"We teach people how to treat us." ~ Phil McGraw

Safety is your number one priority. People who are emotionally healthy feel safe. That's why the 5th journey is about safety. *You should always feel safe.* Safety is when you take it upon yourself to ensure any hazards or conditions which may be harmful to your physical, psychological, emotional, or mental health are controlled, reduced, or eliminated. It's your responsibility to keep yourself free from harm or danger. That means you learn to see potential danger, unsafe people, and risky situations and avoid or otherwise handle them.

No doubt you have already become a master at attempting to keep yourself safe in unsafe situations. You could likely teach a course on how to navigate dangerous environments and survive. Your survival skills have been put to the test and you succeeded.

Sometimes we don't take time to reflect how much we have survived to be here today. If there were a badge for bravery, you would have been honored with it. If there were a medal for sacrifice, it would be pinned to your vest. If they gave out the highest honor for courage under fire, you would have been awarded. You've been through a lot. Never forget the sacrifices you made, the battles you've survived, and the sheer courage it took to get here. That alone is to be celebrated. So, whenever you start to doubt what you can do, just reflect on what you've been through already and you will remember how brave and strong you really are.

When you experienced fear or a threat you likely chose the flight, fight, freeze, or fawn response. We discussed this in the 2nd Journey. If you remember, when someone experiences intense fear, their response might be to take flight or run away. Sometimes this is the best idea. For example, if there is a large threat to you, it may be better to flee the scene and get away to live another day. Sometimes we choose to stand our ground and fight. Sometimes we freeze and are not able to do anything. Some people use the fawn response where they try to please the person who is a threat to them. Most often people have a dominant response which they use across many situations. For instance, the "freeze" response may be someone's dominant response. They become so overwhelmed with fear they can't or don't respond. The abuser, exploiter, or perpetrator has complete control, and the victim complies. What has been your dominant response to fearful situations?

Now we are going to add some skills and replace some dysfunctional responses with a healthier process. Whenever you are confronted with a fearful or scary situation, there are some biological responses which should occur first. Remember to breathe and try to keep your brain from going numb. Grab something small and squeeze it with your hand over and over or just open and close your hands over and over. Research says this technique may keep your brain alert and focused. Then go through the SAFER Process.

The SAFER Process is an acronym. Human beings use the SAFER Process all the time when they are under threat. For some, it's as automatic as blinking your eyes. For others, particularly those who have been traumatized, their response may be either overexaggerated or non-existent.

Those who often miss the signs of an imminent risk or threat can learn the SAFER Process to re-learn how to recognize risky situations and people. The SAFER Process takes place internally. The first step is to see the situation or person as potentially risky. Typically, when someone has been abused in the past and was denied the power to keep themselves safe, they learned that tapping into their instincts hasn't resulted in increased safety. Over time they began to numb out and no longer listened to the instincts which told them trouble was nearby. It's important for some who have been victimized in the past to tap back into their instincts and relearn to listen to what their gut tells them. Tuning up your gut instincts and paying attention to your feelings of uncomfortableness is the goal. You will need to turn-up that little voice inside telling you danger could be close. This takes time. Slowing the process down and relearning it is important to recovery. Below is the SAFER Process that may be used to recognize and respond to a threat.

S - *See the potentially risky situation or risky person.*

Instead of dismissing any uncomfortable feelings related to where you are, who you're with, or where you're going, tap into your instincts. If something doesn't feel right to you, turn-up your inner voice. Trust your instincts. Widen your lens and look at the situation, taking all actions of others and the physical space into consideration. Is this a risky situation and/or is there a risky person with a motive that isn't clear?

A - *Ask yourself, "What is going on here and how risky is it?" Assess (think about) the situation or person involved.*

With what you see, think about the situation, the people involved, and how that makes you feel. What are they doing? What are they talking about? Where are they? What is their body language saying? What is the risk? Are you uncomfortable? Do you feel like you don't want to be in this situation? Pay attention to your instincts. Who else is around who may be positive and helpful? Who else is around who may be negative and hurtful?

F - *Focus and find the best solution.*

What are the possible solutions or ways you could get away from this person or out of this situation as safely as possible? Focus and find the best solution.

E - *Empower*

Empower yourself to act. Based on your possible solutions, which one is the best solution? Could you walk away? Involve someone else? Scream? Run? Talk your way out of it? Make an excuse to leave? Confront the situation? Make a judgement call. Be ready to put it into action.

R - *Respond based on your assessment and solution.*
Your response should be one which offers the best chance for you to be safe.

Sometimes when a survivor has experienced trauma-inducing violence, instead of numbing their ability to see future risk, they become hypervigilant. Hypervigilance is an elevated state of consistently assessing for a potential threat, even where there are none. Hypervigilance can negatively affect one's quality of life because it becomes difficult to relax when you are constantly anxious and looking for a potential threat.

If you are experiencing hypervigilance, consider stopping and breathing deeply to ground yourself. Look for objective evidence which supports your fear or anxiety. If there is evidence, follow the SAFER Process. If there isn't evidence, pause and acknowledge the fear and anxiety you are feeling, but don't give into it. Discuss these feelings with your therapist and ask for some coping skills and remedies to address it.

Emotional Regulation

"What happens around me I can't always control, but what happens within me, is what I control. Because I have not given that freedom to anybody, no one can make me angry; I choose anger. No one can make me happy; no one can make me unhappy. I choose sadness. These privileges I own. It's time for you to own your emotions because if somebody else can decide how you will feel at this moment, isn't that the ultimate slavery?"
@ishashivshanti

This may sound strange at first, but as you reclaim your own power, choice, and voice, we realize no one can make you mad or sad. Indeed, no one can make you feel anything. Those feelings are inside of you and only you can control your feelings.

People we call "Reality Therapists" say most people choose anger, sadness, and joy. Now there are some instances where the mind is not in control. In those instances, therapy and sometimes medications can help. However, many of us have the power to choose what we want to feel.

When you say, "he made me so mad," you have given total control over to someone else, so much so this person wields the power to make you feel something you had no intention of feeling. When someone has that type of power and control and uses it whenever they'd like, that is the definition of emotional slavery. When someone can take your day and ruin it whenever they want, then you have given over too much power and control.

Picture a person fishing. They fling back their fishing pole and throw their line into the water. They hope some dumb fish believes the worm they dangle in the water will be a great meal and takes the hook into their mouth. When that happens, they are caught up and the fisherman can then tug at them, swing them around the water, and do whatever he pleases. He is in total control. He will eventually reel-in the fish. Once he hooks the fish, it is his to do with whatever he pleases.

Think of yourself as a fish. If someone casts out their fishing line and you bite it, they can swing you all over the place. They can reel you in. They have all the control over you. Because you bit down on the hook, they can make you mad, sad, happy, jealous, or anything they want to make you feel because they have the power.

The moral of the story is to not bite the hook. What is the hook? In real life, your friends, partners, and family members know you. They know how to push your buttons. They know how to instigate a fight. In other words, they know how to cast the line and dangle the worm hoping you'll bite it. They know how to get through the emotional boundaries you have set up. If you want to be in control of your own emotions, don't bite it. Don't catch the hook. Stay in control. Instead of being swung across the pond at the will of someone else, don't take the bait.

Think about what they are trying to do. Don't just jump into it. Sit back inside yourself and consider how you would like to respond. Be strategic. Once you have thought about what they are doing, why they might be acting this way or saying what they are saying, think about how you would like to respond, then respond accordingly. Doing this puts you in the driver's seat and allows you to own and choose the emotion you would like to express.

Some examples of someone trying to hook and reel you into an argument might be: "you always...," "you never...," "I hate it when you...," or any comments that can tempt you to choose anger or sadness. Other hooks might be to try to get you to do something you don't want to do or shouldn't do. Those comments will make the activity sound so good, or nostalgic, or so fun it will be hard to resist. They may be designed to make you feel left out if you don't join, or you will gain so much and lose very little if you do join. Before taking the bait, think about it. Is what they are convincing you to do in line with your recovery? If not, realize it is the hook and bait and confidently let them know you are not interested and your life has changed. If your friendship with this person or group starts to grow distant, it is because you are on a new path, a path they are not on. You will soon meet healthier people on this path who are moving in the same direction as you are moving.

Emotional Enmeshment and Disengagement

Another component of learning to emotionally regulate our own selves is to understand and practice the appropriate amount of emotional distance and closeness to someone else. When someone is too emotionally close, to a point where it is unhealthy, we call that being enmeshed. When someone is too emotionally distant, we call that disengagement.

Enmeshment means you are too emotionally involved. When you are enmeshed, their emotions become your emotions. If they are having a bad day, you are having a bad day. If they like something, you like it. If they don't like it, you don't like it. If you were happy all day, but they come in sad, all of a   sudden you become sad. You cease to be an independent person in a relationship with a friend, child, or romantic partner and you become a clone of the other person. Enmeshment is closely related to being codependent. Instead of allowing them to feel what they feel, you become obsessed worrying about what they are feeling, thinking, and doing. You become over involved and they have little privacy or opportunities to experience consequences and personally grow.

When someone you care about is upset, it doesn't mean you need to automatically be as upset as they are. If someone you love has a bad day, it doesn't automatically mean your day has to be ruined. You can and should emotionally separate yourself enough so you can empathize with their experience, but not succumb to it. Practice being understanding, but not being swept up by their experience. That's *their* experience and not yours. Being enmeshed is like the fishing example by being hooked where someone else dictates how you feel. In the case of enmeshment, the person who is influencing your feelings may not be casting out an emotional fishing line to get you to feel a certain way. You may be doing this yourself. In being enmeshed you have given control over to someone else. Whatever they feel, you feel, anytime total power and control is given or taken, the result is going to be unhealthy for you.

Disengagement is the opposite. This is when you are not emotionally involved enough. You remain aloof and it comes off as being cold and unconcerned. You may share physical space with others, but not emotional closeness. You may say you're in a relationship, but don't have a strong emotional connection. If you have disengaged, think about it. Why have you disengaged? Address it with your therapist. Decide whether or not it's healthy for you to re-engage or not and if so, when and how? It may be not healthy for you to re-engage at this time or ever. If so, that is a decision you must make, including how you will emotionally process the loss.

Processing Your Emotions

Learning to regulate your emotions is a process. When we feel we are about to go to "10" emotionally, walk away. Process your emotions until you can get to a "4" in how much it is upsetting to you. Come back and have a conversation when you have command over your emotions and can talk about it in a reasonable tone. It helps if you sit down while talking because it will bring the temperature in the room down. Express yourself without using curse words. Look the person in the eye. Use a calm voice, but be direct and matter-of-fact. If you find yourself getting out-of-control or way too angry again, let the person know you are going to take a break from the conversation. Let them know when you might be ready to talk again. That can be in a few minutes, a few hours, to a few days. The important thing is you continue the conversation so it doesn't just stay out there unresolved in the universe.

A-B-C Technique

Another technique to help you regulate your emotions is called A-B-C, developed by Albert Ellis. It is particularly useful in helping you shift your emotional state from one in which you feel and exhibit an extreme response to one in which you feel and exhibit a reasonable emotional response. For instance, using the A-B-C technique may help you shift from being furious to being upset or from being devastatingly depressed to being moderately disappointed.

The technique is to first look at the "A" or Activating Event. The Activating Event is the event which upset you. The second component is your "B" or Belief about what happened or why it happened. The third component is the "C" or Consequences or how you responded as a result.

Therapists say it's not always the actual event that was so horrible, it's your belief about the event which makes you act out in ways that are negative and have bad consequences. For example, if a partner comes home from work with the expectation the house will be clean and a cooked dinner will be waiting, but instead comes home to a dirty house and no dinner, the partner is not happy. The unhappy partner can choose to feel rage. Rage can turn into yelling and screaming. How it is handled is largely based on the unhappy partner's "beliefs" about why there is no dinner nor a clean house. If they choose to believe their partner is a lazy person who doesn't care about doing their part in the re-lationship, then the yelling and screaming will likely commence. What if, however, the partner spent the day at their child's school because their child was in some trouble. Perhaps the partner spent the day in the emergency room. Maybe the partner was taking care of other things that needed to be done which supported or contributed to the running of the household like going to the laundromat, getting an oil change, or numerous other daily duties. Or maybe the partner laid around all day smoking weed and playing video games.

Often what happens is one partner has a "belief" about the event that happened causing the destructive consequences. Those beliefs might be "my partner is lazy," "I feel used," "my partner doesn't care about me or the relationship," or "I should get rid of them and find someone else." Thus, it's not the event itself causing destructive conse-quences, such as the yelling and screaming. It's the "belief" about it. But what if instead of jumping to conclusions, the unhappy partner chose to suspend their belief about why this happened until they communicated calmly with an open mind. It's important to discuss and understand the reason so your reaction aka the "C," "consequence," is in line with the offense. The same thing could be said about how we interact with our children. If we "believe" our children's motivation for doing something or not doing something is egregious (aka they are lazy; they are stupid; they don't care), then our reaction or consequence may be destructive, over the top, and even verging on abusive.

Before assuming you know the motivations or reasons for someone doing or not doing something, and then feeling justified in causing a fight, take time to ask questions to uncover their reasons and openly and calmly discuss what your expectations are. Compromise and come to an agreement that is clearly communicated and understood. Using the A-B-C model will help you regulate your "belief" about what is hap-pening without assuming you already know. It will help you adjust your perspective.

In the event your partner chooses to let you down over and over, or you believe they are not feeding and seeding the relationship to help it grow, then yelling and screaming about it will likely not create the change you want anyway. In doing that, it becomes a relationship of verbal abuse and dysfunction. Given what you now know about yourself and how you would like to be treated, you may consider if this is the relationship for you. Does this relationship fit how you see yourself now and who you are now? take time to deeply ponder this question.

Fair Fighting

Fair fighting is a way of confronting an issue and resolving conflict. The idea is instead of accusing, blaming, and using "you" statements, each person describes their own feelings in a calm manner. Someone may describe what is bothering them using "I" statements. Thus, instead of saying "you always," "you never," "you need to stop," instead turn it around and describe "your" feelings, "your" thoughts, or "your" behavior. Try using "I" statements e.g., "I feel frustrated...," then describe what frustrates you such as, "I feel frustrated when I come home and the dishes aren't done." Another example might be, "when I'm expected to pay whenever we go out, I feel used." Another one might be, "I don't feel appreciated when..."

In fair fighting, you are expressing what you are feeling and thinking in an honest and nonjudgmental way. You only discuss one issue at a time, and you do it calmly. This way of expressing yourself is less threatening and is honest. It may decrease defensiveness and increase opportunities to communicate problems less judgmentally and resolve them.

Physical Regulation

Acting out physically also usually stems from our beliefs about a situation. If we believe someone has hurt us, betrayed us, or is a threat to us, then we believe we have the right to "go off" and be physically destructive and abusive. There is NEVER a time when you should give yourself permission to get physical with anyone unless you are attempting to physically protect yourself or your dependents who are unable to physically protect themselves from someone.

For some, learning to physically restrain yourself may mean you need to retrain yourself. If when you are angry, sad, stressed, guilty, anxious, irritated, or feel threatened you act out physically - then this section will be helpful for you. For example, do you hit, kick, punch, or throw things? To change your behavior, you'll need to first assess yourself. Know that unless your life is at risk, you are acting in an abusive way. Right before you become violent, tune-in to what are you experiencing physically? Does your jaw tense? Do your muscles get tighter? Does your heart start racing? Does your face get flushed? Does your body or hands shake?

What are you thinking? Has your mind taken over and filled with anger or anxiety to the point where you can't think of anything else? Get in touch with these feelings and experiences. Learn your signs. At the very first sign that any feelings, thoughts, or physical reactions begin to overtake you, stop. Don't react. Count to ten and breathe deeply. It may sound silly, but this will help you regain control. Breathe in deeply, way down in your stomach, not from your throat. Breathe in for four seconds, breathe out for four seconds. Slowly regain control of your physical and emotional senses. Do this as many times as necessary. Try saying a calming word or phrase to yourself like "calm down," "relax," "take it easy," or "regain control." Walk away until you can come back to the situation or topic at hand and have a discussion about it. Practice this each and every time. Spinning out-of-control physically can be destructive. Let your therapist know what is happening. Ask that you both spend concentrated time helping you restrain yourself and approach problems in a healthier way. It is difficult to establish and maintain healthy relationships as long as you continue to violate someone else's boundaries.

The Child, Parent, and Adult Inside Us
The way in which we communicate, act out, or express ourselves largely comes from the way we grew up watching our parents/foster parents and those in our family. If our parental home was unhealthy, we didn't

have a healthy model upon which to base and judge our style of communication and self-expression.

When we are able to regulate our emotions, we can more clearly see problems and are better able to create solutions to best meet everyone's needs. Being able to regulate ourselves is a major leap forward in living the life we want to live. Even in a healthy world, you get what you give. In order to create life spaces where we feel safe, we must learn to express ourselves in ways emotionally and physically safe for others. If our communication style is healthy, we will create and maintain healthy connections with others.

How we interact with people, particularly during times of stress can undermine our safety. Some therapists say we operate from one of three internal states: a child state, parent state, or an adult state. Taking control of how you communicate with others is a part of the 5th Journey because poor communication and inappropriate reactions can put your safety at risk. Below, we discuss each state and provide some scenarios related to each one.

Our internal child or "child state" is someone who is demanding and wants what they want now. The child isn't much concerned with other people's feelings or needs. When or if you choose to act in the child state and don't get what you want, you may throw a tantrum. Children who don't get what they want may yell, scream, hold their breath, fall on the floor kicking and throwing their arms around, or they may cry, hit, kick, pinch, or act out in any way possible to let someone know they are not happy about not getting what they want. An adult who channels the child state may yell, hit, kick, and take what they want. They may be mad and spin off in their car squealing the tires to make sure everyone knows they are throwing a child's tantrum. They may scream and cry and throw things. They may hit other people, take things from others, and slap and scream at others. Often, it's not just because they are out of physical control, it's often because they lack the emotional tools to choose differently. When stressed they will choose to release the angry inner child who stomps, fights, holds their breath, and yells "Mine!" It's a child-like state, but not childish. They are adults in an adult world, but acting in a child-like state.

The "parent state" or internal parent part of us is the voice inside which tells us to parent ourselves or to parent someone else. When we act as a parent, we are taking into consideration all the years we spent listening to parental figures, even if we didn't have a very good one. We heard from our parents, aunts, uncles, grandparents, teachers, police officers, probation or parole officers, security guards, and our bosses at work. It's the voice we picked up and absorbed over the years of listening to parent-like authority figures. The inner parent reminds us about how things should be handled or done. This is the part of us which knows the rules and tries to follow them and the one who reminds and helps others, like our children, to follow them.

The inner parent will help us feel guilt when we've done something wrong and helps us to stay safe and do the right thing. When we approach an issue from our parent state it sounds like this: "you'd better clean that up," "oh, you messed up now," "you're in trouble," "I'm not going to listen to one more minute of this," and so on. We may act as a parent when there are rules to follow, and we believe or agree the world should be ordered in a certain manner, and we carry those rules, roles, and decisions in certain ways. If there is too much inner parent however, we can feel anxious a lot of the time, feel guilty, feel shame, and be regulated to follow too many rules and even listen to others we should not or no longer be listening to because it is against our own well-being.

The "adult state" is ideally where we want to come from when we are interacting with others. Adults weigh things out. They make rational decisions. They make safe decisions. They consider their own thoughts and feelings and other's thoughts and feelings. They make sound decisions based on what they know. Our inner adult is the part of the self that can think logically, reasonably, and rationally and is the one who mediates between the child and parent. The child often acts in ways connected to their past. The parent often acts in ways which might be future oriented. The adult however expresses themselves in ways related to the present. The adult takes in the facts, the context, rational

thoughts and reasonable feelings and expresses themselves accordingly. The adult also regulates between the parent and child, and keeps
both in check. The adult should always be in charge, allowing the parent
self to take over when needed and releasing the inner child when it's
time to be playful, imaginative, to dream, and to see the future possibilities. When we are free and healthy, we can "choose" to act in ways that
are beneficial - given the situation.

Now, let's take a look at some scenarios where the person can
choose to respond as a child, a parent, or an adult.

Scenario #1: After hearing one of your favorite department stores
won't allow you to return the shirt and give you your money back, you
have three choices- to respond as the child, the parent, or the adult.
Here's what each might look like:

*Response as the Child: "This is ridiculous! You'd better give me
my money back or else I'll be back here when you get off work
bitch," (This person is clearly choosing to yell and fight. If she were
an actual child, she may have fallen to the floor and kicked and
screamed).*

*Response as the Parent: "I don't know how you sleep at night. I
don't think not giving me my money back is the right thing for you
to do. You should learn how other stores do it and do the right
thing by me," (This person is clearly out to parent, punish, and
make the clerk feel guilty).*

*Response as the Adult: "I wasn't aware of your policy to not re-
fund customers when they return merchandise. Can I speak to your
manager about this? If this is the case, I will keep the shirt, but I
will not be shopping here again," (This person decided to be honest
about not knowing about the store policy but decided to advocate
for herself. If it doesn't work out, she will use one of the powers she
has and that is to not shop there again).*

This is how it might look in an intimate relationship:

Response as the Child: "He really pissed me off so I flattened his tires and cussed him out. Let's see how he will get around town now!"

Response as the Parent: "You know better than that. I'm going to teach you a lesson. Find somebody else to have sex with because it won't be me."

Response as the Adult: "I'm really upset by what happened and I'd like to discuss it and work through it with you."

Not only is communicating in an adult fashion the most appropriate and beneficial for you, but approaching life as an adult will help you to live a happier, healthier life because you will have power and control over life and yourself.

Mind-Fields: Choosing and Cheating

When you make the choice your safety is not important, you are choosing to put yourself at risk. It's another way of saying your life isn't valuable. When you allow someone to violate your boundaries, you are saying you are not important enough. You are cheating yourself out of the opportunity to feel happy and safe. Needing to feel safe is a fundamental need everyone has. Demanding you feel safe is not selfish. Maintaining boundaries isn't rude. It's what everyone who loves themselves does.

People who truly care about you and are healthy human beings will want you to have boundaries. They will worry less about you if you have boundaries. They will love you more if you have boundaries because they will realize you love and care about yourself as much as they love and care about you. Without boundaries you are not safe. Without safety you are a walking victim. Don't choose to cheat yourself out of a fulfilling life.

In choosing to operate as an adult you will find and maintain healthy relationships with your intimate partner, your children, and your friends. Without feeling safe and choosing healthy relationships, you'll be cheating yourself out of the quality of life you deserve.

Transformation: *"I maintain emotional and physical boundaries and am safer".*

Remember you are the architect of your life. You have the power to design it the way you would like to design it. You decide who is in your life and who is not. You decide the quality of those relationships. If your life were a movie, you would decide who would be in it, the parts they would play, how big the part is they get, and you decide if the movie is a big hit, or a big flop. The power is yours. As you take on the 5th Journey, those choices are yours.

When we have power and control over our lives, we can experience joy. The difference between happiness and joy, is happiness is fleeting. It comes and goes, but joy is something internal to us. We experience joy regardless of whether everything is perfect or not. A part of joy is internal satisfaction with who we are. Feeling safe and in control is an important part of joy.

There will be some in your life who won't celebrate your transformation. They won't appreciate it. They may even try to sabotage it. Never dim your light or change your course to make them happy. Never give up your safety, boundaries, and physical and emotional control. Just remember you'll rarely be criticized by someone doing better than you. You'll likely be criticized by someone doing less well than you (Asif Ali). Read the poem below and stay on your journey to live the life you want to live.

Let them judge you
Let them misunderstand you
Let them gossip about you
Their opinions aren't your problem

You stay on the journey
You stay the course
Committed to your freedom, truth, and transformation
No matter what they do or say
Don't you dare doubt your worth
Or the beauty of your truth
Never dim your light to make others feel better
Just keep on shining like you do
~ adapted from Scott Stabile

6

6th Journey: *The survivor engages in an open and honest self-examination to understand the past.*

6th Truth: *My past explains my present but doesn't dictate my future.*

6th Transformation: *I know how I got here and where I want to go.*

Trigger or Validation:
For some, the material in this Journey may be triggering. If it triggers you, reach out to your support system including those you trust and appropriate members of your Bomb Squad and/or engage in some self-care activities. For others, this information will be validating. In those cases, use the material to help validate you and affirm what you are or have been experiencing is real.

CHAPTER 6: SELF-EXAMINATION

"Owning your own story is the bravest thing you'll ever do."
~ Brené Brown

Congratulations! You have completed some amazing work. It wasn't at all easy, but you summoned up the courage to dive in and do it. No matter how long it took you, the timing was right for you. No need to rush a good thing. Celebrate a little and treat yourself to something nice and something special. Once you've done that, let's continue our journey from survivorhood to thrivership. We do that by helping you dig into who you really are, which is rooted in where you came from.

Working on getting to know YOU is critical to your recovery. As survivors, so much has happened in our lives we likely have not had time to reflect on who we are, what we've been through, and where we're going. When we stand in our truth, we allow ourselves to uncover our wounds and scars, along with our desires and goals. There is nothing wrong with standing in your truth. In fact, your truth is ultimately what will set you free from your own self-imposed barriers.

In the 6th Journey, you examine your life. You take an honest accounting of your life. Why is it important to engage in an honest and open examination of your life? Because recovery is about changing the way we live. We can only change what we understand. Our work through this journey is to bring into the light what has been hidden in the darkness so we can understand it.

Our thoughts, feelings, expectations, past, hopes, dreams, desires, and experiences were shaped by our family and our relationships. These experiences are imprinted on us. Sometimes in order to move forward we have to go backward and examine who we are. This examination will help us understand our risks, our patterns, and perhaps why we've been successful in some things and not in others.

The goal for this journey is to use the tools provided to identify patterns in your life and then to examine each piece by piece. A professional therapist can help you process what you find and will let you know if it's safe for you to do that. If it's not safe, work with your therapist to strengthen yourself so you will be ready and able to take this journey.

You will begin by looking at the people who have been in your life beginning with your family. Our family heavily influenced who we are today. They had a lot to do with the way we think, behave, and feel today. When we were kids and even teenagers, we picked up on everything. We were like little sponges absorbing all the family's good will and all of the family's dysfunction. Some of us may have been in foster care being bounced around to places and with people we did or didn't really connect with in a deep and meaningful way.

Perhaps we even ran away from home at some point to get away from our family. If we did, we were either running from something or to something. Maybe we couldn't articulate all the internal turmoil we felt at the time. We just knew we had to get away. As a result of these experiences, some of us didn't do well in school. We may have been involved in activities which got us in trouble with the law and we ended up in juvenile court. We weren't bad, we were troubled. But we couldn't exactly articulate it to the adults because we didn't have the capacity to understand it ourselves, let alone explain it to someone else. Or maybe we did share what was happening in our home and no one really cared. A few of us knew something was terribly wrong, but we dutifully stayed in our families suffering and putting on a brave face.

Truth: *"My past explains my present but doesn't dictate my future".*

Why bring up all these experiences? After all, these are experiences that happened in the past. The past has a great deal to do with who and what you are today; how you feel about yourself, why you keep getting yourself involved in bad relationships that don't work out, or why you don't trust others and share yourself openly and completely with someone else. All these experiences took a toll on us.

We have to go back in order to move forward. The past helps us understand our present. But let's be clear, our past in no way dictates our future. As we reclaim our own power, choice, and voice, we are the ones who decide what the future holds for us. We decide the directions we will take and the decisions to be made. That is why it is so important to understand our past, because our past holds unspoken beliefs and patterns. Without revealing them and understanding them, we are doomed to repeat them.

To begin, go back to look again at the most relevant core beliefs and schemas you identified from the 4th Journey. Keep these core beliefs and schemas in mind as you travel through this journey.

Think about your childhood and answer these questions. Was your childhood a happy one? Likely there were both happy moments and sad moments. Our childhoods are filled with a complex medley of experiences. How were you treated for the most part? Who in your family was there to love you and protect you? Who did you look up to and want to be like when you grew up? Who provided for you? Who gave you the love you needed? Who didn't? What did you love to do for fun? What did you hate doing, but had to do? Who was your best friend? What did you and your best friend do together? What was your favorite game or fun activity?

Now let's look deeper into your childhood. There are some universal promises owed to children regardless of who they are, what they look like, where they live, or what they do, did, or didn't do to please their parents or guardians. These universal promises are that children are to be loved and protected. Children should always feel safe. A child's need for food, clothing, shelter, and safety should always be met. There is nothing a child has to do or should do to have these basic needs met. Emotionally, children should not be afraid in the spaces designed for them to be safe. They should be made to feel like they are precious and they have good hearts and intelligent minds. As they grow, they should be given age-appropriate tasks they can master so they begin to feel strong, competent, empowered, and good about themselves. They should receive positive feedback when they have accomplished life tasks necessary to support their emotional, intellectual, physical, and spiritual growth. These are the universal promises made to the children we raise.

Now let's discuss the opposite. There are several different forms of child maltreatment. Child sexual abuse is probably the most studied. Child sexual abuse may or may not involve physical touching or physical force. Some abuse involves physical sex acts or attempted sex acts, but may also involve non-physical assault including harassment, threats, forced exposure to pornography, images, filming, or photography. The victim may or may not be aware they are being victimized.

Approximately 1 in 4 girls and 1 in 13 boys are reportedly sexually abused as children (CDC, 2021). Over 90% of children are victimized by someone the child or family knows. The peak age of vulnerability is between 7 and 13 years old, but abuse can and does occur with much younger and much older children (Finkelhor, 1994).

Sexual abuse is highly traumatizing and can negatively affect the way we view ourselves and others. It impacts our core self-esteem, violates our boundaries, colors our future relationships, and can destroy our trust in others. Being a victim of child sexual abuse is devastating to our very being, but with support we can learn to process it and become emotionally healthy.

Child physical abuse is also an experience which can negatively impact us. When someone devalues a child to the point of physically lashing out at them, the message the child receives is they are unworthy and unlovable. Instead of understanding the adult is wrong, deep down a child often feels something must be wrong with them.

Child neglect is more prevalent than both sexual and physical abuse. In child neglect, instead of doing something to a child, there is failure to do something needed by the child. Neglect may include failing to provide food, clothing, or shelter for the child. Neglect also means failing to properly supervise the child, provide a safe environment, or provide an education. Children may be physically, medically, educationally, or emotionally neglected. They are left to sometimes feel unsafe or unsure, and in survival mode asking, taking, begging, or stealing what they need in order to survive.

Parents or guardians who neglect children may fail to provide because they don't have the financial means to do so. However, not all parents who are neglectful are poor, and not all poor parents are neglectful. Parents neglect children for a variety of reasons. They may be ill equipped to parent. They may be preoccupied with drugs or alcohol. They may have untreated depression or a mental health diagnosis preventing them from adequately parenting. They may have consciously adopted values about parenting that support their neglect. Finally, they may be unable to adequately parent because they are being controlled by someone else.

Emotional and/or verbal abuse is by far the most prevalent form of abuse because it is a part of all other forms of abuse. However, some children can and do experience emotional abuse without experiencing other forms of abuse. Emotional violence is just as powerful, and in some respects more powerful and longer lasting than physical violence. It may involve name calling such as calling a child "stupid," "a loser," or other names taken to heart. It may include persistently comparing a child to another child, mocking a child, shaming them, threatening to embarrass them in front of others, leaving them or threatening to leave them, making them the butt of a cruel joke in the family, making them feel responsible for any abuse they suffered, and expressing to them they are unwanted and/or no one else would want them. Other forms of emotional abuse include distancing children from other loved ones, disconnecting them from needed socialization with others, or purposefully withholding food, clothing, shelter, or safety to control the child. Finally, killing a family pet is another form of emotional abuse[1].

Familial abuse and neglect of children occurs from parents or other family members, including siblings. When sibling abuse occurs, partic-

---

[1] Center for Disease Control 2021 https://www.cdc.gov/violenceprevention/child-sexualabuse/fastfact.html

ularly in a severe form, it is often an indication of family pathology. Of course, family members are not the only abusers of children. Anyone can abuse a child. When this happens, it is most often someone the child or the family knows.

The common denominator among children who experience abuse is the feeling of shame and the experience of trauma. Abused and neglected children often believe they are not lovable or worthy of genuine love, care, and concern. Without help, survivors of childhood abuse may engage in behavior, thoughts, and feelings which continue to tell them as adults they aren't valuable. Often this is where we first heard, believed, and began to adopt some negative core beliefs about ourselves which we learned about in the 4th Journey. This is why it's important to visit our past. We can't fix what we don't understand. In learning where we came from and our experiences there, we can work through them and move into our future, taking intentional and healthy steps along our life journey.

No childhood is perfect. Even when you have loving, engaged, and good parents or guardians there are some things that happened in your childhood which may have been damaging to you. Perhaps you were ostracized by friends or bullied. Perhaps you were different because of your sexual orientation or identity, or your culture or ethnicity, or perhaps who you were and what you valued didn't match the family and/or friends you shared space and time with, and you felt different and "othered" as a result. Perhaps your parents separated, one of them having to leave the home. In some instances, a family member had a devastating illness or disability and/or died, a family member had to go to prison, or as a child you witnessed domestic violence. Any of these experiences can be emotionally traumatizing and can shape what you thought about life and yourself in the process.

As you grew up, these experiences shaped your teenage years. Being a teen is already awkward as we are growing into our bodies. Our feelings about ourselves are heightened and our friends and social identity become extremely important. If we had any friends, we were significantly shaped by our experiences with them and we believed who they were was indeed who we were.

Even though our friends and our social experiences in adolescence shaped who we are today, we have been most heavily influenced by our family. In fact, not only did any type of trauma or abuse affect us, being in a dysfunctional family can set the course of our life. Why? Because there are often repeated behavior patterns throughout generations of families. If we were to examine our family tree, we might see certain patterns repeat from generation to generation in our family.

Tools: Self-Examination through The Family Tree (Genogram)

The easiest repeatable pattern to see across generations is when it comes to our health and disease. For instance, if your great-grandfather suffered from diabetes, it is likely diabetes will show up in other family members. The same is true for other diseases passed down from generation to generation, like heart disease, hypertension, arthritis, some cancers, dementia, and Alzheimer's disease to name a few. Just like some health conditions are passed down from generation to generation, so do behavioral patterns.

The most important lesson here is that knowledge is power. If I become aware my great-grandfather had diabetes, my grandfather had diabetes, and my two aunts have diabetes, then I already know that I'm at risk for diabetes. I also know diabetes can be chronic, and I may experience life-long issues requiring me to watch what I eat and take special care of myself if I am to remain healthy. If I ignore this knowledge, not only might I get diabetes, but if I continue to ignore it, I will run the risk of losing my eyesight, losing limbs, and eventually dying earlier than expected due to complications related to diabetes. Knowledge really is power, because if I act on my knowledge, I may be able to prevent myself from even getting diabetes, or I can learn to manage it and live a longer, happier, healthier life.

The same is true when other problems run through families. Not only can medical conditions put your health at risk, but there might also be patterns in families affecting your emotional health and well-being, mental health, addictions, and other patterns of dysfunction. These patterns impact your family in ways that put you and other family members at risk to suffer lifelong consequences. With this knowledge, however, you can work to lower your risk and change the trajectory of your life to one happier and healthier.

As a part of this journey, we will develop and examine our family tree. Another name for your "family tree" is called a genogram. A genogram, developed by Murray Bowen in the 1970s, is a written diagram or picture of your family tree including all the important experiences in the family. Using a genogram, you look over at least three generations of your family. It might include your parents, you, and your children. It could include you, your parents, and your grandparents. A genogram is something you draw using symbols and arrows. You'll find out how to do this in your workbook.

The main purpose of a genogram is to map out various patterns in your family. Someone doing a genogram may map out the number of people in their family who have had addiction issues. An addiction includes anything persistently done, causes the person to be obsessed, and renders the person emotionally and often physically unavailable to the family. It can be an addiction to a substance, thing, or activity. This may include abusing drugs or alcohol, or being a work-aholic, shop-aholic, church-aholic, having a gambling addiction, and more.

Another important variable is to look within and across generations for abusive and violent relationships, and patterns of child abuse and neglect. When using a genogram, you can map out practically anything of interest to you, particularly anything which placed you and your loved ones at risk, left you vulnerable, or was emotionally disturbing. These might include medical conditions or issues that run through your family, mental health diagnoses, disabilities, and more. You can map out any emotionally devastating experiences such as who in the family has been to jail, the number of abortions, the ages at which family members have died, or if there were arguments or fights which changed family relationships. You can also map out happy occasions like the ages when family members married and had their first child, those who graduated high school and/or college, and ages when each moved away from their parents or bought their first home.

You may map out the manner in which children, women, or men are treated in your family, or how people who are different because of sexual orientation, sexual identity, ethnicity, or disability are treated in the family. Once you have decided which experiences you will focus on, you begin mapping. While you are mapping your family tree, you are looking for repeated patterns throughout your family from generation to generation, as well as across family members, to include your sisters, brothers, aunts, uncles, cousins, and others.

There are also "themes" you may discover in families. A family theme is an idea which keeps recurring through families. They may be repeated family feelings and sentiments through time. For instance, "shame" might be a family theme. Did your family members experience "shame" because of who someone was in the family or what they did? Is there a "theme" of shame running through the family with more than one family member being shamed? Is there a repeated theme of "anger," "sadness," "accomplishment," or "success"?

Did your family have certain expectations others in the family didn't live up to like, "everyone goes to college" and you didn't, or "everyone gets married" and you didn't, or "everyone has children by a certain age" and you didn't? We call those "family rules." Family rules are interesting to map. Family rules are regulations and understandings about what can happen and not happen, be said and not be said, be done and not be done in your family. We are not talking about a family rule where someone has to take off their shoes before they walk through the house. Those are not the important rules. In a family, the rules we are talking about are deeper than removing your shoes, keeping your elbows off the table, or saying grace before every meal. These are the real rules and the most meaningful rules. These are the rules which make a difference in whether as a family member, you are a part of "us" or not a part of "us." These family rules are rarely spoken about, yet everyone understands them. Some family rules are "we don't marry people outside our ethnicity or race," "we have our babies early," "we never divorce no matter what happens," "as long as we go to church, anything else happening in the family is ok," and "what happens in our family, stays in our family." There are numerous unspoken rules families have. It will take deep thought and time to figure out what some of your unspoken family rules have been.

When an unspoken family rule is broken, the person in the family who broke the unspoken rule has to pay emotionally, financially, or physically. Whatever the violation, there will be a cost associated with it. Sometimes the rule violator may be ostracized by the family, blamed for other family problems, no longer invited to family events, or in extreme cases, kicked out of the family. Sometimes they pay by being labeled and blamed for several family problems. The level of cost paid is often in relation to the level of rule broken. For instance, a white person within a racist family who marries someone of a different ethnicity may no longer be invited to the family's holiday dinners. If the rule is everyone in the family graduates high school and someone doesn't, the family may view them differently and then attach beliefs about this person's intelligence, character, or ambition. If someone was abused and no one else in the family acknowledges it, that person may be seen as a troublemaker, a drama queen, or a liar who wants to embarrass the family. Why? Remember it may be more important to follow the unspoken rules of the family then it is to tell the truth. Breaking rules embarrasses the family and risks exposing some ugly truths many family members don't want to face. Exposing them would disrupt some of the family lies others built their life around.

In addition to family rules, there are also family roles. Each member of the family assumes a role or a number of roles. Some classic family roles might be the "hero," or the one who is the good or successful, responsible child. The "mascot" is the child who deflects attention away from the family problems by being cute or funny. The "scapegoat" is the person who is acting-out in the family. This is the person who the family can blame for many of their problems. Just like the mascot, the scapegoat takes the family away from its real problems so they can focus on blaming, fixing, or worrying about the scapegoated family member. The "lost child" is the quiet one, the dreamer, the invisible one. This child keeps to themselves for the most part. They are not willing to cause the family any more problems than they already have, so they sacrifice their needs and wants for the family. Indeed, each of these members with significant roles have taken them on at a price. Each resents taking on their roles because of the family problems. Other family roles might be the "mediator," or the one who works to solve disputes in the family, or the "switchboard operator," who communicates among parents, siblings, or other family members - or in foreign families, they may be the one who translates for the family. "The garbage man" is the one in the family who cleans up the family's emotional messes. The "power-broker" manages major family deals, whether emotional, physical, and/or financial. There is the "cheerleader," the "clown," the "truth teller," the "keeper of the family secrets," the "rescuer," the "successful one," the "most impressive worker," the "most impressive mom," the "most impressive man," the "couple with the most impressive marriage," the "college graduate," or "smart one," and so on. Even those with seemingly successful roles may feel stress and may not be succeeding *because* of the family, but *despite* the family. There are numerous roles family members assume. As you think about people in your family, what roles did they play? What stressors did they face as a result? What might they have been resentful about? What sacrifices do you think they made? What role(s) did you take on? What stressors and resentments do you have? What sacrifices did you make? What did your family teach you that was positive and can use in your future? Who are you thankful for in your family? What are you thankful they provided to you?

Having spent time in foster care complicates things because children in foster care may have to learn different rules, roles, and themes as they move to a new home. This adjustment can be confusing and causes foster children added daily stress trying to fit in and relearn different themes, rules, and roles. If you have spent a significant amount of time in foster care, you can choose the family you want to focus on for this journey, or you can choose to do both or all the families where you spent time.

Constructing a family genogram (family tree) can be a powerful experience. Right in front of your very eyes you can see the patterns of dysfunction and risk. You can predict, just like you can with diabetes, if these rules, themes, and risks will be passed on to your children or grandchildren. Once you have clearly examined your family and see them, it will help explain why you struggle. It may give you the motivation to stop any pattern you don't like. Perhaps you make the decision that the pattern of dysfunction will stop with you. You will end it and create a life for yourself and/or your children you want. Once you see the patterns you don't like, you have the power to change your life for the better.

Mind-Fields: Creating and Constructing

When you don't acknowledge and examine your past in a truthful and honest way, you will build your new life on an unstable foundation. If the work on self-examination isn't done, the subsequent work you put in may be flimsy, weak, and subject to be destroyed by any major problems or future disasters. It's like building a house. If I build a house on land that is not solid, I run the risk of my house caving in, crumbling, or falling apart. The same is true for you. You want to build the life you deserve on solid ground. To build a solid joyful and empowered life, we need to first reinforce areas of the foundation that are weak or have been damaged before we bring in the wood to frame the house, hang curtains, and bring in the furniture.

Some of us indeed would love nothing more than to avoid our past, believing that the past should stay in the past. We don't realize the brokenness of our past is present with us, festering within us, poisoning our lives with the toxins of the past. Sometimes we minimize our past as if it was no big deal, or we attempt to block out our past. However, our sub-consciousness remembers, and without ever consciously thinking about it we become compliant and are doomed to repeat the past. Without dealing with our past, we will unconsciously sabotage our happiness and will repeat the family's pattern. We can't avoid working through our past if we want to have a future as one we control and are happy with.

In neglecting to heal the wounds of the past, the danger is you may inadvertently create and construct a life bound to repeat the patterns of the past. The other danger is in not taking an honest and truthful journey, you run the risk of creating and constructing alternative truths, half-truths, and fantasies about your past in order to justify why you should stay where you are or why you are unable to repair the past or strengthen your current foundation. In creating and constructing truths, half-truths, and fantasies, you will set yourself and your Bomb Squad off on the wrong path. This will prevent recovery. To avoid this, challenge yourself to be as honest, raw, and as real as possible. Ask other family members about your family so they can fill in the gaps for you. Ask for and accept when your therapist challenges your reality about your family and your experience. Your therapist will help you put these things into perspective.

In examining your past honestly, you provide yourself with opportunities to heal from the past and to repair relationships which may need to be repaired. Therefore, major internal construction begins now. Do not take this journey without having your therapist involved, seeing them at least once a week. Know, that in taking this journey, you are in the good fight for your own health and well-being. Take the time to heal the wounds of the past so you are strong enough to build the life you want on a solid foundation. With your therapist, in your Survivor's Journey groups, and in writing in your workbook examine, repair, and strengthen those areas which need to be repaired and strengthened. You can't change the past, but you can understand it so you can stop repeating cycles and change old family patterns passed down from generation to generation.

Next, let's take a look at your friends and the type of friends and associates you have had throughout your life. As teenagers, our friends became so important they influenced who we were and what we thought about ourselves, our lives, and everyone and everything in it. They imprinted on us the viewpoints we formed about what is good and not good, what is cool and not cool, how we spend our leisure time, and what is fun and not fun. They influenced our preferences and shaped our lifestyle. Take a look at your friendships as you grew older. How did they change? Everyone has a need to belong. Friends provide us with a sense of belonging. They influence the way we feel about ourselves. Friends can shape the course of our life. What kind of friends did you have? What did you and your friends consider fun?

The past intimate relationships we had also greatly affect who we are today. If you want to know how emotionally healthy you've been, look at your past relationships. If you want to know how emotionally healthy you are right now, look at your current or most recent relationship. Is it healthy? Are you proud of it?

We learn how to have relationships by watching and learning from the first relationships in our lives, those of our family members. What was the relationship between your parents like? How did your sisters and brothers treat each other, and how did they treat their girlfriends and boyfriends? How did family members treat you? Many of us came out of unhealthy and dysfunctional families and we learned how to set up and engage in unhealthy relationships with others. If what we witnessed was dysfunctional and abusive, we likely got into dysfunctional and abusive relationships. If they were loving and kind, we sought out loving and kind relationships.

What you have to understand is even though you have these risk factors as a result of being in your family, you can change the pattern. You can keep the living and healthy parts of your family and end the negative patterns. You can begin a different pattern, re-route where you have been headed, and change the trajectory.

When you understand your family tree and the risk factors there, you can make the decision NOT to follow the family rules that you are now aware of. You can decide to NO LONGER assume the role you were given or took on. You can make life decisions that lower risk, and you can change direction or set the future course.

When you understand the type of friends and intimate partnerships you've been involved with, you can decide YOU will no longer get involved in dysfunctional relationships.

These are all called choices and each of them is within your power. You can decide which family rules you will and will not follow. You can choose to adopt new rules for you and for your children. You will decide if the roles you have assumed are too burdensome for you and if you need to drop them and/or assume a different role. This is more easily said than done, because you have to work through all of the guilt associated with giving up the dysfunctional and unspoken agreements you made with friends, family, and intimate partners. We will focus on those agreements in more depth when you take the 9th Journey. For now, just know with time and practice you can change all the unhealthy patterns, themes, roles, and rules you have submitted to and create new ones. The power is yours.

As you begin to identify and change negative patterns, you can begin to think about what you want for your future. This Journey is not only about what to identify and stop doing, but it's also about what to identify and start working toward. To do this, let's examine your goals, values, motivations, strengths, weaknesses, and source and level of confidence. Let's examine those issues holding you back from living out your desires and achieving your goals. Think about these questions as you work along in your workbook.

Sit with yourself and reflect deeply on your desires. Get in touch with what you really love doing and love thinking about. Reconnect with that part of you inside who would dream and be excited about the dream and the fantasy of who and what you wanted to be.

Many survivors have dreams beyond their wildest imaginations, but they are afraid to pursue them. Most are afraid to even acknowledge them for fear someone else will ridicule them. Read the poem by Marianne Williamson:

Our deepest fear is not that we are inadequate. Our deepest fear is that we are powerful beyond measure. It is our light, not our darkness that most frightens us. We ask ourselves, 'Who am I to be brilliant, gorgeous, talented, fabulous?' Actually, who are you not to be? You are a child of God. Your playing small does not serve the world. There is nothing enlightened about shrinking so that other people won't feel insecure around you. We are all meant to shine, as children do. We were born to make manifest the glory of God that is within us. It's not just in some of us; it's in everyone. And as we let our own light shine, we unconsciously give other people permission to do the same. As we are liberated from our own fear, our presence automatically liberates others.

Note: If you are reading this and you're under 18, or are over 18 and still live with your parent(s), there are certain explicit rules you must follow. Parents/Guardians who care about your well-being establish rules to keep you safe and prepare you for life. Until you are living as a more independent adult, you will need to follow those rules and allow them to guide you. If for any reason you believe their guidance is inappropriate, discuss it with your therapist.

Transformation: *"I know how I got here and where I want to go".*

Understanding your past and some of the general patterns of your family helps you become more knowledgeable and clearer on who you are. Knowledge is power because once you understand the patterns you can make a conscious choice to break those patterns you no longer want and not pass them on to the next generation. This opens you up to become the person you choose to be and have the health, family, friends, and relationships you choose to have.

Transitioning into the more evolved you takes courage and hard work, but achieving your goals is like nothing you can ever experience in life. Victory is sweet and it's all the better because it's self-affirmation which you can indeed do what you put your mind to. This in turn gives you even more motivation to achieve the next step on your list of goals. Remember, as you are considering your future goals, only you have power over what you can change about you. You don't have the power to change someone else's heart, mind, or behavior. Use your workbook to dream about who and what you want your life to look like. Do you want to put energy into pursuing a loving intimate relationship? A better relationship with a family member? A great job? Your own home? To enter school? To open a business? The bigger the dream, the harder the work, but you can certainly get there. Follow the prompts in your workbook that help you map out what you want to do and where you want to be in the future. Work with your case manager to get there. There are local, national, and international programs who support survivors in achieving their goals. Talk about it in your Survivor's Journey group. Speak it into existence with those you trust. Make a decision to put your energy into it. Go through the workbook exercises. Don't be afraid. Be excited. Be determined. This is a new chapter in your life. The level of energy and hard work you put into achieving a goal is relative to what you get out of it.

7

7th Journey: *The survivor learns to trust and engages those who are trustworthy.*

7th Truth: *Trust is demonstrated in action, not words.*

7th Transformation: *I trust people who are nurturing and trustworthy, and I remove those who are toxic.*

Trigger or Validation:
For some, the material in this Journey may be triggering. If it triggers you, reach out to your support system including those you trust and appropriate members of your Bomb Squad and/or engage in some self-care activities. For others, this information will be validating. In those cases, use the material to help validate you and affirm what you are or have been experiencing is real.

CHAPTER 7: TRUST

"It's hard to trust when all you have from the past is evidence why you shouldn't." ~ Anonymous

Jeanette's Story: "I was in pain. I just felt inadequate, incomplete, not good enough, and it hurt. I wanted to be loved and to love someone in return. I wanted to live the life I saw other people have. As long as I can remember I felt like I was outside of something and that something important was missing from my life. I didn't really fit in, and I knew it, but I wasn't sure if anyone else knew it. I was good at hiding it. So when I met him, he was talking that good shit, you know, that kind that makes you want to follow him anywhere. He literally said I was sitting on a gold mine and that together we could make a lot of money. He said that I could make easy money just using what God gave me and doing what I knew how to do best. We laughed, talked, made love, and he complimented me all night. I wanted to do this for us. I wanted to do this for him. His roman-ticized version of the hustle wasn't anything close to reality. When you put your face in the lap of a trucker that has been driving for 10 hours, you realize this isn't easy money. The way to get through it is to put your mind somewhere else. Pretend your man didn't just send you out here to be with another man. Pretend you are ok with everything that is happening in your life. Pretend you want this life.

John's Story. "He as a priest; a man of God. Of course, I trusted him. He abused me sexually and he said it was ok."

Beverly's Story: "I married a successful man. He knew how to make money. He knew how to make everything, including us, look good. Everything was about him and I knew that reality going into the relationship. I knew that if I supported him emotionally that I would be taken care of financially. I hoped that he would love me and be faithful to me. In the relationship I would take care of all of the things he needed to feel secure. I made sure our house looked nice and that I looked nice. I made sure that I stayed by his side and was loyal to him. If he said or did something that I didn't agree with, I tried to figure out a way that I would be ok with it. My thoughts became his thoughts. His politics and his beliefs are what I learned to believe. The way he saw the world is the way I tried to see the world. I no longer said "I" when talking to others. I said "we" because in my mind we were one. I had long forgotten what I liked to do or who I really was. My world became his world. I left my individual identity to become his. The day I finally learned that he didn't value all that I did and everything I brought into the relationship was devastating. He looked down on me. He thought I took from him and didn't bring anything of value to the relationship. He thought I was lower than him. That I used him. He believed he was smarter than me and better than me. He began to tell me that I was stupid and an embarrassment to him. He started to treat me as less than a human being. He no longer cared about my feelings and would openly ridicule me in front of our children and in front of his friends. His disdain for me was evident. He accused me of cheating on him. He started slapping me and choking me when I didn't do what he wanted. I started finding receipts of him purchasing motel rooms and buying items for his lovers. When I confronted him about it, we had a bad fight. He told me I had no right to question him when he was providing so much for me. This went on for several years. I even began to agree with him about me. I believed that no one else would want me. I believed that I couldn't take care of myself without him. I began to believe that what I brought into the relationship was worthless and that I was worthless. Today I no longer believe that. I understand that what I experienced was abuse. I was abused emotionally and physically. I do have value. I worked to remember me and to regain my self-worth. Never again will I give myself away so much so that I lose who I am. Today I understand that someone who loves me, wants to be with me, my personality, and all of my flaws. That's what a healthy life partner wants. I will no longer give up who I am to be with someone I love."

Harold's Story. "She was my foster mother. She didn't have to take me in, but she did. I was grateful at first, but over time she just got really mean and just stayed that way. She never hit me, but she would do weird things like tie me to the bed at night. I learned that this was also a form of abuse."

Why Trust is so Important

Not trusting others is a normal response given what you've been through. Everyone understands why you do not trust. No one would blame you for never trusting anyone again. You would be rightly justified. But there's one critical thing about trust. It's the main ingredient in every meaningful relationship. Trust is so vital to thriving and truly living as a human being that it is the essential element needed in the most important desire we have - to give and receive love. Trust also involves elements of safety and belonging. We are less lonely when we trust. We can be more authentic when we trust. Life seems less challenging, and our problems are less insurmountable when we trust because we have someone whom we can share our thoughts, feelings, problems, hopes and dreams with. When we can trust someone, we know there is at least one person in the world whom we can put reasonable faith in, who understands, and who truly knows us.

Your Past Experiences

For some of us, our past experiences made us vulnerable and contributed to our lack of trust. We have learned to follow twisted, unhealthy rules, and to keep secrets for a very long time. What you need to know is that secrets keep you sick. As people in Alcoholics Anonymous say, "You are only as healthy as your secrets." It's true. If you were a victim of child abuse or neglect, you need to know you had no power or control over what happened to you. If you got involved in relationships which were violent or emotionally abusive, you had no power or control over their behavior.

Your childhood experiences are where you first learned about trust. If someone violated your trust, you learned you can be fooled. You learned if fooled, you could be violated emotionally, physically, and/or sexually. Perhaps you were bullied or pressured to engage in ways which made you uncomfortable. The result is you learned not to trust others and learned not to trust yourself.

When someone violates your trust, trauma-math occurs. This means not only do you no longer trust the person who violated you, your mistrust is multiplied exponentially. You no longer trust males, or adults, or people who live in a certain community, and so forth. Survivors who don't resolve their trust issues assume the characteristics of what we call the porcupine, the possum, or the pig.

Not Trusting: The Characteristics of the Porcupine

Without the tools provided on this journey, you may choose never to trust anyone. Just like a porcupine, if anyone gets too close to you they will be stuck, poked, and hurt. They will be hurt by you. This is your way of keeping people at a safe emotional and physical distance.

The porcupine already assumes betrayal will occur and then acts accordingly. You await betrayal. Regardless of how someone behaves, you assume they will betray you and you look for evidence of such in every single trust building encounter. You will search for any crumbs of evidence and when there are none, you will make them up to justify why you shouldn't trust. You will even be suspicious of your Survivor's Journey facilitator. Anyone trying to help you will become suspect.

Even though you have seen and read about people who are trustworthy, deep inside you believe most people betray others. You expect it. You may even unconsciously set it up or sabotage your friendships or relationships so when it happens you can say, "See, I told you."

You distance yourself from others. You are no longer carefree because you have to stay on high alert, just in case you may be fooled again. You may physically be with friends or family, but you are not emotionally invested. You are guarded and just waiting for someone to say something or do something that will confirm you shouldn't trust them.

A sure way for the porcupine to never trust anyone is to avoid commitment. You can't commit because something could go wrong or someone could be wrong. You'd rather stay home, stay distant, say no, and try not to achieve any level of emotional commitment or closeness because it is terrifying to you.

It is within your full rights as a human being to conduct the life you want to live. Never trusting anyone is the best way to never get hurt again. It is also the best way to not live a genuine and fulfilling life. Going through life not trusting anyone is a lonely way to live. You will appear as if you are functioning in a healthy way, but when people try to get close you have a hard stop. The consequence is you deprive yourself of genuine human connection and authentic living.

Pseudo Trust: The Possum

Some survivors who have trust issues assume the characteristics of the possum. When a possum doesn't trust, they play dead by fainting or freezing. They play possum in hopes a deadly predator will move on and not try to harm them. Getting too close to someone who is like a possum scares them and they are at an emotional stand-still frozen by fear. The hope of the possum is to make the person believe they do trust. In reality, they are pretending to their own detriment.

Pretending to trust someone is not trust. It's playing possum and making others believe you have the ability to trust, when you don't have the tools to genuinely trust again. It puts you in the same position as a con artist because you are playing a con-game. You are pretending you trust someone else, but you really don't trust anyone. You are lying to them and setting the friendship or relationship up to be fake from the start because it is built on a lie. You are playing possum.

You confuse other people because you are pretending to trust, but you don't. You *act* as if you trust and then you *show* them you don't trust. You may say you trust, but act in a way where you are never emotionally vulnerable or available. Your heart is wrapped in plastic and placed in a vault, and you have swallowed the key so no one can get to it. You become quick to say no to anything emotionally risky. You avoid genuine intimacy.

You may date others who are asymmetrical or incompatible to you. For instance, your intimate partners or friends are beneath or above you financially or emotionally. Your ages are very different. You live in geographically different locations. They are married. They are addicted. They lack the intellectual capacity you have. It's obvious you would never take them seriously and/or they couldn't possibly take you seriously as a potential life partner.

Pseudo trust sometimes shows up as overprotection. Possums keep people at an emotional distance so they can't get hurt. They make sure their children are overly protected so nothing as bad as what happened to them, happens to their children. In many ways they don't allow their children to grow and experience life because they are afraid their children will be hurt the way they were.

Another way to pseudo trust is by pretending trust is not a big deal, when it is everything to the person. One thing the person will trust in is their fear of trusting anyone. The possum will put their own self down in front of people before someone else can. They will make a joke about themselves before anyone else has a chance to hurt them. They are playing possum with themselves and other people.

Chance vs. Trust: The Pig

Someone who assumes the characteristics of a pig jumps full force into a relationship or friendship without a clue of whether their new friend is trustworthy or not. Because of our vulnerabilities based on our past experiences, we may miss the red flags that tell us this person is not trustworthy.

Taking chances without tools to determine trustworthiness is like playing Russian Roulette. When you've been deeply hurt before, opening your heart to fully embrace someone and trust them feels like putting a bullet in the revolver, spinning the cylinder, and hoping it doesn't fire. Fully opening yourself up and placing your heart in someone else's hands feels like emotional suicide. Without the tools to assess trustworthiness, it is a gamble without the odds being in your favor. But instead of wagering money, in this game of chance you are playing with your feelings. When your trust has been violated, it's important you learn who you should practice trusting and who you should not. Trust is a gamble we all make, but with the correct tools, we can tip the odds in our favor.

When someone assumes the characteristics of the pig, they do not employ any tools to assess whether the person they are engaging should be considered trustworthy or not. They jump into friendships and/or relationships with both feet and worry about the consequences later. Just like the pig that jumps into the slop and begins eating without ever recognizing the pig pen they are in and what they were willing to eat. When they finally raise their heads to see what has happened, they realize they've given their heart to someone who hurt them and who wasn't trustworthy.

Because of your past victimization, you no longer have the luxury of just blindly giving your trust to whoever shows up in your life. The life and times when you could bring someone close to your heart will no longer become a game of chance. You can't afford a game of chance. You will no longer engage in pseudo trust either, where you are lying and making others believe you trust, when you don't. If you use the tools provided in this Journey, they will help you make logical decisions about who will be in your life and why, and who will not. Without being logical about it, you will no doubt attract those who are not the type of friends and relationship partners you can trust. Leave those who take chances about who and how someone is in their life to the romantic movies you might watch. Your life and happiness is too important to throw away on blind chance. Your life, love, and friendships will be fulfilled because you purposefully designed them that way.

The 7th Journey is all about learning to trust again. This Journey is not about just trusting anybody; it's about helping you screen and determine those who are trustworthy. To do this, you need to assess others using your head and not your heart, and have the appropriate boundaries in place. But before we do that, let's reveal the type of people you should NOT trust.

Types of People you Shouldn't Trust: Recognizing the Game

"Be careful when a naked person offers you a shirt."- if they don't trust themselves, you shouldn't trust them ~ African saying

We talked about risky people and situations in the 5th Journey and taught you to use the SAFER Process, which is to <u>see</u> risk, <u>assess</u> it, <u>focus</u> and find the solutions and respond to it, <u>empower</u> yourself to respond, and then <u>respond</u>. When you are at immediate risk, the SAFER Process will help you stay focused and search for ways out of the risky situation and away from the risky person. However, the process of understanding and determining a course of action, when there is not an immediate threat, is not the same. Even though trusting the wrong person or people puts your heart and emotions at risk, the process of understanding who is not trustworthy is different and takes time. Using the information provided in this Journey gives you the tools you need. There is never a guarantee, but applying these tools increases the probability you will be able to see more clearly who you should trust and NOT trust. Overall, there are four types of people who you shouldn't emotionally connect with or trust. They are known as the Con Artist, the CEO, the Guerilla, and the Broken. Each of these are dangerous to you because they are out to harm you either emotionally, financially, physically, or all three.

The Con Artist aka Narcissist

Con Artists (aka Narcissists) come in all types of shapes, sizes, ethnicities, and genders. They are great storytellers and liars. They show up as boyfriends, girlfriends, husbands, wives, friends, family members, kind strangers in need, and those there to help you. They weave a narrative about who they are which makes you feel comfortable with them. They manipulate you so you bring them close to your heart. They might show you they have potential and so you take a gamble with them. Whatever it is that brought them close enough to you, they made you believe they could be trusted with your heart.

In reality, Con Artists never take anything from you; they manipulate you so you give them what they want. A Con Artist will not take your trust, you will give it to them. They won't take your love, you give it. They won't take your empathy, compassion, loyalty, kindness, or generosity. You give it. When you are in the grasp of a Con Artist, you will work against your own best interest to give them your most precious internal gems, such as your love and trust, and then perhaps your material items like your money and creature comforts of life. The hallmark of a Con Artist is they will end up being taken care of by you, sometimes both emotionally and financially. In this relationship you will do most of the work and take the hits to your credibility and self-worth.

Con Artists understand your vulnerabilities and your expectations. They present themselves to you in the likeness of someone you should trust and right when you are vulnerable and invested enough, they turn the tables on you. They present to you the image you already want to see in them. What does your idea of a most trustworthy friend, family member, intimate partner, husband/wife, or guardian look like? What might they say and do? What might they promise to you? The Con Artist will mirror all of these things to you, but deep down past the façade, they are not who they say they are. There are very easy ways to see the Con Artist for who they truly are and we will talk about those later in this Journey.

The most precious thing that a Con Artist takes from you is your trust. And they don't even take that. They convince you to give it to them. That is the basis for the confidence game. It's a game of trust.

Once they have your trust, they move forward to use it against you. With your permission they chain your heart and your mind. They convince you that listening to them, what they need, what they say, what they believe, and what they want you to do is what you should submit to. They gain your commitment to them. Over time they gain your loyalty to them. A Con Artist will not often physically hold you against your will. You stay and participate in your own victimization or someone else's with them. There are times when they are lovable and you want to stay and times when they are incredibly scary and will frighten you back into submission. There are moments when your good sense breaks through and tells you to run and get away, but the con is inside and it convinces you to stay and endure more.

In the world of sex trafficking, Con Artists are otherwise known as finesse pimps. They finesse their way into your life and con you into the life they want to live. Many people consider sex traffickers or pimps to be people that snatch and force victims into trading sex, while they take the money, but that is rare. Most sex traffickers manipulate their victim into trading sex and giving them the money. There are less likely to be chains around their victim's wrists and ankles. There are chains around their victim's mind and heart.

The same is true for those who are victims of domestic violence. Prince/Princess Charming presents themself to you almost in the exact package in which you'd like them to appear. They say most of the right things and offer you the life and the love which is not perfect, but is good enough for you. They get you to give them your love, your trust, and your loyalty. In time, they get you to stop thinking about your needs, wants, and desires and instead to focus on them and what makes them happy. Eventually you can't even remember much about what you liked or who you were. You are focused on their needs. When they are violent the first time, whether it is verbal or physical, they beg for forgiveness. Since you know no one is perfect, you forgive them and you experience a honeymoon period where everything is good. But tension starts to build and when you least expect it, they become angry again and you are once again victimized.

You notice their protective nature you first thought was flattering turns into control. Their jealousy which was endearing before, becomes scary as they attempt to isolate you and possess you. You first try to appease them, believing they are insecure, stressed, overworked, sensitive, and whatever additional terms you have to explain away their behavior. You try even harder to accommodate their needs and be sensitive to their feelings. Each time you are inching closer to suspending your freedoms, giving up who you are so they can feel safe and assured you love them. You grow more distant from your friends and stop talking to some in your life who upset them. Over time you try and predict when there will be a bad day. On these days you try to say the right things or do the right things, but the right things are not enough. This person is violent. They are abusive. They are disrespectful. They are accusing you of things you are not guilty of. They tell you they wouldn't be acting this way if it wasn't for you because it is your fault. You can't do anything right.

So you try harder to live by their rules and standards to make the relationship work. At this point there may be physical violence, verbal assault, and perhaps sexual violence. In their eyes there is something inadequate about you. Over time and because of the slow and steady torture you experience, you are now unsure of yourself, unsure how you got here, and unsure why you stay. You keep secrets about your relationship. You question your own intelligence, your beauty, your self-esteem and anything else they have consistently attacked.

The same thing happens when children are abused. They place their trust in someone who takes advantage of them. Their abuser takes their trust, their self-esteem, their self-confidence, their childhood, and sometimes their internal joy. They ask their victim to keep secrets so dreadful it eats them up inside. Some of us started out as victims of child abuse. Because these early abusive relationships are so familiar to us, we repeat them over and over through our adolescent relationships and into our adult relationships.

Have you ever seen the movie *Get Out* directed by Jordan Peele? The movie is about a young couple in college. The female college student takes her boyfriend home to meet the family. Little does he know her family has mastered the ability to place an old person's brain into a new young body giving the older person the opportunity to continue to live their life with a new, young, and vibrant body.

The mother in the movie hypnotizes the young college student so the father can eventually perform the surgery to place the old brain in the young body. Any time the mother gives the cue originally used in hypnosis, the intended victim falls into a trance. When they hear another cue, they awaken from the trance. During a party the family holds an auction, cleverly disguised as a bingo game, with the highest bidder paying to receive the body of the young, college boyfriend who is visiting. One flaw in the family's design is the occasional ability of the hypnotized victim to have a brief breakthrough to their past selves (If you saw the movie, this happened when the maid was confronted by the boyfriend). It lasts for a brief moment before their thoughts and feelings are once again taken over and they fall back into the trance they call "the sunken place" where they have no control.

Have you fallen into the trance and are under the spell of your abuser or exploiter? If so, use this brief moment of clarity to put some plans in place to "Get Out."

The CEO

The CEO type of exploiter/abuser plays on your need to feel loved, safe, and taken care of. They show up in your life presenting themselves as someone who is powerful, strong, competent, and almost all knowing. The CEO's competence, coupled with the way they handle the world, makes you feel lucky to have been chosen to be in their company. It's their competence and arrogance that makes them so appealing you want to be involved with them.

The CEO comes with an implied contract. This is rarely spoken about in great detail. They have promised either verbally or nonverbally that they will take care of you. In return, they request complete loyalty and allegiance to them.

The hallmark of a CEO is there are differential and unequal rules between the both of you. First, they have all of the power in the relationship and you have little to none. What they believe is what you must believe. They own, possess, and keep you. In return, they expect complete loyalty. In fact, if you violate their trust or break the strict rules they have placed you under, you are subject to severe consequences. However, they do not abide by the same rules they place you under. They will break your trust over and over, believing that because they are taking care of you and have ownership of you, they can ultimately do what they want.

When you enter the relationship, the CEO believes you are not equal to them and will never be equal. Over time, in their minds their self-importance grows and is magnified, while yours continues to diminish. This uneven perspective of theirs deepens and they give themselves permission to see you as someone who no longer deserves respect. Once this person feels justified, they can treat their property, aka you, in any way they see fit. As the abuse sets in, you may be called and treated as if you are stupid, ugly, and worthless. Once you are dehumanized in the eyes of the CEO, they can hit and beat you without much sympathy. They may apologize afterward and seem sincere, but this is not genuine and is done to ease their own conscience.

The CEO loves to capture and acquire things for their collection. Since they've already captured you, you no longer fulfill their needs. When they are not busy spending their time being bored with you, they spend their time being angry and resentful of you. They may also be busy becoming attracted to their next victim. When or if one of you leaves the relationship, their goal is to leave you with nothing or very little, because in their eyes you deserve nothing.

The Guerilla
The Guerilla is someone who may be charming and charismatic from the start, but who has a dangerous edge to them. Unlike the Con Artist (who 'appears' to be trustworthy in the beginning), there is something scary, and in many cases dangerous and violent, about the Guerilla from

the start. They have a power that either frightens you into submission or it is the frightening charisma calling you to them. They have a strong ability to influence other people. People both fear them and admire them because they are self-assured and confident.

The Guerilla may become violent shortly after meeting. This happens in cases of date rape or sexual assault, or in the rare cases of victims being kidnapped and forced into the sex trade. Entanglements with Guerillas not only threaten your physical safety, but it threatens the safety of your children, friends, and family members because they will use anything and everything they can to hurt you and get you to submit.

Some of us didn't get an opportunity to make any choices. We were forced into various situations under the threat of a Guerilla. There was no negotiation, manipulation, or sweet talk. Some Guerillas have neither the time nor the skill to attempt to persuade their victim to do what they need them to do, they force them to do it. The Guerilla style is forceful and violent, and it's indeed scary and threatening to be on the other end of a guerilla pimp, intimate partner, gang leader, or sexual abuser. The Guerilla is not only scary to you, but they are scary to a lot of people in their world. Their motive is to instill fear so they can continue to violate whomever they want, whenever they want.

Something is truly wrong with this type of person. Get as far away from them as humanly possible. They are dangerous and will remain dangerous, because something inside them, which is vital to humanity, is missing. There is a difference between a Con Artist and CEO compared to the Guerilla. The Con Artist and CEO may be scared when the police or others get involved. The Guerilla takes such a threat as a personal challenge. They will not back down no matter what happens. Get far away from them because your life depends on it.

Whether they really are as powerful as you think they are is questionable. However, they have convinced you no matter where you go or what you do, they will be able to find you. In these situations, reaching out for help from the criminal justice system, protective shelters like the battered women's shelter, and members of your Bomb Squad will be important to devising a safety plan and strategy to get and stay away.

For the sake of clarity, Con Artists and CEOs will often use guerilla tactics of threatening and beating their victim when they are out of options, however the Guerilla is somewhat different. The Con Artist and CEO uses violence as a tactic to maintain power and control, while threats and violence ARE the Guerilla's main tactic of engagement.

The Broken

The Broken person is not a Con Artist; they are not trying to take 'from' you or be taken care of 'by' you. They also don't believe they are better than you like the CEO does. They don't seem like they have violence in their DNA like a Guerilla, although they can be very violent and abusive. The Broken person is not really ready for a relationship. They don't understand how to have a healthy relationship. They haven't had any models presented before them of what a healthy relationship looks like and feels like. They want to do the right thing, but they don't have the skills and the level of maturity to do so. When they are stressed, angry, or don't get their way, they don't have the internal tools to deal with their emotions, so they use violence because it seems to work.

You connect with them on a subconscious level. They show you the parts of them which are broken. You understand them because there are parts of you broken. Much like a winged bird, you recognize their pain and you bring them close to your heart. You take care of broken things. Your brokenness connects with their brokenness. You understand being wounded because you've been wounded, and you emotionally reach out to them. You hope your love will save them. If they can be healed, maybe you can be healed.

You will not heal the Broken. The power of your love is not that powerful. In reality, what you are looking for is your own healing. However, you haven't had the self-esteem to go after it for yourself. You haven't placed enough importance on yourself to seek out your own healing. Your low self-esteem is what brought you to this place and to this person. If you woke up, you would see it is your need to save yourself and not your need to save them which is your true motivation. But you believe you don't deserve someone better. So instead, you are fighting to create a person you can love, because you don't think anyone who is already healthy and wonderful would want you and your brokenness. The truth is when you work to become emotionally healthy, you will find a love that is healthy and fulfilling to you.

The Broken typically don't have relationships, they take emotional hostages. They will threaten their victim, threaten to take their own life, use the children, manipulate, or use violence. They can become desperate. Because they lack internal tools and are emotionally unhealthy, they will do anything they think might work to keep their partner. These may be some of the tactics you have also used in your past relationships or friendships. The Broken will use any means necessary to take back control and make sure their victim never leaves them. This is not a relationship. It is a hostage situation.

The hallmark of all of these victimizers is they aren't initially who they say they are and they can't deliver a healthy and satisfying relationship because they are not healthy. Early on in the friendship or relationship they show you one side of themselves. But there is another side which eventually shows up. In reality, it's likely you see a bit of your relationship in each of these characters presented. However, unlike the Con Artist who is finessing their victim into a position where they can use and abuse them, the Guerilla shows their other side fairly quickly and in full force. They can change into a very dangerous and scary person in a matter of moments. It can be as fast as turning on a light switch. This happens in cases of date rape or sexual assault by someone you barely know. It happens when or if someone becomes the target of a Guerilla. It happens in relationships when, seemingly out of blue, a partner becomes violent. This person is truly dangerous because when they unleash their violence and hatred, you are witness to something extremely horrifying. Their actions let you know they have moved beyond all reason and in making the wrong move you understand you could be seriously hurt. In some cases, others may not believe you when you attempt to reveal who the abusers truly are. Others have seen what they can do and are also afraid of them. The CEO will never see you as an equal and will continue to find ways to elevate themselves while belittling you. Your 'never being good enough' will always be their justification for abusing you. Finally, the Broken doesn't have any emotional tools or relationship strategy. They lack the internal coping skills needed to solve problems, and without these, when they are frustrated, stressed, or don't get their way, they will continue to become violent.

Whether it's a Con Artist, CEO, Guerilla, the Broken, or a combination or elements of each, it's likely you have revealed much of who you are including those more tender parts of you. This means they know how to deeply hurt you because they understand your hopes, your dreams, your desires, your needs, and your secrets. You may have shared what scares you with this person, what makes you feel safe, and what makes you most happy. They may know who and what you care about most. They may know where you are broken. They may know how to hold you emotionally and/or physically hostage and they do. They may use what you love and fear the most against you. They will do anything to keep you emotionally hostage.

These abusers have one thing in common, they don't know how to express genuine and healthy love. Even though you know you need to leave them, you may still feel a deep attachment, which is confusing. Your mind is telling you that you can no longer share time with someone that hurt you so much, but your heart is telling you to stay connected. Know that this is more about your previous victimization and current vulnerability than it is about your love for this person. It's because there are spaces where you and your abuser fit together like a glove since you both have been wounded. You bonded over that. You are unconsciously connected. But connecting where you are wounded is not healthy. What you are grieving is not love. You grieve the loss of this connection. You grieve the time you shared. You grieve the parts of yourself you gave to them. You grieve leaving behind the future you fantasized about with this person. That is what you are feeling. It's not love. It's the work. It's the time you put in. It's the part of you which you shared. It's the history. It's the fantasy. It's the woundedness. In reality, you are confusing that for genuine love. If you gave up the fantasy of what you wanted the relationship to eventually become, and looked honestly at what it was and what happened during the relationship, you would clearly see this wasn't love.

But in order to grow, you have to let go of those things hurting you in your life . There is a life ahead for you. Go to the end of the book and read the Survivor's Journey 12 promises. There are people who are waiting to enter your life. Life can't change and they can't enter when you continue to hold on to your past. There are two parables about letting go we will share with you.

One is about a trapeze artist. A trapeze artist swings in the air hanging from one trapeze. Their goal is to grab hold of the other trapeze. In order to do that, you have to let go of the first trapeze. The moral of the story is you can't move forward without letting go and being willing to grab the next trapeze. For a brief moment, however, you are in the air not holding onto anything. It's during this time you must learn to trust in yourself the most.

Another way to think of letting go is to remember that change is inevitable. The wisdom is to know who in your life is a root, a branch, and a leaf. A tree has a lot to teach us. There are some people in your life who are like the roots of a tree. They ground you. They send you nutrients to help you grow. They keep you standing straight and tall. They have been with you and will be with you until the end. Then there are people in your life who are like branches on a tree. They will be in your life for a long time. Some of those branches will be there for years and then some will rot and break off. Some will break during a bad storm. Finally, there are also some in your life who are like leaves on a tree. They are meant to be there for a season. They will fall away as they are supposed to do as the seasons in your life change (*Tyler Perry*).

Your job is to understand who the roots, branches, and leaves are in your life and treat them accordingly. Remember, if the leaves don't fall away, the tree can't continue to thrive. If the rotten or dying branches don't break off, the tree can't continue to grow. Allow those branches and leaves to fall away so new branches can grow and you can become stronger. Finally, identify those roots in your life and cherish them. They will be with you forever.

Violated Agreements

"A true friend knows your weaknesses, but shows you your strengths; feels your fears, but fortifies your faith; sees your anxieties, but frees your spirit; recognizes your disabilities, but emphasizes your possibilities."
~ William Arthur Ward

When you have a friend or an intimate partner, there are implied and unspoken promises to one another. When these are violated, trust can be damaged.

These agreements involve proximity, frequency, support, and non-judgmental attitudes toward each other. Proximity means you like to be in the company of each other and you like to spend time together. You support each other and are honest with each other. You normalize each other's experiences, accept each other, and invest time in one another. As your friendship grows, so does the level of trust you have in this friend. The same is true for intimate relationships, with the addition of emotional and physical intimacy and the expectation each will remain true to the sexual and emotional agreements you made to each other.

Trust is broken when any of the agreements above are violated. It is particularly triggering for someone who has suffered trauma. For someone who has suffered trauma, a violation might not be seen as a slight or moderate betrayal, but as a major violation. Because trust is the attribute you use to interact with the world and feel safe, when trust is violated it is crippling to the victim. It is the ultimate betrayal.

Truth and Tools: Trustworthiness

"Trust is demonstrated in action, not words".

Words vs. Actions
When we are vulnerable or have experienced any past trauma, we tend to trust words and ignore actions. In other words, we will trust what people say and not pay attention to what they actually do. The first and most important tool in your toolbox is to learn to separate someone's words from their actions. You will begin to separate and compare what

people do from what they say. Maya Angelou said, "When someone *shows* you who they are, believe them." You will notice Maya Angelou did not say "When someone *tells* you who they are, believe them."

We have to learn to separate the words from the actions, because it is the actions that tell us who someone really is. If they tell you that you are important to them, but they continue to be late, not show up, or tell you something else came up and they can't be there, they are showing you they do not value you. If their actions were put into words, their words would be, "*You cannot put your trust in me, because I am not trustworthy.*"

Someone may tell you, in many ways, they are trustworthy. However, when they fail to show up, fail to complete the task they told you they would do, or act in a way toward you or others that is opposite of what they said, they are showing you who they are. Trust in their actions, not their words. Their actions will always tell you who they are. The truth lies in their actions.

They may verbally tell you what they believe in. However, if they act in direct opposition to what they said they believed in, believe their actions, not their words. If someone tells you they are a lover, not a fighter, and then argues over almost everything you believe in, they are more of a fighter.

They may tell you about their behavior and then act in the direct opposite of what they told you. Of course, these people will give you a logical reason for why they acted the exact opposite of who they told you they were. They will give you a reason for why they said they believe in this, but acted very differently. Instead of listening and believing all they tell you, pay attention to how they act and what they do. For instance, if someone tells you they are generous and will give anyone the shirt off of their back, but you watch them say things like, "*I'm not picking them up. They can walk.*" It is their actions which tell the true story.

Sometimes people won't even tell you who they are, you just assume they are kind, nice, and loving. They show you through their actions that they are not the person you assumed them to be. Believe what is shown to you.

What people do, not say, is the measure of their character and their actions will tell you who they really are. For instance, if someone tells you they are faithful to you, but has sex with someone else, they are not faithful to you. It doesn't matter how many times they explain the circumstances, the reasons, or the situation, their words said "faithful," and their actions showed "unfaithful." If someone tells you they are kind, and then ridicules you time and time again, it doesn't matter why they did it. They are not kind. If someone tells you they are responsible, but they are continually late, they are not responsible. It doesn't matter how many excuses they attempt to get you to believe. If someone tells you they love you, but they make you do things you aren't comfortable doing, they don't love you. They may even think they love you, but they don't know what love is. If someone tells you they will keep your secret, but then tells your secret, they are not to be trusted no matter their excuse.

These people are not to be trusted because their behavior does not match their commitment. Their words don't match their deeds. Their intent doesn't match what actually happens. However, we may become confused because of their words. No doubt your partner or friend will provide you with lots of reasons, feelings, and thoughts, and may even try to blame you or someone else for their own character flaws. In the end their behavior did not match what they promised, and they are not to be trusted. They haven't earned your trust and don't deserve your trust.

Some people who are not to be trusted don't just show up in our lives as friends and lovers, these people can also be in our families. A parent who says they love you, but does not use the money they have to make sure you have food, clothing, and shelter you need, is not someone whose words match their deeds. Likewise, a family member who borrows money and fails to pay it back, or who says "I love you" and then frequently hurts you, is not someone worthy of your trust.

A neighbor who says they will help your child to get off the bus, but instead drives off to go shopping, is not to be trusted with your child. Their words don't match their actions. Even if they tell you that they love children and they smile in your face. Their actions do not match their words. Don't trust them.

But let's go deeper than the simple examples above. Let's talk about relationships and dating. Let's say you have an expectation if you give your heart to someone, you are trusting they will hold your heart in their hands, their minds, and their heart, and keep it safe. When you make that decision, you are being vulnerable. In turn, the person in a relationship with you is also being vulnerable with you. What you do with your partner's heart will reveal a lot about your character and in turn what they do with your heart reveals a lot about their character. Will you choose to keep their heart safe, or will you abuse it, play with it, tease it, make it jealous for your own satisfaction, hurt it, and throw it away whenever you are upset? If you will, then you can expect the same in return.

Because your heart has been wounded in the past, you will have to take special care of it. Your heart is not like other hearts. It's been broken and you have suffered trauma as a result. In this case you can't afford to just throw your fragile heart out there to anyone to potentially hurt it. Because it's wounded, you will need to be extra careful and choose wisely. The tool which helps you choose is to pay attention to their actions. Their actions will always tell you the truth.

Listening to Your Intuition

The second tool you can use in learning to trust others is to begin to trust your intuition. Your intuition is your gut feeling. It is your thoughts and feelings about people, places, and experiences. Listen and turn those thoughts and feelings up, instead of down. Do not dismiss them. No doubt some of your thoughts and feelings will be rooted in fear and your past experiences. Indeed, they may be off center because of your past trauma. That doesn't mean you should stop using your intuition. Discuss and process your intuition with your therapist and in your Survivor's Journey groups, and process in your workbook. When you do this consistently, what you are doing is learning a few important lessons that will carry you throughout your life. First, you are learning to talk about your genuine feelings. This is a form of trust. Second, you are learning to process your feelings with others, particularly your therapist. Third, you are learning to accept wise counsel from others who may be trustworthy. Fourth, you are learning to compare your thoughts and feelings with the wise counsel of others and make adjustments. If your feelings and thoughts are vastly different from most others' advice, you can learn to regulate your own thoughts and feelings to come in line with what is reasonable. Lastly, not only are you comparing your thoughts and feelings to the overwhelming majority, but you will also begin to learn how to separate the good advice from the bad advice you'll receive. And because you have more information from various sources, you may feel a lot better about the choices you end up making. In other words, you can trust a lot more in what you believe you should feel, do, or think because you have sought out and received sound advice from people who do not have a reason to manipulate or steer you in the wrong direction.

Taking the Time to Trust

The third most important tool is to take your time. Trust is earned. It takes time to trust. Have you ever heard someone say, "let's slow this relationship down," and you couldn't figure out why someone would say that, or you thought they must mean they are not interested? Even if someone is genuinely interested, they may slow the friendship or relationship down because it takes time to figure out if someone is trustworthy. It will take time to assess if someone's words and actions match. Healthy people will take the time to figure this out because they recognize how precious trust is. They value their heart and their feelings, and they won't frivolously give their trust to just anyone. They also won't expose themselves and their loved ones to someone in any meaningful way until they have determined the person is trustworthy.

If you have taken the time and determined this isn't a trustworthy person, you can choose to walk away. If walking away isn't what you want to do, make sure you DO NOT bring this person into your heart space. Keep them at a comfortable emotional distance. This is someone who you should not trust wholeheartedly. Do not trust them and do not introduce them to others who are vulnerable.

There is a definite process to determine if someone is trustworthy. They include assessing if their words match their actions, using your intuition, and taking the time needed to understand them. And even then, trust is something that has no guarantee. People aren't perfect. Trust can be broken. However, learning what to look for in assessing whether someone is trustworthy is possible. Using the Four C's below will guide you to make logical decisions on whether or not to take another step toward trusting a particular person. Understand that trust is about being vulnerable. Making a conscious choice on whether to move physically or emotionally toward or away from someone trustworthy will help you surround yourself with those who are healthy and who support you emotionally.

The Four C's of Trust

> *"If the least they can do is the most you can expect,*
> *it may be time to move on."* ~ Rigel J. Dawson

If your suitor or friend wants to become emotionally close quickly, back them up. This is a red flag for you. If they want to see you every day and spend all day together, slow them down. If they want both of you to share your deepest, darkest fears and desires too soon, slow them down. You need time to assess and judge their actions accordingly. If they are using the "L" word, meaning love, or the "B" word, meaning "best" friend, slow it down. Instead of this initial feeling being a great feeling, make it an uncomfortable feeling for you. In any other time in your life, when have you ever experienced someone rushing in and it all worked out? Think about it. When this happens, it's usually a salesman trying to make you sign on the dotted line today! If someone is trying to overwhelm you by rushing in and confusing your senses, it should feel uncomfortable and the response should be to slow down. They don't even know you yet and you don't know them, so what is their motive? Slow it down so you have a chance to implement the strategy we are about to teach you. If they are truly interested in you, they will slow down and respect your wishes. If they threaten to walk away, let them.

Here is your new rule of thumb. If someone is in a hurry and they need you to make a decision now, then the decision is "no." If they won't wait, consider them to be a shooting star. Like a shooting star they propelled themselves across your life like a bright hot shining light, but as fast as they moved in with a light so bright it heats up your heart, they may likely fizzle and burn out.

The strategy to use to find out if someone is trustworthy is called the Four C's. Those are consistency, compassion, capability, and communication. You can use this method to assess your friendships and your intimate relationships. You can also use it to look across any interactions with agencies and members of your Bomb Squad.

Consistency is the idea that the person you are attempting to trust is consistent, meaning they present themselves the same way day after day and time after time. If someone is nice one day and yelling the next day, they are not consistent and you would be in your right mind not to trust them. If they are on time most of the time, you should begin to trust they will be there most of the time because that is what they are showing you. If they promised something and fulfilled that promise and they do this consistently, they are earning your trust. If they borrow money and pay it back each time, they are showing you they are consistent. If they promise to pick you up and are often late or don't show up at all, this person can't be trusted. If they say they love you and they consistently act in a loving manner, they are earning your trust. If your best friend holds your secrets, they are showing you they may be trusted. On the other hand, if they share it with someone else, they are showing you they cannot be trusted.

Part of being consistent means having integrity. Having integrity means you are who you say you are and you do what you say you'll do. It takes time to assess for integrity. You have to see them across time engaged in various activities in order to judge their integrity. This is the very reason it's important to never rush into a relationship or best-friendship, or to hand over or give access of precious items to someone too early. You have to have time to watch them and assess them.

Compassion is the idea that someone's heart is in the right place. Someone with compassion has concern for the suffering and misfortune of others. They are able to have sympathy or to feel sorry for others. Perhaps they have empathy, or the ability to be able to put themselves in another person's shoes in an attempt to understand their experience.

Compassion in action might be when you see someone practice acts of kindness in order to help someone else. Other examples of compassion might be when someone spends time with their family or children, when they say something encouraging or supportive to someone, when they hug someone, say thank you, or shake someone's hand. Other ways to see compassion in action is when they offer to help someone without the expectation of pay or praise, when they open the door for someone, or motivate others to do better. Being a good listener is a sign someone may be compassionate.

Assessing for compassion means to watch for how well-meaning and kind someone is. There are plenty of opportunities each day to choose kindness. Do they? Do you? When someone needs a dollar and they have it to give, do they give it? Or do they make excuses? To see compassion in action here is a great exercise. Go to a restaurant and see how your new friend treats the waitstaff. If you think about it, wait staff at restaurants are paid under minimum wage to wait on you. They run and get everything you need. No matter how you treat them, they must smile and be kind. If you send them back to the kitchen three times, they have to do it for you. In essence, the people at your table have total power over this other human being. You can choose to treat them in any way you would like to treat them because the wait staff assigned to you are completely powerless to stand up for themselves. How does your friend treat them? How do they speak to them? How many times do they run them back to the kitchen? How dismissive of them are they? Do they tip them? Nothing exposes character more than how you treat people you think you don't need. This is a window into how you might be treated sometime in the future. When they have you and assume you are powerless, how might they run you around in the future, expecting you to give and give and give. Will they value what you are doing for them and with them? How dismissive will they be of you? This is just an experiment you might try.

Capability means to trust that the person has certain abilities. This is the easiest form of trust to have. For instance, if I hire a plumber, I can trust the company that hired the plumber has determined the plumber has the skills to do the job. If I am learning from a teacher hired by a school or program, I trust they know how to teach me the subject I want to learn. These are the signs I use to tell myself whether I believe someone is capable or not. If I hire a babysitter for my children, I should have some indicators which help me determine whether they have the ability to care for my children in a safe and loving way. Maybe they provide references from other families. Perhaps I've seen how they interact with children.

However, when it comes to friendships or relationships, we aren't given a manual or references. People don't come with a seal of approval. There are some people in the world who for whatever reason aren't capable at this time in their life of forging a genuine friendship or intimate relationship. They may be stunted in that they are not able to show the emotion you need. They are not able to be as open as you would like. They are not able to communicate as transparently as you need. They don't have the power and/or the ability right now to be as healthy as you need them to be. This can be because of some experiences they have had in the past, or it may just simply be who they are. If this is someone of value in your life or someone you would like to be of value in your life, you can suggest they seek help to become more emotionally present and available. But don't sell yourself short by connecting deeply with this person, because you will not be satisfied with what they have to offer. You will experience frustration and will struggle through your connection with this human, because they are not ready. If they are emotionally stunted, they will not connect emotionally in the way you need them to connect.

Communication is the key to any good relationship, whether it's a friendship or intimate relationship. Someone who is transparent is someone we can learn to trust. They share their thoughts, beliefs, opinions, and past experiences. This person is more of an open book when it comes to who they are. They will talk with you on a feeling level. Communication helps you connect to them because you believe you know who they are.

As you go through this Journey and others to come, give people the opportunity to earn your trust. Allow them to show you who they are (not tell you). Watch carefully and assign them accordingly. If they show you they are consistent, compassionate, capable, and communicative, allow them some trust. Over time, allow them more and more trust as you feel more and more confident about them. Don't expect miracles because no one is perfect. Everyone stumbles now and then, but if they are earning your trust, give it. When someone shows you they are not to be trusted, it doesn't mean you have to stop talking to them, but it does mean you should not place any faith in them which hasn't been earned. You should not give them power and control over anything precious to you; not your heart or emotions, nor any tangible items, like access to your children, house, car, or other friends and family.

Nothing is Perfect and No One is Perfect

No one is perfect. People make mistakes and they should be forgiven for a mistake. If someone breaks a trust, depending on the trust being broken, you may decide to forgive them. The reason you forgive is because the violation was a mistake and is out of character for the person being forgiven. To show someone grace by forgiving them means you show them empathy, compassion, and understanding. These things are gifts you give to people you care about. It's when mistakes keep happening and forgiveness has to be given over and over, that the lessons aren't being learned by either party.

Transformation: *"I trust people who are nurturing and trustworthy and I remove those who are toxic".*

Because of our previous trauma, deep down inside we may not trust ourselves anymore. There may be a part of us which blames ourselves for our own trauma. Somehow, we believe we should have seen it coming.

We should have stopped it. We should have had the power to avoid it. Because we didn't see it coming or couldn't stop or avoid it, we believe we failed ourselves. That failure caused us to be hurt. We can't trust someone who fails us ever again. That means we can't trust ourselves. When we think deeply about our experiences, we find ourselves saying "if only" we had known or known better, or "if only" we could have done something about what happened. We torture ourselves with the notion we should have seen it coming or "if only" we had been smarter, more powerful, stronger, or more insightful. Those two words "if only" haunt us.

The truth is, we can't always see what's ahead or around the corner from us. We aren't psychic and can't predict our future. The truth is, we have blind spots preventing us from even seeing some things right in front of us or others can see more clearly. The truth is, we aren't always powerful and all-knowing. The truth is, sometimes we are vulnerable and can't see risky situations or risky others. The truth is, we trusted in the wrong people and the wrong situations.

Today we may blame ourselves and torture ourselves with "what ifs" and "whys," as in "what if I would have...," "why didn't I see it," "why couldn't I stop it," or "why did they do that?" We obsess over these thoughts and they get stuck in our brain and play over and over and over. This is part of your trauma. When this happens, it's our brain and our heart trying to understand and reason through what happened. When this is happening, let your therapist know at times your brain will get stuck in this groove, playing those thoughts and questions over and over.

The fact is, others in our same situation may have done the same thing. We do the best we can with the thoughts, feelings, and beliefs we had then. We survived and that is what is most important. Because we survived, we have the time to work on our healing. That means we have to learn to forgive ourselves and understand we are human.

So how do we learn to trust in ourselves; the very person we believe has let us down in the past? We don't. We pretend we trust others when we don't. We pretend we trust ourselves when we don't. We pretend. Because we don't trust ourselves or other people, we have found one way to deal with this. Trust no one. Let no one in. Be a fortress where no one can enter. Be your own island disconnected from others.

Learning to trust yourself means you also have to practice the Four C's of trust. It's the best way to have others begin to trust in you. You have to become consistent. When you say you are going to do something, do it. When you say you are going to be somewhere, be there, and be on time. When you say you are going to make a decision, make it. When you say you are going to talk to someone about something important, have the conversation. Make yourself consistent.

Be compassionate. Don't only talk about how much you care about something or about others, show it in your actions. Make sure your words match your actions.

Become capable. If you love someone, don't just tell them, show them. Love is an action word. It means both saying and doing things which show the person you care about them. If you care about an issue, don't just talk about it, take action steps to get involved in fighting for or against the issue you are passionate about. If you have knowledge and skills to share capably, share them with others.

Become more communicative. Say what you really mean and mean what you say. Be transparent. Let other trustworthy people know your thoughts and feelings. Don't hide them. Share them with who you believe you can trust. Begin to slowly share with them and assess whether they can handle your feelings and if they can be trusted.

Trusting in yourself also means learning how to make wise decisions. Before you make a decision, seek wise counsel. In other words, seek advice from people who have traveled the path and know what lies ahead. Talk to people who have this wisdom, not because they say they have it, but because you have seen them struggle through certain decisions. When you get advice from people who are wise, you will be best informed. You can also check on the Internet or seek the advice of an expert associated with the issue at hand. These ways of collecting information will allow you to search your feelings and your thoughts and make the best decision possible. In doing this, you will begin to trust in yourself more each day because you will rely heavily on first collecting as much information and various perspectives on the issue, and you will take all of this data into consideration, allowing you to make the best decision.

Game Recognizes Game

True character is what you do when no one is watching. We all have character flaws. But if you want to know who you truly are, watch what you do and who you are when no one is looking. I'm not talking about how often you scratch when you're alone, your masturbation habits, the fact you skip cleaning your house, or bathing yourself. I'm not talking about how much of a slob you can be or how much you binge watch television when you should be doing something else. Those things are all normal.

True character is whether you are willing to swindle, cheat, or steal someone else's trust. For instance, if you could get away with stealing from a friend, would you do it? If your grandmother was no longer able to understand what she owned and didn't own, and no one would find out, would you have her sign her brand new car over to you? If you had the power to deny your partner the free choice to be with you, and you could make them be with you for life and give you everything you wanted, even if you knew they would be unhappy, would you do it? These are the signs of true character. If you secretly answered yes to any of those questions, then it's your character you first have to work on if you are to be in the company of those who are trustworthy. Why? Because game recognizes game. Others who are trustworthy want to be around those who are trustworthy. Healthy people have the uncanny ability to sniff out someone who is not trustworthy and they will politely distance themselves. If you want to be in the company of trustworthy friends and have trustworthy relationships, then you have to be trustworthy.

Those who are trustworthy will not authentically engage with those who are not trustworthy. If you are attempting to run a game on someone who is wise and woke, they may fall for your tricks once, but they won't do it again. People who have integrity and good character want to be around others who have integrity and good moral character.

Some of us say we want to have loving relationships and trustworthy friends, but we are not in a place where we can offer that in return to others. If we want to love and trust others, we have to become loving and trustworthy. One way to do that is to shed the fakeness of us and rid ourselves of the game. That means we have to become genuine and authentic if we are to be trusted by those who are healthy, genuine, and authentic.

To demonstrate what we mean, hold both of your hands up in front of you at shoulder's height so your fingers face each other. Spread your fingers. Bring them together so both hands are together and the fingers interlock. That is how a good relationship, whether it is a friendship or intimate partnership, comes together and stays together. Now unlock them. Take one of your hands and hold it higher than the other. This hand represents the friend or partner who is healthy. The other hand is lower. It represents the friend or intimate partner who is not emotionally healthy and trustworthy. Now attempt to bring your two hands together and interlock your fingers in relationship. You can't because they don't go together. They are on two different levels. If you want a trustworthy, loving friendship or relationship, you have to work on yourself. If you don't, you will only meet someone who is on your emotional level. If you want someone who is emotionally healthy and trustworthy, be that person. The only way you'll find and connect with those people is by being one. Otherwise, they will see your sickness (game recognizes game), they will distance themselves because they are looking for the same thing you are looking for.

Components of trust also include commitment, character, and credibility. If you want to trust more in yourself and become trustworthy to others, show your commitment. If you said you are committed to something or someone, show it. Take care of your responsibilities in a way others trust in you to do.

In order to trust someone and be trusted by others, they have to believe you have integrity or good moral character. Just so you are clear about your work through the 7th Journey, the best way to be trustworthy is to be true to your word. When you're true to your word, you don't make promises you don't keep. You honor your word. You show up when you say you will, and if you can't you call or text right away to explain.

Trustworthy people are transparent. They communicate their thoughts and feelings. They say what they actually mean, and they mean what they actually have said. They are honest in that way. The person they show you is in fact the person they are.

They are trusted because they demonstrate over and over through their actions that they are where they said they would be, they do what they said they would do, and they behave in a way that is predictable. They don't say one thing and do another. They don't *assume* you know what they are thinking or feeling. If it's important, they communicate their thoughts and feelings.

I know this is hard for you to believe, but there are people in the world today who act exactly like that. They are trustworthy people. They do exist. And it takes one to find one. You have to be trustworthy in your thoughts, feelings, and actions in order to attract someone who is the same way.

If you are not trustworthy, you will not attract trustworthy people. There is a lot of wisdom in the sayings we grew up with: "game recognizes game," "if you lie down with dogs, you wake up with fleas," "you are who you hang around," and many other sayings all designed to tell you that you become who you associate with. If you are not trustworthy, those who are trustworthy will see it in you and will distance themselves from you.

There are also other sayings, including this one by Denzel Washington: "If you hang around five confident people, you become the sixth. If you hang around five intelligent people, you become the sixth. If you hang around five millionaires, you become the sixth. If you hang around five idiots, you become the sixth." It can also be said, "If you hang around five trustworthy people, you become the sixth." Why? Because you begin to pick up the attitudes of your friends. Why? Because the average human being is highly influenced by who they hang around.

They begin to pick up their beliefs, thoughts, feelings, and behaviors. Thus, we have to consciously decide who we want in our lives and how close we want them to be. We do this by actively designing who is in our lives and not just accepting whoever and whatever happens. When we have power, choice, and voice we use them to design and construct the lives we want, and who is in them is a part of that construction.

In turn, you attract who you are. If you want to know how trustworthy you are, look over your friends and associates. Do you trust them? You are a reflection of the five people you hang around and know the best. Look over this list of the qualities of a trustworthy person. Do you have those qualities? If not, start to work on being a person who embodies these qualities. As you become healthier, you are changing. Your friends will reflect who you are as you create change.

You'll Become Truth-Worthy

When you are trustworthy, you become truth-worthy. That means a select few will confide in you. They will trust you with their most intimate secrets, thoughts, and feelings. Becoming truth-worthy is an honored position. Not many people receive such an honor. When someone shares their vulnerable selves with you, it is a gift and you must treat it delicately and with care. They trust you will not share their information with anyone else. They trust you will not judge them negatively. They believe in you. Sometimes it's because they are chance takers and they don't know any better. Sometimes it's because you have proven yourself to be trustworthy. In either case, recognize this gift and honored position and treat it as sacred as it is.

Choosing Not to Trust

Choosing not to trust is an option when you have freedom over your choices in life. Continuing not to trust is within your power and it's the one true way of never being disappointed again. If you never trust in anyone, then your trust will never be broken. However, never placing your trust in anyone is a very flat, lackluster existence. Still, the choice is 100% yours to make.

Boundaries

In taking back your power, choice, and voice, you have to learn who to trust and with what information. In other words, you don't need to tell everyone everything. Make conscious decisions about who you will trust with what type of information, and who you will trust with your children, your material possessions, and your secrets.

The second way to learn to trust again is to approach your friendships and relationships with caution.

Mind-Fields: Conviction and Corruption

One of the mind-fields we can experience in relation to trust is to repeatedly convict others. Once we learn the components of trust and how to assess it, we can very clearly see who is and is not trustworthy. However, just because we know someone isn't trustworthy doesn't mean they are void of all value. Everyone has value. Allow me to present a short story to you which was told to me as I began to create change in my life. Someone told me about a woman who quit living her life in a way that was unacceptable to her. She used to smoke, drink way too much, have sex with whomever and whenever, and cuss like a sailor. She stopped smoking and drinking, she had sex only when she really desired sex, she stopped cussing, and she started going to church. She sat on the front pew of the church every Sunday. While the change in her life suited her just fine, she also thought it a good idea to judge everyone else who didn't live like she now did. She made sure she pointed out how awful she thought it was that her friend still slept around and didn't take any man seriously enough to be in a relationship. She made sure to cough loud enough whenever she was around a smoker. She preached how alcohol was the devil. She became unbearable to be around.

The lesson here is just because you decide to create changes in your life doesn't mean you have the right to convict others who are not living the way you choose to live. Just because you've made healthier choices, doesn't mean everyone you know should do the same. Quit convicting people based on rules and a lifestyle you have decided for yourself. Others are allowed the free choice to live their lives the way they choose to live them. It doesn't mean you should give your heart away to someone who is not trustworthy or to allow them past the emotional boundaries you have set up to protect yourself, but you should not become judgmental about them either. You may be excited to share what you are learning, and the way the Survivor's Journey is changing your life. Please do share, but recognize everyone is allowed to make their own decisions and choices in life. That's what living free is all about.

Finally, some people have not grown emotionally and have been this way for several years. They may not even recognize life could be different for them. Perhaps you watch them move between relationships and friendships, not being around people who are good for them and getting hurt over and over. Perhaps you see them hurting others and not being a very trustworthy person. Because of your growth you can clearly see it. It evokes emotions in you. They can stir up feelings inside you like anger, sadness, and frustration! Remember, this healing journey is for you. All of your time and energy should be spent on you. It's not your job at this stage to help them change who they are. You cannot put on your cape and play superman or superwoman and save someone from themselves. I know it seems selfish to worry about yourself and not others and is against your nature. The Survivor's Journey is an extremely selfish set of Journeys. And while selfishness has been seen as a bad trait to have, it's a trait you need right now. You have given and given and given. It's time for you to move inward and give to yourself. This is your time right now to engage in your own healing. You can't give away what you don't quite have yet. Continue to focus on yourself and your healing. There will be plenty of time for you to help others once you have focused the time you need on yourself. In reality, in helping yourself you are preparing yourself to show up in a more healthy way for others.

8

8th Journey: *The survivor pursues healthy and supportive relationships.*

8th Truth: *Unhealthy relationships keep me sick.*

8th Transformation: *I build and sustain healthy and nurturing relationships and support systems.*

Trigger or Validation:

For some, the material in this Journey may be triggering. If it triggers you, reach out to your support system including those you trust and appropriate members of your Bomb Squad and/or engage in some self-care activities. For others, this information will be validating. In those cases, use the material to help validate you and affirm that what you are or have been experiencing is real.

CHAPTER 8: HEALTHY RELATIONSHIPS

"Their eyes meet across the crowded room. They instantly connect. They make their way toward each other. It was love at first sight."

"The man was looking good from his head down to his toes. He smelled good. He walked like he had all of the right parts in the right places. Like the world was at his feet. He spoke with confidence. I melted."

"Look at her. She is someone I need in my life. I would love to just be in her company today, tomorrow, and forever."

"Oh my Lord, why did God make such a wonderful creature. This is a person I could love forever, or at least for the night."

What do you think about the comments above? Have you ever felt an emotional or sexual energy from someone and knew an attraction existed? Many of us have. *However*, you will not solely be led by what you *feel* without paying attention to what you *think*. Because of your past experiences, you will no longer solely rely on your heart and your feelings to choose a potential partner. You will include your brain. Indeed, it's your brain that will do most of the work. It's your brain that will assess the situation and determine if you have a potential candidate to spend your life with.

A Healthy Relationship with Yourself

But before we focus on a relationship with other people, let's first focus on your relationship with yourself. The relationship you have with yourself is one of the most important relationships you'll have on earth. The relationship you have with yourself is a good measure of how healthy you are. So, how do you treat yourself? Do you tend to treat others better than you treat yourself?

In order to be involved in great friendships or a fulfilling intimate partnership, you have to be a healthy person who attracts healthy people. Even the best of us get busy or preoccupied and often neglect ourselves. Neglect, which goes on too long, has serious emotional, mental, social, spiritual, behavioral, and physical health consequences. Thus, it's important to engage in regular self-care addressing all the parts of you.

It's Not Selfish. It's Self Care

What is self-care? First, let's talk about what it isn't. Self-care involves more than doing things that make you feel good in the moment. It's more than taking a bubble-bath, although that might be a good start. It's more than going to a party, painting your fingernails, or watching a good movie, although those are great mood-boosting behavioral activities. Because self-care involves caring for all the parts of you, it requires taking care of your emotional, mental, social, spiritual, behavioral, and physical self. Self-care is the practice of taking an active role in protecting your own well-being and happiness, particularly during periods of stress.

The benefits of self-care are improved mood and overall well-being. Self-care can reduce stress and anxiety, increase patience and resilience, improve your physical health, and encourage greater compassion for others and self. Let's get into the different types of self-care and ideas to practice when stress arises or you feel a need for self-care.

Emotional Self-Care

Emotional self-care helps during emotionally stressful times. Learn to tap into yourself and become aware enough to identify those times when you are feeling emotionally stressed. Allow yourself to feel the feeling long enough so you can identify it. Recognize the feeling, despite how terrible and uncomfortable it may feel to you. Remember, it is temporary. Understand when you meet your therapist, you are working on your overall emotional health. Go to Survivor's Journey groups and complete your workbook. You will soon learn the power you have over what you choose to feel, and why. Remind yourself it is temporary and there will come a day and a time in life when you will have power over what you feel and you will be able to better handle those feelings.

Here are a few ways you can connect with your emotions and process them in healthy ways:

- Contact your therapist and process your emotions.
- Discuss your emotions with your case manager or NA/AA Sponsor.
- Talk about your emotions in your Survivor's Journey group.
- Write in your workbook and process your emotions there.
- Find and use your favorite positive affirmations.
- Meditate.
- Practice yoga, preferably trauma-focused yoga, online or in person.
- Use the power of positive thinking by focusing on the more positive aspects of your life.
- Practice recognizing what you can be grateful for; Gratitude Practice

Gratitude Practice is a technique some use to remember what they are grateful about. It is a powerful way of focusing on the gifts you were given. Gratitude changes your mindset and helps you focus on what is right with you and in the world. The fact that you are working on your own healing and health is something to be grateful about. Your ability to attend Survivor's Journey groups and experience recovery with others is something to be grateful about. Having a friend, food, clothes, and the opportunity to live another day can make you grateful.

Writing yourself a gratitude letter, explaining things you are grateful about, is a powerful way to help you shift your focus. In a study conducted at Berkeley, participants wrote gratitude letters daily for four weeks, and after 12 weeks felt significantly better as a result. Try writing a gratitude letter every morning and keep them in your workbook, or better yet, tape them on your refrigerator to consistently remember what you are grateful about. Be intentional about it. Establish a gratitude habit. People who are intentional about their gratitude typically have better emotional health.

There are two to three things in everyone's life of major importance to them, even if everything else is taken away. Those two or three people, situations, or things being disturbed or lost would rock your emotional core and would cause you to have to do some deep, emotional work. Identify what those two or three things in life are to you. Become aware of what those are. It could be your health, your children, or even a loved one. Know, other than those things critically important to you, everything else pales in comparison. Know, everything else is small. Know, if something goes wrong emotionally, it will be uncomfortable for you, but it's not strong enough to rock your world. Some of us forget there are some things much more important than others and by default we hold everything to the same level of priority and then emotionally fall apart about anything that goes wrong. We then become overly dramatic because we have forgotten life happens and not everything that goes wrong should be equally painful.

We need to put it into perspective, even those elements connected beyond our life, to our very soul. Those elements are valuable. Everything else, while it could be emotionally disturbing to us, won't be life-altering and will be ok because we will get through it. *And if* or when there comes a time when one of our soul-altering losses occurs, we can rely on the support system around us, namely our therapist and our Journey members who will help us through it.

Improved Mental Health as Self-Care
Self-care also involves taking good care of your mental state. Seeing your trauma treatment therapist regularly is a great self-care habit to keep. Read and learn more about trauma, self-care, or anything you might be diagnosed with or dealing with emotionally. Become as educated as possible about your struggles. Not to sink even deeper into poor mental health, but to become educated and empowered to act in your own best interest. If that involves a diagnosis and taking mental health medication, take your meds. Taking your meds is a big part of

self-care. Work with your psychiatrist and therapist until you find the treatment in your best interest, short and long-term.

For improved mental health, it's also important to eat well and eat regularly. It's important you get enough sleep, and you surround yourself with people who support you. Also, begin your daily gratitude routine. One of the keys to gratitude is not comparing yourself to others. Focus on what *you* have accomplished today, this past week, or this past month.

Work on stimulating your mind. Read a new book, visit a historical museum, walk in the park, write a poem or a short story, paint or color in a coloring book, have a bubble bath with candles, watch a movie; the options are endless. Do those things you love to do. If going to the museum is boring to you, go to a concert instead. Do what you enjoy and what stimulates your mind.

Spiritual Self-Care

Having a connection to something greater than yourself is a proven great source of healing and inspiration. Spiritual connection means nurturing your soul. It honors and connects your soul and your belief in God, Allah, the Great Spirit, nature, and/or humanity. Nurturing your soul means you engage in prayer and/or attend spiritual services and ceremonies, connect with nature, perform meditation, read religious or philosophical texts, or do what inspires your spirit. You might volunteer for causes you care about. Feeding your soul is a fulfilling practice. By connecting with something loving outside of yourself, it fills you with a sense of calm and peace. Practice feeding your soul and increasing your spiritual well-being. Make this a daily or weekly self-care practice.

Organizing for Daily Life

Organizing for daily life is also a part of self-care. The more you are organized, the greater and more productive you feel. An uncluttered space often equates to an uncluttered mind. Thus, cleaning your home, work, or school space, or tidying up your car is a great way to feel less stress. Writing your appointments down in a calendar is important and will help you stay on top of your responsibilities.

Taking care of yourself also involves turning off your cell phone and limiting your time on social media to spend more quality time with yourself or your loved ones. Investing time into your personal and professional growth by taking classes, listening to podcasts, or reading self-help books is also a good way to feed your growth.

Financial Self-Care

Some of the most stressful times in a life arise during financial uncertainty. As authors of the Survivor's Journey, even we have lived in poverty. We've experienced living on $100 a month, surviving domestic violence, life with a drug abusing alcoholic partner, homelessness, and addiction recovery. We understand what it means to have little to nothing by the end of the month. Ensuring you can take care of yourself financially reduces chances of stress. It's an important part of self-care and without it, you will consistently live life in survival mode and when that happens, it becomes difficult to invest in any other parts of self-care.

Safety

Emotional and physical safety is also a critical part of self-care. Making sure your space is safe and shared with safe people is important to maintaining good mental health. Without it you will find yourself feeling hypervigilant and almost always focused on ensuring your safety.

Truth: *"Unhealthy relationships keep me sick."*

Earlier, we discussed the idea of becoming who you associate with or hang around. Take account of the people you spend the most time. Do you have an emotionally healthy relationship with them? If not, consider distancing yourself from those who are toxic and invest more time into those relationships more healthy. In fact, the rest of this Journey is devoted to social well-being as self-care aka healthy and unhealthy friendships and intimate relationships.

In our lives we usually have a mixture of those who are toxic and those who are nurturing to us. We might also refer to toxic people as

"Basement People" because their toxic habits bring us down, while in contrast, we refer to nurturing people as "Ceiling People" because they lift us up. The goal is to distance toxic people from our lives and bring nurturing people closer to us. In order to do that, we have to first determine who in our lives is toxic and who is nurturing.

A toxic person is someone that reminds you of the mistakes you've made in the past. They tell you in a number of ways you "can't do it" or "you shouldn't try." They want you to stay where you are in life because it makes them feel more comfortable. The reason is, if you turn out successful, where will that leave them? If you become emotionally healthy or do better in life, they would have no more excuses for their lack of motivation or execution. Basement people prefer you to ruminate with them about how unfair life is. They love spending time with you, reminding you why you can't or shouldn't change. They stomp on your dreams and kill your ambition. They work hard at making you feel you can't do it. And when you try, you'll hear them tell and show you, again, in many ways, why you should give up. When you are busy working on yourself or your dreams, they will give you examples of when you tried and failed. As you work towards your goals, they will call or visit and distract you from your goals. Not because they are deliberately trying to sway you away from those goals, they simply lack respect for your dedication or assume you would never be successful anyway.

A toxic person is harmful to your emotional and mental health, and even bad for your physical health. Repeated engagement with a toxic influence is just like a silent killer. It can run your blood pressure up, upset your stomach, and thin your hair, just from the prolonged biological stress of being around them. Engaging with "basement people" can make you feel stressed, apathetic, frustrated, and can cause you to question yourself, what you believe, and your likes and dislikes. This person can confuse you and try to make you feel bad about yourself.

A nurturing person, or "ceiling person", is someone who reminds you of why you are a good person, despite what has happened in your life. They remind you of your good qualities. They show you they are available for you. They love you and they like you. They encourage you to improve yourself. They help you find the time to improve yourself. They support and nurture you. They understand your heart, even when you have made past mistakes. They help you grow as a person. They forgive you. Your progress excites them. They see past your past and embrace what you want to do with your life.

Understand a nurturing person in your life isn't always someone who sings your praises. A nurturing person can also challenge you to do and be better. The difference between a nurturing person's challenge and a toxic person's goal is a nurturing person has your best interest at heart. They are speaking truth to you so you will see your barriers and challenges and can make it through them to victory. The toxic person's goal is to get you to give up.

Sometimes it's difficult to decipher which person is toxic and which is nurturing. Sometimes the toxic person appears nurturing, while the nurturing person that is challenging you appears toxic. You'll need to consider the differences and come to a conclusion about who is who. Once you understand who in your life is toxic and who is nurturing, you'll need to determine the direction in which the flow of the toxic or nurturing energy works. Complete the exercise in your workbook. In essence, if you have a toxic person in your life and a lot of the toxic energy is flowing from them to you, then this is very damaging to your emotional, mental, and physical health. If you are receiving a lot of toxic energy you will remain sick. It takes a lot of emotional, mental, and spiritual energy to counter toxic energy and repel it. You may wonder why you aren't motivated or don't have the energy to do all of the things you want to do. One reason might be the number of toxic people in your life and the flow and level of toxic energy you have flowing in your direction.

"There was a time in my life when I was trying to go back to school and be successful. However, I was in an abusive relationship and no matter how hard I tried, I couldn't study hard enough to get good grades. I thought I just wasn't smart enough. I couldn't focus. I wouldn't take the time I needed to sit and study. I had too much negative energy in my personal space and I was too worried about

when the next fight was going to break out and how I was going to pay the bills once my partner drank or smoked up all of our money. Once I got rid of him and worked on my emotional trauma, I realized that I was smart. My grades got a lot better. I was able to focus and learn a lot faster. I decided to get my master's degree and continued on to receive my PhD."

~Celia

Also recognize when *you* are the toxic person making someone's life miserable. If you spew toxic energy, it is because you are not well emotionally. Participating in Survivor's Journey groups will be particularly important for you. The last thing you want to do is be toxic to anyone else. In some cases, both people engaged in a friendship or relationship are toxic toward each other. This is a recipe for disaster. If you are in a toxic relationship, you will make little to no progress because your goals will continually be sabotaged or disrupted. You may even find yourself putting little to no energy towards your goals because much of your energy will be used up from navigating your toxic relationship.

Toxic relationships can be very exciting and even intensely sexual if intimate. These relationships are rarely even keeled. There are maximum highs and maximum lows. The levels of love and anger in these relationships have high peaks and low valleys. For example, one minute you love your intimate partner and the next you hate them. You break up, and get back together. It is a rollercoaster of a ride. The level of energy required to maintain these kinds of dysfunctional relationships is quite consuming. Many people become addicted to the extreme emotional highs and lows in the relationship.

Nurturing people are those who inspire you and have your best interest in mind. They are rarely judgmental and genuinely like you. They try to support you. They are truly a friend to you. Nurturing people don't always make you feel perfect, but they can challenge you to be better. It's because they know you can be better and do better. Nurturing people are honest. They may have higher expectations of you. And because no one rises to low expectations, they can sometimes make you believe you can achieve your goals. If you have a nurturing friend, family member, or relationship, consider yourself lucky. Is this person perfect? No, nurturing people make mistakes, sometimes hurt your feelings, and take missteps, but all-in-all they are great for you. They don't belittle you and aren't negative towards you. They try to help you and try to help make your life better. The energy flow coming to you from a nurturing person is like your life's blood. Recognize it and cherish it.

If you are a person who is supportive and nurturing to a friend, a family member, or in a relationship, know that you are inspiring and helping to lift someone up.

To successfully make it through the Survivor's Journey you need *(and deserve)* a supportive group of people who are in your corner. Your "Bomb Squad" are supportive people who are in your corner. Your Bomb Squad is what we call your "formal support system". Now you need to make sure you have a healthy "informal support system". Your informal support system may be made up of your friends, family members, co-workers, neighbors, and intimate partner.

In your workbook, you will list those in your life who are toxic and those who are nurturing. If you have at least one toxic person in your life, you will design an intervention to start placing physical and/or emotional distance between you and them. You are somewhat familiar with this because we discussed boundaries earlier in the book. Let's discuss how to begin the process of distancing yourself from them.

Physical and Emotional Distancing from Toxic People

Distancing toxic people is usually done over time. You can also choose to cut them out of your life immediately, but that usually isn't a strategic decision. It's usually an emotional decision which doesn't last. Typically, they will be right back looking to regain the relationship they had with you. Once you soften, you will be inclined to accept them back into your good graces.

There are many ways to effectively distance toxic people and begin to remove them from your life. For instance, your cell phone ringing is a suggestion. You don't have to answer it every time it rings. You can choose not to answer. Let it go to voicemail. If someone texts you, you don't have to respond right away, or ever, if you don't want to. Remember you teach people how to treat you. If every time someone calls or texts and you respond right away, you teach them that you are always available. But when you don't respond right away and you choose a time when you are ready to respond to them, you teach them that you will control if and when you want to interact with them.

You can also inform the toxic people in your life that you don't accept visitors who don't get permission to come over first. If they show up unannounced, don't answer the door. It may sound cruel at first, and it will be hard to do, but once you do it they will get the message. If they want to interact with you, they will learn to do it in a way acceptable to you. In doing this, you are designing your life and the people in it to suit you. You are engaging in good mental health and important self-care. This is not selfish, it's self-care.

In most cases you can begin to distance yourself from spending in-person time with toxic friends and family members. You owe no loyalty to anyone who doesn't help your self-esteem and your mental health. In most cases, it's really out of some sense of love and obligation you are connecting with this person. You love them and they are family. For instance, you may feel obligated to take care of your mother or your aunt or uncle because they are family. You believe they need you and you are the only person in the world who can take care of them. You may feel guilty if you don't. The truth is, you are not the only person in the world who can help them. There are plenty of formal services in communities who can help with food, clothing, shelter, medical care, socialization, legal services, mental health services, in-home care, case management and more. There may also be available informal helpers like neighbors, friends, other family members, including their siblings or your siblings who can also help. You are not everyone's savior. You can invest in others when you are emotionally healthy enough to do so. That would be you practicing your old, bad habit of trying to help others before you can help yourself. This is especially true if this person tries to make you feel bad about yourself, reminds you of the mistakes you made in the past, tries to make you feel guilty, ashamed, or leaves you feeling empty, depressed, angry, or broken. They are not someone who is good for your recovery. As you begin to distance yourself, it is more than likely they will find someone else to latch onto for support. You can point them in the right direction to receive the support they need. And that is okay, they will do what is best for them.

Re-read the paragraph above. Meditate on it. Let it sit with you for a while. Use these words to become empowered to put a plan into action. You can begin by slowly implementing your plan. You don't have to cut these toxic people out of your life immediately or completely. You start by choosing when you will talk to them, what you *will* talk about, *won't* talk about, and *where* you will talk to them. If they begin a conversation which is unhealthy and demeaning to you, you can stop them. Kindly let them know this is not a conversation you are willing to have. Use your "I" statements by saying things like, "I am not comfortable talking about this with you." Feel free to reiterate it as often as needed without getting emotional or raising your voice. If they decide to treat you in a manner that is upsetting and toxic to you, let them know those types of conversations are no longer acceptable or tolerated. Use your "I" statements to explain. For instance, you can say, "When I hear that type of talk, I feel 'include what you feel', so I would appreciate it if that didn't happen." If it continues, leave the conversation. What you are doing is teaching them how to approach you and engage with you. If they don't learn then you will have to make a decision about how, when, or if you engage them again.

It's emotionally taxing to continue to do this. Part of becoming healthy is distancing yourself from toxic people. However, in rare cases there are family members you simply cannot physically distance yourself from. Perhaps there is a situation where you absolutely have to engage with them and they will not change the way they engage with you. In these cases, you can emotionally distance yourself from them, even though you are physically in proximity to them. You do this by not allowing what they say affect your emotional self. Don't allow their words or tone to enter into your heart space. Practice politely tuning them out. It may hit your chest wall cavity, but don't let it enter.

To become healthy, you'll need to distance those toxic people and eventually remove them from your life. This is critical if you want to begin to become a healthier person and live the life you want. You can run with 100 healthy people who are striving for health, or you can spend your life trying to drag one toxic person along with you down the road to improve your health and happiness. Do you want to go through the pain of distancing yourself from them now, or experience smaller doses of pain across your lifetime? The choice is yours.

When someone is emotionally toxic to you, it's like carrying a 50 lb. sack of someone else's burdens on your back. Consciously choose not to carry it or to own it. Know their burdens are not yours to carry. When you are truly able to do this, others will notice. They will wonder why these things being said don't bother you. And it will be because that burden is no longer yours to carry and you know that deeply in your spirit. When you do this it will feel like a breath of fresh air. You will feel lighter, and happier. When you can do it safely, limit your time with this toxic person to the minimum time you have to spend with them. You will be surprised at how much better you will feel and how much emotional energy you will regain to put to use on your own emotional health.

Qualities to Look for in a Potential Partner

"It's a good thing if your palms are a little sweaty and you have butterflies in your stomach. It means you're growing." -Jill Blashack Strahan

What is it you are looking for in a relationship? Think about the qualities you are looking for. Don't think about the external characteristics (e.g. great looking) or material possessions (e.g. a nice car) someone should have just yet. Consider the internal qualities and characteristics. We understand physical attraction is also critically important; It's hard to stay in a relationship with someone you aren't physically attracted to, but do that last, after you have identified the qualities you are looking for in a potential partner. You can also use this list to assess the partner you are currently with.

Sit down and create a list of the qualities and characteristics you are looking for in a mate.

Here are some general qualities to consider in a potential partner:

- *Maturity:* They learn from their past experiences to evolve as a human being. They are not easily swept away by emotion. They think before making important decisions.
- *Openness:* They are emotionally open. They don't hide who they are, who is in their life, and their past experiences. Taking into consideration no one is willing to be 100% vulnerable until they trust, this person shows you a willingness to be vulnerable with you.
- *Honesty and Integrity:* They are who they say they are. They are where they say they'll be. They are dependable.
- *Respect:* There is a level of respect they have for you. Even when you argue, which happens within the best of friendships or relationships, there is a level of respect. Respecting someone in a relationship means to find their partner valuable. It means they believe their partner's thoughts and opinions are valuable. For instance, they wouldn't make a decision affecting their partner without consulting them first. They also respect and encourage their partner to fulfill their dreams.
- *Interdependence:* There is a mutual dependence on each other. In turn, each also has activities or an identity that is an addition to who they are in the relationship.
- *Empathy:* They feel for other people. They can put themselves in the other's shoes.
- *Affection:* They show an adequate amount of emotional and/or physical affection.
- *Sense of Humor:* They understand their partner's sense of humor. They can laugh with their partner.

- *Trustworthiness:* They have reasons to trust their partner. They behave in ways that are trustworthy.
- *Attractiveness and Intimacy:* They are attractive to their partner, and are interested in being intimate with or affectionate toward them.
- *Self-Discipline:* They display a level of maturity and are able to act in healthy ways. challenge themselves to overcome their weaknesses and pursue what they think is right despite those challenges.
- *Clear Communication:* They clearly communicate their thoughts and feelings. This is what leads to trust.
- *Emotional Regulation:* They know how to regulate their own emotions. They don't lose emotional control.
- *Positivity:* They have the ability to see the good in things and in life. They aren't always negative.
- *Ambition:* They have goals and are working on them.

Do you find it interesting that it takes time to see many of these qualities? That's because when you are healthy, you realize it takes time to get to know someone before committing to a relationship. Once you realize a person possesses many of the qualities you decided were important to you, do you pursue them or push them away because of your past trauma? Do you figure out why it would be impossible to date this person? Do you make excuses? Do you find the one thing about them you can't stand and give up pursuing the relationship? Understand no one will be perfect. Great relationships are made when the person finally understands this. And when you decide the thing which is wrong with this potential partner is something you can look past, you may have found a solid potential partner.

But where do you find such a potential partner? Take a look at your list. Does the list give you any clues about where such a person may be located? Where might such a person physically spend time having fun? Where might they be working? Enjoying their hobby? Which of your friends or acquaintances might know such a person? Where might they be present online? Because in-person safety and online safety is critically important, where might you be able to engage new friends or a new hobby or interest in a place that is safe? If you are looking for a potential partner, try new things. If there are poetry readings, attend some of them. If you are a big sports fan, gather with others and go to a game. The main point is to consider reaching and putting yourself in safe, yet fun settings. You may meet new, healthy friends and you might just meet someone of special interest to you.

If you do happen to meet someone, it's not the physical attraction which will be the deciding factor for you. There should be some physical attraction which interests you, but it will be the other qualities you are looking for that will give you the green light to continue to see where this leads or stops you from pursuing anything further.

No one is perfect. The person who is connecting with you won't possess all of the qualities you desire. But if they are matching many of your desires, they may be someone to consider.

Also understand, because there are no perfect people, there are no perfect relationships. If you were to have an honest conversation with someone in a long-term relationship who you consider healthy, you'll find this to be true. You will find they have accepted the flaws in their partner because of the abundance of great qualities their partner has. You will find their relationship, much like other long-term relationships, are like the stock market - there are good days and bad days. There are days when the stock is high and is paying great dividends and there are days when the stock drops and you are paying the price (not in abusive ways, however). In great long-term relationships, there are great weeks and great months and bad weeks and bad months. If you were to ask a person in a healthy, long-term relationship if they liked their partner all of the time they would say no. When the stock is high, they would say they like their partner about 90% of the time. When the stock is low and there are problems, they would say they liked their partner about 30% of the time. This fluctuation in healthy relationships is normal. There can be a period of time where life is good, and the relationship is stable. Then there are times when inside the relationship there are problems which need to be resolved. These may swing from small annoyances to large issues. People who stay together have learned to weather the storm. They know it's likely problems will be resolved if they just hang in there and work to get the relationship back on stable ground again. It's when there are lots of consistent days where one partner is unhappy with the overall relationship that the foundation can begin to crumble. Problems which don't get resolved can cause cracks in the foundation that sets the stage for an end to the relationship.

People involved in healthy relationships try and share their lives together. They work to weave their lives together in ways that complement each other and make each other feel loved and cared for. However, people involved in healthy relationships don't lose their identity or who they are because they are in a relationship. There are parts of yourself you should maintain because they are a part of who you are. For instance, perhaps you have a hobby or you have personal or professional goals you are pursuing and you would pursue those whether or not you were in a relationship. Stay true to yourself and do some things without your partner. Continue to pursue your goals and engage in your hobbies. Your partner should complement who you are and should want and encourage you to pursue your dreams and goals, and vice versa.

Relationships to Avoid

There are numerous types of intimate relationships. If both adults in a relationship are happy with the relationship, no one should tell them their relationship is dysfunctional or they should end it. It functions the way they want it to function. We can't get caught up in trying to make our relationship or someone else's relationship adhere to the standards of whatever an idea of a relationship is supposed to look like or feel like. We cannot define ourselves or our relationship by someone else's standards. If we are satisfied with our relationship, if we are loved and feel respected in the relationship, we should continue with it. If it is a loving relationship which just needs a little help - we should work on it. Before giving up on a relationship, try to fix it. Perhaps, go to couples counseling or book a relationship coach and try to improve the relationship where it needs improvement.

It's only when the pain in the relationship consistently outweighs the pleasure that we should consider ending a relationship. Sometimes we stay because our identity is wrapped up in the relationship. We think who we are is who we are in relationship to this person. Sometimes we are afraid to leave. These are relationships which we are not happily involved in. The fear may include fear in which our partner will find someone else, fear in which they will physically hurt us if we try to leave, fear in which the children won't be well adjusted if we leave, and fear in which we will lose our social standing or financial support as well as other fears. When maintaining an unhealthy relationship is based on fear, it will be difficult to remain healthy and happy.

There are certain relationships we want to avoid. They include being in relationship with someone who is truly unattainable, is emotionally unavailable, is an emotionally wounded soul, or is a partner who is completely unfulfilling to you.

The Unattainable

This person is "out of your league". Your social self may have convinced you in being with this person you will be placing yourself in a higher social and financial status. You'll begin to think you would feel so good about yourself *if only* you could get this person to commit to you. And that's exactly what you'll do throughout this would-be "relationship". You'll spend a lot of energy trying to get this person to focus on you and to give their heart to you. In the end it won't work. For one reason or the other, you won't have the place in their heart you desire. Instead of dreaming, plotting, and wishing, think about the reality of where you are now in this "relationship". If you're honest, it's not even a relationship. You are pursuing something which, for whatever reason, isn't going to happen for you.

In all honesty, you like the persona of this person. You like their success, their social situation, their physical looks. You want what they have. If you think about it, you don't really want them or who they are as a person. You find it easier just to be with them than it is to achieve what they have achieved. Hoping to be with them, however, is often an empty, fruitless pursuit. Chasing them will keep you thinking about the future. You'll live in the fantasy. Stop thinking of the fantasy and check your emotional self in the present. How do you feel right now when you are with this person? Is there real hope of a future with this person? Are they attentive to you in a way that sets the stage to build a genuine and caring relationship? Are they showing genuine interest in you? If so, consider pursuing the relationship. If not, let's live our lives in reality of what is, not what is probably impossible.

But don't just let it go. Find out why you are so attracted to someone who is so unattainable. Think about it. Sit with it. These thoughts may give you valuable feedback you can use for your personal growth.

The Emotionally Unavailable

This person is not emotionally available to you and will not be there for you when you really need them. They have shown you this over and over. Perhaps they may be married. Maybe they are emotionally unavailable because they are preoccupied with addictions. They may have become consumed with church or work or any number of reasons they can't or don't make themselves emotionally available to you.

They leave you wanting and will always leave you wanting. They will never be enough or give you enough because they are placing their emotional energy somewhere else. Just remember a person's attention is placed on what they consider important.

Ask yourself why you are pursuing someone who is not available to you. Check your self-esteem. You might find the answer there.

If this type of relationship is worth saving, have a serious conversation. Communicate your needs. Give them a chance to step up to the plate and be there for you. You can even go to couples counseling and get your relationship on track in ways which are mutually satisfying and mutually beneficial. Sometimes emotionally unavailable partners come with all of the exterior or social trimmings you want in your life and you settle for that. Perhaps this person tells you or shows you they are emotionally unavailable, but you believe you have the power to change them. You secretly say to yourself, "I'll take that challenge" and you go about trying to change them into someone who is interested in an emotional relationship with you, despite reality. Maybe they told you or showed you they were obligated elsewhere and weren't interested in anything more than a sexual relationship or friendship. Even if they deny their true intentions, watch their actions. Is what they're doing emotionally satisfying you? That is a valuable question to ask. When you are done stringing yourself along hoping, fantasizing, and dreaming, you can move on with your life. Hanging onto the thought of trying to change someone into the person who will love you - will, in fact, leave you heartbroken and with lower self-esteem than you started with.

The Wounded Soul

Everyone has been emotionally wounded at some point in their lives. However, there are what we call wounded souls. A "wounded soul" is a person who suffered such deep past emotional wounding they develop pain-based identities. They take painful past experiences and define themselves by those. They see the world through their pain. They can see themselves as victims and as shameful and broken.

Some of us who have suffered trauma can relate to this because we are wounded. If we don't heal our trauma, we run the risk of connecting to another wounded soul. When this happens, it becomes another form of trauma bond. You can go back and familiarize yourself with the elements of trauma bonding discussed in Part I of this book. What you may be mistaking for love is a form of a trauma bond. When you are mutually trauma bonded, you don't *want* each other, you *need* each other. Or one person in the relationship "needs" the other. Taken to extreme, you'll see one partner who begins to stalk another after a break-up or to threaten suicide and other dangerous types of threatening and desperate behaviors. When there is an open wound, one partner, or both, believe the other is the only person who can fill the void and without them they believe they can't make it in life. While people in relationships connect on a deeper level, the connection among wound mates is their connection is rooted in trauma.

Confusing Soul Mates from Wound Mates

When you meet someone special, you are drawn to them like a candle to a flame. You have a somewhat strong unspoken desire to connect. What you have to figure out is what draws you to them. Is it a strong sense of love or is it that your trauma related needs are deeply and strongly connected to theirs? Are you meeting them in love or are you meeting them where they are wounded?

If you believe in a soulmate, then you are looking for someone who is meant for you. It is less likely that there is a soulmate designed specifically for you. However, there are people with qualities and needs who deeply connect with other people desiring those qualities and needs. A love connection, or soul connection, is something which deeply and uniquely connects two people. Their temperaments, attitudes, beliefs, and feelings connect with each other. They balance each other out. They agree on important things. They have empathy for each other in deep and meaningful ways.

Confusing a soulmate for a wound mate is common. If you both were abandoned at some point in your lives when you really needed someone, you may be connecting around your abandonment issues. If you have addictive behaviors or attachment issues, you may be connecting around your need to possess another and hold them emotionally hostage.

If this is of deeper interest to you, read more about wound mates. Particularly because of the trauma you experienced, we advise against getting into a serious relationship. Unless you are already in a relationship, avoid it until you feel emotionally healthy enough, and you are in the 10th, 11th, or 12th Journey. However overall, here's how to tell the difference between a soulmate and a wound mate. When your emotional wounds surface, a soulmate will allow you to explore those issues and will support you through them and help you resolve them. A wound mate will feel threatened and desperate. All they want to do is stay together. They don't want you to get healthy because they are threatened with the fear that you will leave them.

Casual Relationships When You Want More

Some of us will agree to casual relationships, but we really desire more. If you are in any of these types of arrangements, make sure you clearly understand the benefits to you. Often those who have been victimized, rejected, or have lower self-esteem will submit to these types of arrangements, but are left wanting. If you desire much more, then search for what you really want because you're worth it. Spending time with someone who is giving you less than what you desire is like feeling half full most of the time. Find someone who will fill your cup and give you all the love, time, and commitment you deserve. Here is a list of those types of casual relationships we might find ourselves in.

Situation-Ships

Situation-ships are relationships that aren't defined. There is no consistency or seriousness to them. It seems you make last-minute plans or you casually get together whenever it is convenient. You don't really spend time with their friends and they don't spend much time with yours. There isn't talk about a future together. You might be anxious or nervous about when you're going to see them again because nothing is defined. They aren't available to you emotionally and may tell you they don't want to get serious. If hanging out occasionally with someone is what you want and need right now, situation-ships can be fun. They can be a nice distraction from life. But if you are interested in a relationship, situation-ships will not be fulfilling to you. If you are not sure if you are in a situation-ship or not, ask yourself if you met and know their friends. Ask yourself if you know on a regular basis when you're going to see them again. If or when you call them because you really needed something, are they available to you? Do you regularly see them and can you count on them? In situation-ships you don't really feel single, but you're not in a relationship either. You're sort of in an undefined space.

It can be extremely comfortable for those who want that arrangement and uncomfortable for those who want more.

Friends with Benefits

Friends with benefits (FWB) is different from a situation-ship because in a FWB relationship, the relationship has been clearly defined. Certain things will happen and certain things will not happen. Two people may get together to satisfy each other sexually, then separate to resume their lives. It's only when one person begins to have feelings for the other person when problems arise.

Side Piece

Having a side-piece is a way of saying someone has another romantic partner they are committed to but desires a secret romantic relationship or arrangement with someone else. Because they are already involved with someone else who serves as the "main dish", this other person on the side serves as the "side piece", "side dish", or the "dessert".

Cat Fishing

Cat fishing is when someone pretends to be someone they are not. We may present an identity to a potential love interest, but it's not who we really are. We may present a picture of ourselves online, but it isn't us. We may pretend we are employed somewhere we aren't, or live somewhere we don't, or present ourselves as single when we're not. We may pretend to be a certain gender which we're not or weigh a number of pounds that we don't. We may present ourselves as a professional with certain degrees, a certain level of income, and pretend we own a large home or a certain car when we don't. Cat fishing usually involves stringing someone along and enjoying the fantasy for as long as we possibly can. Of course, most of these relationships never work out because they are built on grand scale lies.

Overall problems can occur in these casual relationships when one partner desires to change the relationship. When one partner desires to change the dynamic, the other partner may end the arrangement. The other problem occurs when one partner doesn't openly communicate their desires to change the dynamic of the relationship.

In the end, relationships can be complex. No one really knows what is happening in a relationship outside of the two people involved. Only they know what is truly going on and even their sense of what is truly happening can be misunderstood. Through the 8th Journey, we can evaluate our relationships based on the level of toxicity or poison present. The exercise in your workbook on *Toxic and Nurturing Relationships* is an important one to do and repeat doing each year. This exercise is not just for people involved in an intimate relationship, it's a great exercise for people involved in close friendships and involved with close family members. The essence is to understand the number of nurturing relationships and the number of toxic relationships you have in your life. The goal is to actively design your life in a way that you consciously choose to bring nurturing people closer to you and learn to distance toxic people.

Abusive Relationships

Abusive relationships are defined as relationships in which at least one person believes they have the right to control another person's life and restrict their freedoms. An abuser typically works to isolate their victim from friends and family and maintain power and control over them. Abuse can happen suddenly, out of the blue like an immediate physical slap or other physical or verbal assaults. It can happen over time as someone develops disrespect or becomes overly jealous and then gradually becomes more controlling and abusive.

At the beginning of the relationship, all of this focused attention on you can seem flattering, but over time it becomes difficult to maintain any level of independence. It can become frightening because whatever you do, or no matter how much you try to accommodate an abuser, they continue to exert more and more power and control over you. In contrast, they do not hold themselves to the same level of loyalty, accountability, and perfection they demand from their victim.

Although physical abuse is horribly victimizing, all abusive relationships don't involve physical abuse. There are numerous ways someone can be abused while in an abusive relationship. Many people have seen the Power and Control Wheel. This very well-known wheel provides you with the key areas and ways abusers victimize while involved in a relationship. As you look around the wheel, determine if you are or have been a victim of any of these types of intimate partner abuses.

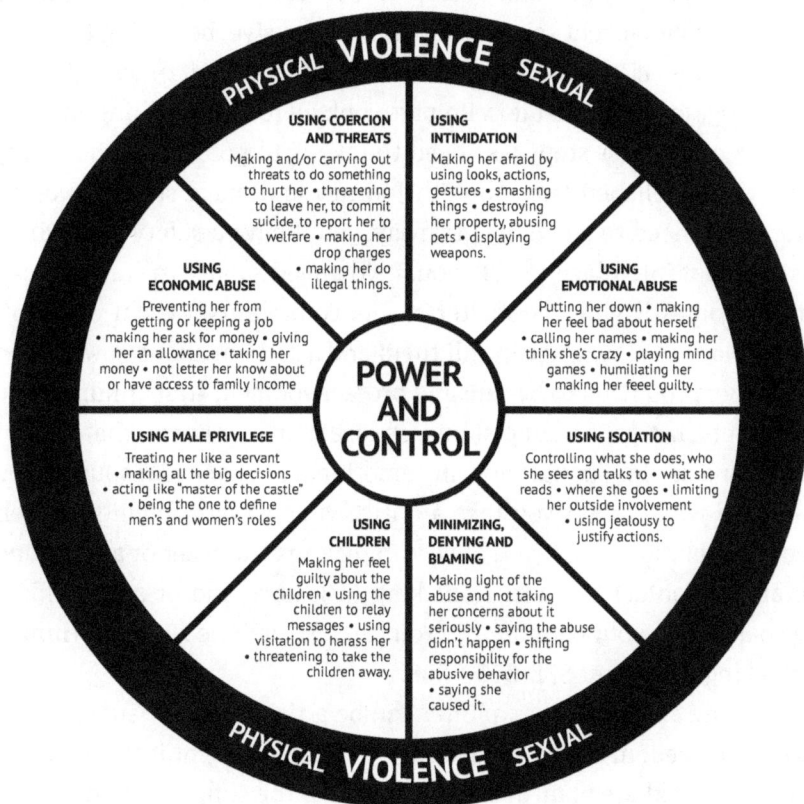

The elements of emotionally violent relationships include: being hypercritical, ignoring boundaries and invading privacy, being possessive and controlling, being manipulative, being dismissive of you or minimizing your feelings, and blaming, shaming, and embarrassing you. People often ignore this part of violence as if it isn't as harmful.

Emotional violence is a violent act and is often more violent than the physical, because as physical wounds heal, emotional wounds can hurt and cause damage for a longer amount of time. The victim of emotional violence can begin to lack confidence, become angry, and (without support) can have a difficult time finding a healthy relationship after the abusive one has ended.

Examine the Power and Control Wheel carefully. Do you see any elements of this in your relationship? If so, take it seriously. If you see signs that your current relationship may be abusive, be willing to admit it. Become very clear on what's happening. Don't avoid it or deny it. If it's happening, see it for what it is. Prepare yourself to do something about it.

One of the first steps you need to take is to go back to the Safety Plan you established from the 5th Journey and make sure it is up to date. If you need to suddenly get away, you'll have a safety plan which has been put into place to help you. If you need a place to stay, you can call the domestic violence shelter in your community. Even if you don't need a place to stay, you can call them and ask them about how to gain the support you need to be safe and protect yourself, your children, and your assets. Let your therapist and/or case manager know what is happening and ask for support and any emotional or physical resources you may need when and if you take a critical step toward freeing yourself from this relationship. If you are escaping a sex trafficker or a pimp and are afraid, contact the anti-trafficking task force and/or anti-trafficking coalition in your community. You can also call the National Human Trafficking Hotline at 888-373-7888.

Leaving an abuser or exploiter can be a risky step towards gaining back your freedom and joy. Make sure you have thought it through, devised an immediate plan, and have an idea of the support you need and know how to get it.

Intimate Partner Violence (IPV)

When we think about intimate partner violence, we think of physical abuse. Being physically abused is a horrific experience to endure. It's terrifying, heart breaking, and emotionally traumatizing. We don't want

228

others to know, so we try to hide it. We hate that our children have to sometimes bear witness to our victimization because it teaches them to solve problems through violence. It also teaches them that being a victim in this way is ok. They also learn when people get frustrated, it's ok to hurt the one you love. The people they love do it.

Often when the victim has had enough and fights back, the police will label it mutual combat. This is not mutual combat. One is an act of violence, the other is called "resistive violence", it is the act of the victim trying to defend themselves.

For some families it's frowned upon to even call the police. It may be highly embarrassing to a family in good standing with a solid and wholesome reputation in the community. It may also be frowned upon in communities where bringing the police to the neighborhood or the household has the potential to get other people (in addition to the abuser) in the neighborhood or household in trouble.

Even though they are there to help, once the "system" of police, courts, and prosecutors get involved, they can inadvertently trigger more trauma-related feelings in the victim. The victim, who goes through the process of getting a protection order or restraining order and leaving the abuser, is courageous and will need a lot of positive support from family and friends as well as a responsive legal and law enforcement community. Unfortunately, the response and support may greatly depend on who you are and where you live.

No one should have to endure the violent abuse of another. No matter how long the victim has endured abuse, it's never too late to leave the abuser. Leaving an abuser is a time when the victim is trying to be at their strongest point in life. They know they have to be strong for themselves and their family. It's important that the victim aligns themselves with supportive people and no longer listens to those who encourage the victim to go back and endure one more beating because in their words, "he still loves you". Think about it, could someone who beats you truly love you? Stop making excuses for your abuser and justifying why they abuse. Stop feeling sorry for them. Finally, stop listening to people who tell you to go back "for the kids". Do you really want to teach your kids that it's ok to beat someone whenever you can't control your emotions? Stop listening to those who will say "How else will you live?" What they are hinting at is for you to go home and get beaten so you will have a bed to sleep in. What is the price you are willing to pay for food, shelter, and clothing? Finally, ignore those people who tell you to stay married because you committed your life under God. The truth is, God would never want this to happen to you. And for the people that remind you that marriage is a commitment that lasts "till death do you part", let them know a death did occur. It was the death of respect, the death of kindness, and the death of love and support.

If you are in an abusive relationship and you desire to leave, listen to the people who want you to be free and who want you to have enough self-esteem not to be abused physically, or in any other form.

Coercive Control

Most courts and criminal justice systems understand physical abuse, but many don't always understand coercive control. As a victim of intimate partner violence, you most certainly have also been a victim of coercive control, but perhaps you haven't ever labeled it as such before.

Coercive control is a pattern of behaviors the abuser uses to control their victim. Each pattern may be unique to the particular couple, but the outcome is the same - to use certain techniques to control a victim and prevent the victim from leaving the relationship. There are numerous ways coercive control happens. The perpetrator provides a certain look to the victim. The victim understands the meaning of the look and falls in line with what the perpetrator wants. The abuser comes home late, the victim knows that means the abuser has been drinking and things could become violent. To counter it, the victim tries to fall asleep early because they know what being awake when the abuser returns means for them. The victim knows to time themselves when they leave the house because it is already understood the approximate length of time they can be gone before the abuser begins to get suspicious. Allowing the kids to play in the house right before the abuser gets home may trigger yelling and screaming from the abuser. Wearing certain clothing out in public may trigger a fight. It goes on and on and on. Coercive control is exactly what it appears to be, a way of controlling almost every aspect of a victim's life including the way they think, feel, behave, what they do, will do, won't do, and are afraid to do. The victim loses themselves and becomes the person who tries to keep the abuser happy and keep themselves and their children from being abused. You might remember this as the fawn response discussed in Chapter 2. What they don't realize is, in trying to decrease the physical abuse they might suffer, they have already been controlled to such a level they lost themselves, their joy, and no longer really know who they are anymore and what they like to do. Within the elements of coercive control, the perpetrator's behavior is consistently attacking the victim's sense of safety, self-determination, satisfaction, and joy. Even threats to self-harm, prolonged medical illness, or struggling mental health can all be used as a means of coercive control to keep the victim where they are.

Safety Plan

Every victim of intimate partner violence needs a safety plan. There are many different types of safety plans. You created a simple safety plan during the 5th Journey. But safety plans can get complex depending on the needs of the victim. Some victims will make copies of all of the important papers and identifications and will keep those at a location away from home in case they need them. They will begin moving essential clothing or will buy essential clothing and keep them off site and away from the house. They may begin making friends with someone who their partner never met so they can establish a supportive friend in the event they leave their abuser. Some begin a confidential savings account, planning for the day they will leave. The victim of intimate partner violence decides what their safety plan should include. When the time is right or when the day comes and they know they can't take it anymore, they have established some of what they needed to sustain themselves for a while.

Once the victim leaves the abuser, they should be prepared to receive public apologies, heartfelt conversations filled with tears, attempts to get other friends or family members to convince them to go back home. They should be prepared to receive gifts and attempts to make the victim remember the good times as well as attempts to show the victim that the perpetrator has changed. These are nothing more than surface attempts. If you expect these things to happen then you won't be surprised or duped into believing them. When the perpetrator understands those won't work, expect to receive aggression, threats, and attempts at further violence. Expect to be demeaned or to hear stories about yourself from others or on social media which may or may not be true. Anticipate your abuser will also use the children or family against you or will attempt to make you feel sorry for them. They will suddenly get sick, become reckless, will drink too much, or will become depressed and suicidal. These are the attempts of a desperate person. Recognize the only experience you can control is your own and the protection of your children. You can't control what someone else feels or does. That is not your obligation or responsibility.

Getting Help

Because those who abuse are obsessed with controlling their victim, it's not typical for a victim to inform their abuser they will be leaving the relationship. Doing so can be very dangerous. A victim typically devises a plan of escape. One day when the abuser is gone somewhere, they may pack what they need to take and leave. If they have children, they pack what the children need and inform them that together they are all leaving.

For some victims this event isn't planned. There comes a day when they just can't take anymore. It may be during an abusive episode or right after. They have a moment of clarity and courage, and they leave. For others it is a well thought out plan. Some go to a battered women's shelter, or a place of faith and ask for help, or they move in with a family member or friend.

Leaving an abuser is dangerous. These moments are the most dangerous moments of the victim's life and the lives of their children. They have done something which has shifted the course of everyone's life in a positive way. Even so, it will be necessary for a victim to understand the risk and to put as many safety measures into place as possible. Having the abuser not know where the victim and children are staying increases the victim's safety. When or if the abuser calls, recording any threatening calls will be important. Obtaining a restraining order or protection order is important because it lets the court know this person is dangerous. Although a restraining order or protection order is only a piece of paper, it will be important to have and to obtain the services of a domestic violence advocate who can help you. To locate an advocate, you can call the battered women's shelter in your community, or you can call the court system, explain your situation and ask for names of agencies where you can call to obtain an advocate. The advocate can help you navigate the criminal justice system. They are also well aware of many services you might need. You can also call the United Way organization or something similar in your community to ask for connections to a domestic violence advocate.

There are domestic violence shelters in most communities across the U.S. and many communities around the world. Typically staff at shelters are very kind and helpful because they understand the trauma victims have suffered. Their passion is to help victims of intimate partner violence, so reach out to them if you need a place to stay and support.

Help for the Abuser

If the abuser is serious about changing their abusive behavior, they can enroll themselves into a Batterer's Intervention Program (BIP). A BIP should consist of a weekly group which lasts at least between 26 and 52 weeks. Online automated or pre-recorded programs or those live programs that are only a few weeks are not effective. Likewise, a completion certificate does not automatically mean the abuser has changed their ways. It simply means they attended and completed classes.

Effective BIPs teach abusers to name and own the behaviors they perpetrated. To date, there hasn't been a high level of effectiveness demonstrated in any BIP. However, when it works, the programs help abusers to change their life in a positive way. Good BIPs understand that denying the harm an abuser caused is part of the problem. It's how abusers continue to tell themselves what they are doing isn't a problem and they can continue this pattern of behavior. BIPs are set up to allow abusers to change meaningfully. Abusers need to understand their behavior disrupted and traumatized the entire family and changed the way the family or the two adults interacted with each other and the world.

For some people, reading this section about help for the abuser excites them because they see a glimmer of hope which they might be able to stay with their abuser and continue to love them and become a family or have the relationship they've always wanted. As the victim, you need to understand the deep, life altering changes an abuser needs to make should be independent of you, your life choices, or the relationship. Their choices or changes are independent of you and should not be contingent upon you going back to them. All in all, there should be no expectation involving you because this becomes another form of coercive control. If they get the idea that you may go back with them, they will go through the motions in order to get you back. Their work won't be genuine. You owe this person nothing. Make no promises to them.

In addition, someone who is treated for substance abuse or mental health is not automatically someone who will stop their abusive behavior once they are treated for substance abuse or mental illness. All too often, we blame the abuse of substances or mental illness on abusive behavior. However, once sober and/or fully medicated to treat their diagnosed mental health disorder, it is not a guarantee their abusive behavior will cease. In fact, substance abuse and/or mental illness is very different from abuse. An altered state can enhance what is already present, but typically it doesn't cause it. When an abuser convinces themselves or others it is not them harming the person/people they love, it's the alcohol or drugs or it's the mental health issues, they stay in denial and continue to give themselves permission to abuse.

When children are involved, there are court systems and advocates who can help you sort through the complications associated with visitation, supervised visitation, shared parenting, and/or custody. These require skilled advocates and professionals to help you and your children decide the best course of action while keeping your safety and the safety of the children in mind.

Tools: Healthy Relationships

We've discussed dysfunctional and unhealthy relationships. It's important to also know what a healthy relationship looks like. First of all, healthy relationships aren't perfect relationships. Refer to the Equality Wheel below. Using the Equality Wheel, assess the health of your relationship. This is what a healthy relationship may look like. Communication, agreement, and decision making together is what is important. If there is agreement and both parties are content, the relationship

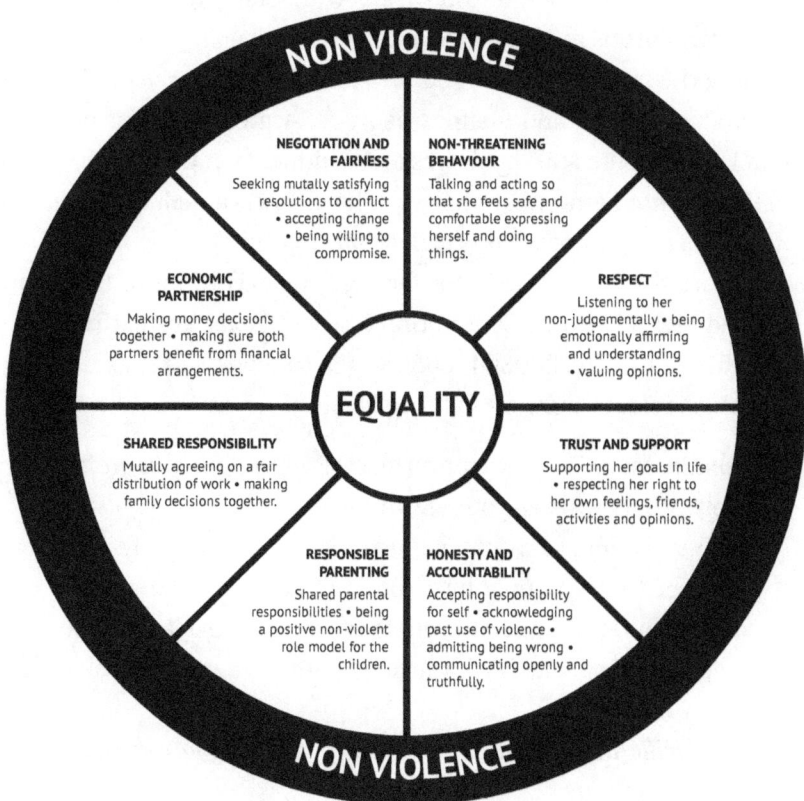

NON VIOLENCE

NEGOTIATION AND FAIRNESS
Seeking mutually satisfying resolutions to conflict • accepting change • being willing to compromise.

NON-THREATENING BEHAVIOUR
Talking and acting so that she feels safe and comfortable expressing herself and doing things.

ECONOMIC PARTNERSHIP
Making money decisions together • making sure both partners benefit from financial arrangements.

RESPECT
Listening to her non-judgementally • being emotionally affirming and understanding • valuing opinions.

EQUALITY

SHARED RESPONSIBILITY
Mutually agreeing on a fair distribution of work • making family decisions together.

TRUST AND SUPPORT
Supporting her goals in life • respecting her right to her own feelings, friends, activities and opinions.

RESPONSIBLE PARENTING
Shared parental responsibilities • being a positive non-violent role model for the children.

HONESTY AND ACCOUNTABILITY
Accepting responsibility for self • acknowledging past use of violence • admitting being wrong • communicating openly and truthfully.

NON VIOLENCE

works for them, and it is likely a healthy one. Learning how to have good communication, agreements, and shared decision making doesn't come naturally. These are skills which must be practiced by both parties.

Fair Fighting

Have you ever run up to two people getting ready to fight? If a punch hasn't yet been thrown, it might be thrown right before the person running up to the fight gets there. That's because the person running up to the fight is bringing added energy to the scene. The lesson here is, when a situation is tense you don't want to bring added energy to it. Instead do the opposite and de-escalate it. Use a calm voice. Try and sit down to talk. Sitting brings the temperature down. Don't use profanity or highly emotional words. Speak clearly and take both the sarcasm and the bass out of your voice before you speak. Avoid blaming the person with "you" statements as in "you make me sick". Avoid using absolutes when describing the issue, such as, "You never..." or "You always..." Communicate your thoughts and feelings using "I" statements. For example, "When I come home and the dishes aren't done, I get upset." Or "When I feel like I'm not being treated like I'm loved and valued, then I am not happy." This is a part of what is called "fair fighting".

Here are the official rules for fair fighting according to the Counseling and Mental Health Center, University of Texas at Austin https://web.archive.org/web/20080418080840/http://www.utexas.edu/student/cmhc/booklets/fighting/fighting.html

- *Remain calm.* Try not to overreact. By remaining calm it's more likely others will see your viewpoint.
- *Express feelings in words, not actions.* If you start to feel so angry or upset that you may lose your self-control, take a "time out" and do something to help yourself feel calm: take a walk, do some deep breathing, play with the dog, write in your workbook - whatever works for you.
- *Be specific about what is bothering you.* Vague complaints are hard to work on.

- *Deal with only one issue at a time.* Don't introduce other topics until each is fully discussed. This avoids the "kitchen sink" effect where people throw in all their complaints while not allowing anything to be resolved.
- *No hitting below the belt.* Attacking areas of personal sensitivity creates an atmosphere of distrust, anger, and vulnerability.
- *Avoid accusations.* Accusations will lead others to focus on defending themselves rather than on understanding you. Instead, talk about how someone's actions made you feel.
- *Try not to generalize.* Avoid words like "never" or "always." Such generalizations are usually inaccurate and will heighten tensions.
- *Avoid make believe.* Exaggerating or inventing a complaint - or your feelings about it - will prevent the real issues from surfacing. Stick with the facts and your honest feelings.
- *Don't stockpile.* Storing up lots of grievances and hurt feelings over time is counterproductive. It's almost impossible to deal with numerous old problems for which recollections may differ. Try to deal with problems as they arise.
- *Avoid clamming up.* Positive results can only be attained with two-way communication. When one person becomes silent and stops responding to the other, frustration and anger can result. However, if you feel yourself getting overwhelmed or shutting down, you may need to take a break from the discussion. Just let your partner know you will return to the conversation as soon as you are able and then don't forget to follow-up.
- *Establish common ground rules.* You may even want to ask your partner-in-conflict to read and discuss this information with you. When both people accept positive common ground rules for managing a conflict, resolution becomes likely.

Parent, Adult, Child Relationships

Sometimes in relationships you'll have one partner who predominantly operates as a parent and one who operates as a child. These relationships aren't healthy because one person is having to set down the rules, hold the other accountable, and dictate what should and should not be done. The other person who assumes the child role must be willing to be dictated to, follow the rules, and is not often allowed to be an adult in the relationship. As a result, the "child" in the relationship will begin to act out passively-aggressively or just aggressively, trying to get away with things and defy the rules. This type of relationship is highly dysfunctional. Besides, no one wants to have an intimate relationship with a parental figure. It's a turn-off.

There are also dysfunctional relationships involving two children. No one in this relationship acts responsibly. When they disagree, it's an all-out war. No one emotionally regulates themselves or their feelings. They yell, scream, and may throw things or even hit each other. When they are hurt, they try to hurt the other person back. They may scratch their car with the car key or put sugar in their gas tank. Nothing is off limits when the child is mad. There will be plenty of fireworks in this relationship. There will be times of great fun and joy so long as both children are happy, and the attention is on them. Once either of the children is unhappy or unattended to, there will be tantrums thrown.

There are also relationships involving two parental types of figures. Typically, both are anxious and overly careful and protective. This relationship often becomes boring because both parties are too afraid to let their hair down and have fun or be adventurous. They want to be safe and can be too careful. They can forget being in a relationship is about taking risks, loving, and having fun. When someone is too much of a parental figure in a relationship, they can also get caught up in finding fault or blaming the other partner. They play the blame game. There is always someone responsible for a problem and the responsible person must be called out and must fix the problem. To a parental figure, the only way people learn is to clean their messes. In always blaming others and providing the lesson to be learned, the parental figure can kill the spice because they are always following all of the rules and are afraid to be vulnerable or silly. They also always have suggestions for how their partner can be better, look better, or do better. They can bring a potentially heated relationship filled with potential to a lukewarm blob of boring rules and excessive caution.

Finally, and hopefully, the two people in a relationship learn to be adults. They can approach the relationship and each other in ways both loving and fun. Adults don't yell and scream when they don't get what they want. They learn to reason through situations and let go of other situations. They try not to hold onto resentments. They understand the importance of both intimacy and fun and they try to do both. They listen to their partner and are empathetic to what their partner may be experiencing. They are not perfect, but they try to meet their partner's needs and be a complement to them.

A good way to determine how internally healthy you are is to look over your past relationships. Were they healthy, loving, and nurturing? If so, then you are likely a healthy person. If not, then you have some work to do. If you have a history of unhealthy relationships, then you are likely used to relationships involving extreme emotional highs and extreme emotional lows where you loved them one week, and hated them the next. It becomes normal to be filled with emotional turmoil. Today you love them. Tomorrow you'd love to throw their belongings into the street. These types of relationships teach us that love is a strong feeling and relationships are filled with strong emotions including love, hate, jealousy and other feelings which keep us on our toes. These relationships keep us interested because something is almost always happening at an extreme.

To someone who is used to communicating in unhealthy ways, a healthy relationship can seem boring. That's because healthy relationships are often emotionally steady and predictable. They aren't filled with a lot of emotional turmoil, and it doesn't take an extreme amount of emotional energy to be in one. Extreme emotional highs and extreme emotional lows aren't normal in steady, healthy relationships. If we have grown accustomed to large arguments and emotionally charged yelling and extreme jealousies, when we don't feel the surge of emotions in a healthy relationship, we think we must not be in love because this is absent. We can determine this relationship is boring and fail to give it the adequate time and nurturing it needs to grow into something fulfilling for us. When there is not a connection, we should end the relationship, but we should stay long enough to know if we are failing to recognize the beauty in a relationship not filled with turmoil. Healthy relationships will look very different to those of us who have been in unhealthy ones.

Do you remember the old black and white movies where the woman sees the man across a crowded room? Their eyes meet and there is an immediate connection? That is no longer the way to approach any relationship. Remember how he walked up to her, grabbed her, kissed her deeply and passionately, and she fell into his arms weak from the power of his love? Remember in Disney movies how Cinderella was taken from her life of abuse with her stepmother and evil stepsisters to be saved by a prince who whisked her away to live happily ever after? Our point is, these stories you've seen are actually just that. They are stories. Made up fairy tales which happen in the land of make-believe. Creating a healthy relationship takes work and it starts in the beginning with how and why you choose to pursue a relationship with this person you are considering.

Relationship Expectations

Relationships are never perfect. People usually come in with certain expectations. An expectation is a strong belief consisting of both spoken and unspoken desires, rules, and roles about the relationship or partner. Everyone has expectations or ways they believe a relationship should unfold. These are the "what's", "when's", "why's", "where's" and "who's" of the relationship. Misunderstandings and arguments occur when one partner misunderstands, miscommunicates, or doesn't fulfill the spoken or unspoken expectations of the relationship to the other partner.

Friendships and intimate relationships involve caring for and about the other person and being there for the other person. These mean different things to different people. However, when boundaries are crossed, or expectations are not met is when issues arise.

Therefore, communicating your boundaries and expectations in a relationship is important. Agreement and negotiation are a part of every meaningful relationship. In these conversations, three possible outcomes occur: (1) An agreement is reached, compromise is made, and the relationship continues, (2) An agreement is not reached, and the relationship ends, or (3) An agreement is not reached, but the relationship continues. In these cases, often the relationship ceases to be healthy particularly when the topic of disagreement is large and significant enough to alter the power, choice, and voice of one partner. As it grows larger, it becomes an invisible elephant in the room. One disagreeing partner grows increasingly unhappy as the problem grows larger. When the partner has power, choice, and voice they will choose to leave the relationship. If they don't have adequate power, choice, and voice they will be controlled by their partner.

Mind-Fields: Cynical and Constrained

Relationships are complicated. They take an investment of your time and attention. Maintaining healthy ones takes daily and weekly work. When you don't consciously practice nurturing your friendships and intimate relationships you may grow more cynical about people and the world. You may get the impression the world is cruel and investing in people and relationships doesn't provide you with the return you want. Without the tools of what to look for in a partner or friend, how to grow a healthy relationship, and maintain a relationship through the difficult times, you may be left without the capacity to guide the relationship in healthy ways. You will become constrained as a result, restricting yourself to only a few relationships, some of which are unhealthy. You will remain afraid to be vulnerable with those you love the most.

Transformation: *"I build and sustain healthy and nurturing relationships and support systems".*

Use this Journey to build and maintain healthy relationships in your life. Avoid relationships with abusive and unhealthy people. As the saying goes: 'if all someone is serving you is disrespect, leave the table'. Seek out relationships using your head before using your heart. Remember, that the best relationship you'll have is with yourself, so be kind and engage in plenty of self-care. Use the tools in this Journey to recognize when someone is unhealthy. Even in the best relationships, people argue. Use the tools of fair fighting when you argue. Try to address problems as an "adult" and not as the child part of yourself. When you incorporate these truths into your life and use the tools provided in this Journey, you are ready to move on to the 9th Journey.

9

9th Journey: *The survivor honors spoken and unspoken commitments which support them.*

9th Truth: *I honor commitments which support and benefit me.*

9th Transformation: *I honor healthy commitments and those which support my growth.*

Trigger or Validation:

For some, the material in this Journey may be triggering. If it triggers you, reach out to your support system including those you trust and appropriate members of your Bomb Squad and/or engage in some self-care activities. For others, this information will be validating. In those cases, use the material to help validate you and affirm that what you are or have been experiencing is real.

CHAPTER 9: UNSPOKEN COMMITMENTS

"Most of us have been trained to take the lukewarm approach to achieving our goals: 'I'll try a little bit and see what happens.' The trouble is lukewarm commitment generally produces lukewarm results. Based on the lukewarm results, people often say, 'Well that didn't work out. It's a good thing I didn't commit myself.' It was, in fact, the lack of commitment that produced lackluster results." ~ Peter McWilliams

You've reached a pinnacle of success and we're so proud of you! You are on the 9th Journey and no doubt you've grown so much emotionally. In this Journey we need to address those spoken and unspoken rules you have that are keeping you stuck and preventing you from moving forward into the life of freedom and health you deserve. This Journey is focused on identifying and letting go of dysfunctional beliefs, obligations, and loyalties you have in favor of adopting those which benefit you.

The life you want could consist of achieving your external goals of having the job you want, the family you want, and the material possessions you want. It most certainly involves meeting your internal goals of living with a level of internal peace, loving yourself, having healthy people who love and care about you, and being able to trust in yourself and a few trustworthy others again. These things are almost worth all the money in the world. They are precious and highly valuable to your sanity and peace of mind.

The main question you need to answer throughout this Journey is: What do I need to give up in order to be the person I want and need to be? This key question will launch you through the 9th Journey.

Taking responsibility to honor our commitments is noble and indeed it's what separates the immature from the mature. That's why we don't send a boy or girl to do a man or woman's job. In honoring our commitments, we demonstrate dignity and integrity. When we remain loyal, we are known to be honorable and earn the right to be respected.

Some spoken and unspoken beliefs, obligations, and loyalties are functional and benefit us, while some are dysfunctional and harmful to us. In this Journey, we will learn how to uncover and no longer pledge allegiance or honor those beliefs, obligations, and loyalties which are harmful to us.

Beliefs, Obligations, and Loyalties (BOLs)

This Journey is about giving up those beliefs, obligations, and loyalties that don't benefit us. The shortened term for beliefs, obligations, and loyalties is called BOLS. When we get caught up and committed to a set of unspoken and dysfunctional BOLs that are unhealthy it eats up our time, resources, and costs us emotionally and psychologically. What we don't realize is remaining committed to BOLs we don't want is a "choice". When this happens we should ask ourselves, "Which BOL of shit am I willing to eat today?" Instead of eating the metaphorical shit which has been placed on our life plate, we will instead learn not to consume it because we will no longer believe in being obligated or loyal to people, places, or things that don't benefit us. For instance, it is believed by some, because of your gender, you are obligated to work a job and are also responsible for cleaning the house, caring for the children, doing the laundry, and preparing the meals. To some this is an outdated idea, for others it's not. The point is from now on you get to choose those beliefs, obligations, and loyalties you want to follow because they are beneficial and healthy for you.

To put it another way, we may be familiar with what some commonly call their "bucket list", or the list of things they want to do before they die. There is also what some call their "fuck it" list. Those are the things we need to give up and let go because they no longer define us and don't benefit us.

These are the unspoken allegiances we've maintained which are just below the surface. We don't consciously think about them. They are just the way things have always been. We have always believed what we believe, behaved the way we behave, and have always remained loyal to people, places, and things to which we thought we should remain loyal.

In this Journey we will uncover those beliefs, obligations, and loyalties and make them conscious to you. Once they are conscious to you, you will have the opportunity to decide which ones you want to stay loyal and committed to and the ones you want to give up. That is what your newly-found power, choice, voice, and freedom affords you. There's no doubt some of the beliefs you have, obligations you've kept, and loyalties you've followed have not been healthy for you and don't serve you well. Your decision will be to keep some and give up others. In addition, in this Journey you will adopt new beliefs, obligations, and loyalties which do benefit you and support your health and well-being.

Truth: *"I honor commitments that support and benefit me".*

The rules which underlie this game of life have not been kind to you, so why keep playing it the way it was laid out? Why honor a dishonorable game? Why follow the rules of a game that hasn't benefited you? As the saying goes "don't hate the player, hate the game." In some respects, let's look beyond the people in your life, the household you come from, and the lessons you've acquired and let's decide to flip the whole script and not play the game the way you've been playing it. Instead let's decide to play this game called life in a way in which you can win. This means you have to reveal the rules you've been playing by and then decide which ones you want to continue to follow and which new rules you will adopt for yourself.

Unspoken Beliefs
Your beliefs, obligations, and loyalties are rules you unconsciously live by. They are not written down or discussed, yet emotionally unhealthy

people know them. They are key rules followed that keep people sick and unfulfilled.

Beliefs specifically are those thoughts we have about why, who, when and how we should think about ourselves, our environment, our experiences, our family, our neighborhood, our community, and other people. These unspoken beliefs were likely embedded in us by others at a younger age. They rule our thoughts, which guide our actions. When our unspoken beliefs deter us from pursuing our own dreams and living the life we are entitled to live, is when our beliefs need to be challenged and changed.

Most people believe just because they are striving to live a better life and they are a good person and putting out good, positive energy, life should be perfect. Everything should work out for them. They don't understand life can slap them in the face after all the hard work they've done to become a better person and improve their life. You may be experiencing what therapists call "Irrational Thoughts." According to the Rational Emotive Theory (RET), there are several irrational thoughts we all have. They are the "musts" and the "shoulds" of life. RET therapists say people "should" aka "shit" on themselves all of the time, meaning they believe they "should" do this, :should" be this, and "should" believe this. These are unrealistic. . These unrealistic beliefs are listed below.

- I must do well and win others' approval or else I'm no good.
- Others must treat me fairly and kindly. If they do not treat me this way, they are not good people and deserve to be punished.
- I must always get what I want, when I want it.
- I must never get what I don't want.
- If I don't get what I want I'm miserable.
- People should always like me.
- I should always like myself.
- I must always be treated fairly.
- Everything I do should turn out well.
- Life should be ordered and predictable.
- If I fail at something, then I am a failure.

- I must be loved and have the approval of everybody.
- I must be rewarded when I put in hard work.
- If I work hard at something, it should work out for me.
- If I am loving and kind to everyone, everyone will be loving and kind to me.

When these beliefs aren't fulfilled, we feel anxious, depressed, shameful, and guilty.

The victim of the irrational thinking errors listed above has put too much faith in the chaos and unpredictability of life. They have placed unrealistic and inflexible beliefs on themselves and are overly concerned with others' beliefs and feelings about them. The best a thriver in recovery can hope for is to put forth their best effort and to take comfort in that. Instead of being devastated, anxious, or depressed when things aren't perfect, allow yourself to feel disappointed in yourself, in others, or in the situation and move on. No one can predict the future, and no one can control an outcome which lies outside of one's control. Take your life one day at a time, doing the best you can and take solace in the fact others are free to think, feel, and behave the way they want because they also have free will, just like you do.

Not only do unhealthy interpersonal beliefs exist, but there are also unhealthy beliefs related to the way we interact in social situations. For instance, there is the belief if the opportunity presents itself, we should take advantage of someone who is vulnerable and unaware. This is very common in business. Famous businessman P.T. Barnum said, "there is a sucker born every minute." The implication is when this "sucker" presents themselves, some believe we should take advantage of them. In some of our twisted psychology it is often the person who is "duped", "tricked", or "deceived" that is to blame. Because someone who is unaware or vulnerable is viewed as weak or naïve, some people will conclude they *should* be taken advantage of or it is the victim's fault for not knowing better. We see this mentality interpreted and played out in social society. When someone takes advantage of the vulnerable, instead of placing blame on the perpetrator, we blame the victim for being betrayed or victimized. For instance, in some communities it is not the married person who is stigmatized for cheating on their spouse, it is the spouse who wasn't sexy enough or available enough to keep their partner faithful. It's not the person who suffered a beating from someone else and is the point of concern, it is the question of what they did to deserve such a beating. It's not the rapist who is the point of discussion and disdain, it is the person who put themselves in the situation to be sexually assaulted and becomes the point of interest.

Another belief is to ignore your hurts in general. Be tough. Be strong. Exist. Survive. Forge ahead and ignore your pain. We watch movies and cheer the hero who ignores their pain to pursue a bigger more noble cause. In reality, this type of dysfunctional belief just keeps people hurt and stuck in their feelings, continually tortured by their past, and emotionally unhealthy. Or they work to bury their pain so deep they behave and react in inappropriate ways and can't figure out why. Finally, some bury their feelings and trauma in drugs and alcohol. Instead, let's believe in acknowledging our pain and work to heal it. Let's place the perception of strength and heroism where it belongs, on the person who is doing the work to heal themselves.

Challenging Your Beliefs

Think about those unspoken beliefs shared above which you may be walking around unconsciously believing. Bring them to the surface of your consciousness. Write them down in your workbook. Meditate on them. Then make choices to give up those beliefs which no longer serve you. Whenever they crop up in your life, in a conversation, in a thought, a feeling, or a behavior, name it, confront it, and give yourself permission to struggle with it. Replace it with the thought, feeling, or behavior you know is healthier for you and for others. It's hard work to do this. It takes someone becoming more conscious of what they are feeling, thinking, and doing. Help others do this. When in your Survivor's Journey group, point out when someone sounds like they are trapped in one of the belief systems described above. Use an example from your own life when you may have believed this way and how this belief pattern didn't benefit or serve you well.

Unspoken Obligations

Unspoken obligations are those commitments and behaviors guided by the rules we adopted and have unconsciously committed to follow. We may be committed because we have been taught to behave in a way which is respectful and accepting of the unspoken rules. We have remained committed without even thinking about them. Even when they don't benefit us, we have stayed committed to them.

The first obligation many of us make is to always take care of the people in our family regardless of how they have treated us. "Family comes first" is the idea that no matter what they've done or have not done we should be obligated to them. It's the idea that we should continue to support them, spend time with them, and stay connected to their dysfunctional ways.

The reality is, there are people in our family who have treated us poorly or treated others poorly. They are engaged in behaviors or the treatment of others which goes against what we believe in. Remaining obligated to support and nurture someone who hasn't returned the support to us and/or others is the definition of dysfunction. In remaining obligated, we are teaching them we don't value ourselves. We teach ourselves we aren't worth more. Finally, we teach younger ones in the family they should remain obligated to people who don't value them. While there is a universal obligation to care for the children in the family, we can choose whether or not we will continue to support adults and in which ways we will choose to support the adults in our family.

Another obligation common in families is to keep the family secrets at all costs. This is the notion that whatever takes place in the family and whoever is hurt, the family image is more important. The family member should keep the secrets regardless of what the secrets are because of the damage they can do to a person in the family or the family in general. Without a concern for the victim and their traumatic experience, the focus is on protecting the perpetrator and keeping the secret.

These family secrets, if exposed, could cause extreme embarrassment to the family or the perpetrator within a family. It could hurt someone's career or their standing in the community. Exposing them or letting the world know about the family secret would expose the family to criticism, shame, or even jail time for some members.

An additional common obligation is to sacrifice one's own needs for someone else who is capable of taking care of themselves or accessing services or others to care for them. Many of us who have lived with trauma are highly sensitive and have a level of empathy for anyone who might be in need. The idea of "being there" for someone and helping them is so strong we are sometimes blinded by it. We fail to see on some occasions and with some people, we are "there for them" too often. We are sacrificing our needs to care for someone who is capable of getting their own needs met. In some respects, we are crippling them with our love. We are preventing them from standing on their own two feet and handling their life. Our sacrifice isn't helping them, and it isn't allowing us the time we need to focus on pursuing our own health and our own dreams.

Additionally, a common obligation is not to try to pursue our dreams because of our past. We say to ourselves we can never pursue our dreams because of the way we look, or the family and the socio-economic status we came from. We can't do it because there is no one in that profession, field, neighborhood, community, or group who thinks like us, likes what we like, or has the past we have. Even though someone's past does not dictate their future, we can use our past as an excuse to not pursue what we say we want.

In reality, fear is a component of our obligations, because if we are busy taking care of someone and/or their obligations, we have a great excuse for not pursuing our goals or living our dreams. Our obligations should be to the children we need to care for and the adults who truly need our help. However, neither of these should be at our own expense or in exchange for our dreams.

Another common obligation is to feel responsible for making everyone feel alright. This role in a family or among friends can be exhausting. It requires you consistently take the temperature among family and friends to find out if everyone feels good or if anyone is uncomfortable, disappointed, or fighting each other. It is tiring always making sure someone doesn't feel bad.

Make a commitment to yourself. If someone feels bad, you consciously *not* try and fix it. You can sit with them in the feeling and be there for them, but don't try and fix it for them. That is their responsibility. Additionally, if someone says something or does something which makes others in the room feel uncomfortable, let them experience the natural consequences of their statements. If you rush in to soften the blow or to excuse their behavior, you prevent them from learning from their experience. Think of it as being disrespectful to forbid someone from learning from their mistakes. If you are there to always soften the blow, they can't learn. When you do that, you are saying you don't believe in that person's ability to learn from their mistakes and grow. Let them experience it. You worry about you and let them worry about them. That's the new commitment you will make to yourself.

Finally, there is often an obligation to live the script you've been given. This obligation encourages you to be similar to everyone else in the family or in the community. Giving into this obligation will prevent you from striking out on your own to be the person you really are inside. It will stop you from pursuing your dreams. It will muffle your voice and stifle your unique expression of who you are and who you want to be. It will stop you from speaking up and speaking out, and from becoming a pioneer who blazes your own trail.

Challenging Your Obligations

Your responsibility whenever possible is to take care of your children the best way you can until they become adults. Other than that, you really owe no one anything. What you become obligated to do should be because you choose it. If you do commit to someone or something, do it because it benefits you as well as others who have helped you and have been positively in your corner. Working a job to pay your bills, being in the company of prosocial others, and committing yourself to other chosen obligations are positive ways of supporting you.

Being there for people who haven't been there for you is unhealthy. Your loyalty should be to those in your life who treat you well – those who are demonstrating their love for you. And because you love yourself and have a standard for yourself, you will appreciate their love and care by appreciating them. When you feel obligated and responsible for taking care of someone with the only criteria being they were born into the same family as you, caring for them will leave you drained, frustrated, stressed, and caught up consistently in drama just because you happened to share some of the same blood and history.

When you choose to give up certain dysfunctional obligations, you'll have room to explore future possibilities. Choose who, what, and why to become committed and obligated. When others ask you why you are doing something or why you are so committed to another person, place, or thing, you'll have a clear and positive reason. In doing so, your life and your actions begin to make sense.

Other recovery programs also focus on having a meaningful life built on good moral character. Those in Alcoholics Anonymous or Narcotics Anonymous don't simply stop drinking or doing drugs. They work on building character. They know why they don't want to spend time with some people or go to certain places or honor certain commitments anymore. And they know why they choose instead to be fiercely honest with themselves and others and why they don't frequent people, places, or engage in things which are unhealthy for them. That's because they lead them back to a place of sickness. The same is true for you. While in your case it's not alcohol or drugs you decide to consume again. It's your BOL of shit.

Think about your hopes and dreams. Take off all your self-imposed barriers and eliminate dysfunctional obligations which take up your time, money, worry, and resources, and just think about the possibilities. Just for a little while, think about *all* of the possibilities. Think about what you really want. If you no longer worry about the obligations you have and could reclaim your time, would you pursue your dreams? Would you go for it? Would you be willing to work hard, lose sleep, and implement a plan to get there?

Unspoken Loyalties

Since loyalties are driven by our feelings, loyalties dictate the obligatory feeling we should have about our family and friends. Remaining loyal to those people, places, and things who have been positive forces in your life is reflecting good character. However blind loyalty to whomever happens to be present in your life is not a healthy practice. We should make conscious choices on who we will be loyal to and why.

For instance, some blind loyalties dictate we "never snitch", meaning we never tell anyone who needs to know the truth or what the truth really is. When we stay loyal to others, particularly those involved in practices which hurt others, we are no longer loyal to our own integrity. Think about it. Who does "never snitching" benefit? When it benefits the person causing harm to someone else, we are on the wrong side of our integrity. Make an empowered choice about what and who you will remain loyal to and under which circumstances.

The second blind loyalty is the idea of giving total forgiveness to someone just because they ask for it. Giving forgiveness is a choice, and *if* given by the aggrieved party, then only when they are *ready* to give it. In other words, forgiveness is given when the forgiver is ready to give it and not necessarily when the requester wants it.

Also, when or if you forgive doesn't mean the person who wronged you should once again receive all of the gifts and privileges they enjoyed with you before. If a friendship or relationship is expected to resume after forgiveness is given, there should be a level of change demonstrated. Your new policy is to be loyal to yourself first and ensure you feel good about yourself and your offer of forgiveness. Never feel you need to be loyal to someone who has deeply hurt you until (if ever) you feel comfortable about it. Forgiving too soon or accepting someone back in your life who hasn't changed will produce a relationship of empty promises surviving until the next violation takes place.

Another common unspoken loyalty some people have is to stay loyal to a life path, even when they are not or no longer interested in the path. Some will remain loyal to a life path to satisfy someone else, or because they believe that is what society has chosen for them, or they feel they are too far down the path to turn around or go in another direction. The truth is, it's never too late to turn around or go in a different direction. That's what the Survivor's Journey is all about.

Family Dysfunctions or Family Virtues

Some of us have decided to cope with their family or friends' dysfunction by turning their dysfunction into virtues. For instance, if family members or friends are great at physically fighting others, we might turn it into a virtue by saying our family members "are bad asses. Don't fuck with us." If they regularly lie, cheat, and swindle people out of things, we might say they "are a group of outlaws" or "they are savvy businesspeople" and then wear it like a badge of honor. When a family fails to take care of each other we flip it and say, "You have to be strong in my family. We take care of ourselves." If this has happened in your family or among your friends, dig deeper than the polished version being told and begin to believe the truth about your family or group. If they bring a lot of drama and fight each other, it's because they don't have the tools to process their emotions. Tell the truth and work to act and be different. If they don't take care of each other, believe the truth. Don't continue to buy into the polished version of why you or others weren't or aren't cared for properly.

Challenging Loyalties

Some of us just refuse to believe our own eyes. Even in the face of concrete examples of dysfunction within our family or among our friends, we will deny what we witness. We will often unconsciously justify why what we know to be true, isn't true. The purpose is so that we can continue to accept their dysfunctional or harmful behavior toward us and others.

We also learn to mis-remember things in a way flattering to our family and friends. We will distort or eliminate those memories rooted in reality which aren't flattering to them and instead paint them with a brush which makes these memories and the people in them tolerable. We learn to justify their behavior in our memories so we can justify why we remain loyal. We need to take off our rose-colored glasses which distorts reality and see some of our friends and family for who they are. Once we see who they are, we can make the choice about who to stay loyal to and why.

Mind-Fields: Compliance and Control

Challenge yourself to consider the types and ways you have remained Challenge yourself to consider the types and ways you have remained loyal to dysfunctional people, places, and things and make a conscious choice about what and who you will commit to and why. If you don't, you will blindly follow a set of unspoken rules and will remain compliant and committed to a set of beliefs, obligations, and loyalties which doesn't benefit or suit you. You will remain controlled by feelings, thoughts, and actions harmful to yourself and other vulnerable people in your family, among your friends, and in your community.

Tools and Transformation: Healthy Beliefs, Obligations, and Loyalties (BOLs)

"I honor healthy commitments and those which support my growth".

Beliefs, obligations, and loyalties have been taught to you by others. However, one of the benefits of being an empowered adult is you get to choose what you will believe in and what you will be obligated to do and not do. Loyalty is associated with trustworthiness. "When I trust you, I can be loyal to you." Before believing in, becoming obligated to, or being loyal, ask yourself the following questions.

1. Which of my beliefs are unrealistic and don't serve me or others well?
2. Am I following rules I want to follow and remaining loyal to those who deserve my loyalty?
3. Will these beliefs, obligations, and loyalties put me in a healthy place or situation emotionally, physically, financially, and spiritually?

4. Am I operating on auto pilot following my old feelings of obliga-tion and loyalty?
5. Am I appreciating and respecting myself?
6. In following these unhealthy BOLs, am I sending the right mes-sage to my children or younger people in my family?

Be empowered to make-up your own mind. Make a conscious deci-sion about which rules you want to follow and which you will not. What will you believe in? What obligations will you commit to? Who will you be loyal to and who will you no longer be loyal to? Which rules will you follow, and which will you give up?

Staying committed to a system which has been rigged against you is not the best way to take control of your life. The best way to honor our families and communities is by honoring ourselves. When we become the manifestation of what's possible, we honor everyone. We become a mentor, a role model, and someone to be looked up to and emulated.

As healthy people, we chose the game to be played. When we do this, the path to winning becomes clearer. It becomes easier to stay emotionally healthier because the rules make sense to us, and the game is set up for us to succeed.

10

10th Journey: *The thriver understands life is good, not perfect, and continually nurtures and forgives self.*

10th Truth: *I engage in daily self-forgiveness.*

10th Transformation: *I practice ongoing daily nurturing and self-forgiveness.*

Trigger or Validation:

For some, the material in this Journey may be triggering. If it triggers you, reach out to your support system including those you trust and appropriate members of your Bomb Squad and/or engage in some self-care activities. For others, this information will be validating. In those cases, use the material to help validate you and affirm what you are or have been experiencing is real.

CHAPTER 10: SELF-FORGIVENESS

"Self-compassion hasn't been a requirement for survival
but is critically needed to thrive." ~ Unknown

W elcome to thrivership! Congratulations on making it this far. You are amazing. The journey you have traveled to get here was no doubt difficult, but well worth it! Have you ever heard the saying "The flower that blooms in adversity is the most rare and beautiful of all"? Rapper and Poet Tupac Shakur wrote a poem about a rose that grew from concrete. In an interview, he talked about how someone who suffered adversity and managed to grow is a marvel to behold, but most people miss what a true miracle they have standing before them. They only see the dirt or dust they might have on them from the battles they've won. He said:

> *"When you become an adult you have sympathy for everything*
> *from animals to whales, to fur, everything- except us... If you saw*
> *a rose growing out of concrete, even if it had messed up petals and*
> *it was a little to the side, you would marvel at just seeing a rose*
> *grow through concrete. So why is it that you see some ghetto kid*
> *grow out of the dirtiest circumstances and he can sit across from*
> *you and make you smile, make you cry, and make you laugh and*
> *all you can talk about is my dirty rose and my dirty stems and how*
> *I'm leaning crooked to the side. You can't even see that I came up*
> *out of that shit."*

Before we talk about the 10th Journey, which is all about self-for-giveness, we want you to first see that you "came up out of that shit".

You really did. You are a marvel to admire. Just take a moment to think about all you have been through. The fact that you are sitting here reading this means you are a marvel to behold. You really are something special and you should celebrate yourself and acknowledge that you are more than a survivor, you are a thriver because what you have been able to accomplish up to this point in your life has been likely some of the hardest internal work you've done in your life.

You are like the rose that grew from concrete. You weren't expected to make it, but not only did you make it, you are blooming. You've been through your battle and won. But unlike other roses, you are the most rare and beautiful because not only did you beat incredible odds to just survive, but you also took your place among other beautiful roses giving off a scent as sweet as any.

By the time you reach the pinnacle of the 10th Journey, you are well on our way to good emotional, mental, physical, and spiritual health. There is a marked difference in you, and other people see it and comment on it. They cannot believe the types of transformations you've made. You even feel pretty good about all that you've done. You should be proud of yourself. Take a moment to think about that.

In the 10th Journey we drill down and do more work on your internal shame. We know and you know it is still embedded deep inside. Shame is like peeling an onion, the more layers you peel the more stink is revealed. While we seem to have our lives in better order, deep inside ourselves we still suffer with shame from our past and it's time to examine it and to let it go. There are parts of our past we feel guilty and shameful about. We need to forgive ourselves, make amends, and move forward with our lives.

If we're honest, when we are alone and thinking about our past, we continue to beat ourselves up about things we did that weren't positive. While we celebrate our progress, there is a part of us that looks down on ourselves because of those things we participated in, and we feel guilty about them. We secretly feel like some of our progress has been an illusion and isn't real. Some of us will even dismiss or minimize our recent hard work and progress we've made and will focus on those parts of ourselves where we still feel ashamed. We have grown too accustomed to seeing ourselves through the eyes of our abuser or exploiter. It may be because we don't truly believe we deserve to love ourselves more. But we do. We need to consciously and purposefully love ourselves more. One way to do that is through daily self-forgiveness.

Truth: *"I engage in daily self-forgiveness".*

So, let's examine those parts of ourselves we still don't like and resolve these issues. To examine our past wrongs, let's first separate ourselves from what we are ashamed of so we can take an independent look at them. In your workbook, write down those critical past experiences which still bother you, the past experiences you believe were your fault and you were wrong. Those things might include witnessing or having knowledge of the victimization or abuse of someone else and/or not stopping it. It might include victimizing or causing the victimization, or exploitation of someone else. In some cases, a victim may believe they were the cause of their own victimization and believes it was their fault. Make sure you have the privacy you need to seriously think about these past experiences and write them down. Also, make sure you keep your workbook in a place which will keep your information private. You need to control what you want others to know and when or if you want them to know. Once you have them written down, let's take a look at them.

As you look through your history of past wrongs more intentionally, let's separate out those things which truly were not your fault or responsibility from those things that were. We will explain how to tell the difference. Those experiences in which you had "power and control" belong in your "past wrongs that were my fault" column. Those past wrongs belong to you.

Those experiences in which you did not have power and control are not yours. These include those experiences you *wish* you had power over, those experiences you *wish* you could have controlled, and those experiences you *feel* responsible for, but without having enough power or control you could not have changed the circumstances or the outcome. Remove those situations from your list. Because you feel remorse and wish things would have been different, we will place these experiences under a different list of situations which were not your fault, but you would like to grieve. We will title this list, "experiences to grieve".

Power is defined in two ways, "power to" meaning the person has the power to change the circumstance or exercise options and "power over" means the power to limit the options of someone or something. Control is the ability to direct people's behavior. Having both power and control are important elements when determining whether any past wrongs truly belong to you and should go on your "past wrongs which were my fault" list.

There are also various elements associated with power and control. Responsibility and accountability are subsets of power and control. It is important to take responsibility for something that you've done wrong. When you have power and control you may be given the "responsibility" to control certain situations and may also be held "accountable" for the outcome of those situations. However, without adequate power and control, a person given the responsibility for something when they are *not* able to control the situation or outcome is a set-up. It is inappropriate and unfair to take or be given responsibility and feel guilty or shameful for something which was beyond your power and control. Again, power and control are key. Think about those times you regret and feel a level of guilt and shame around. Did you truly have both power and control to change the outcome? Separate out those situations where you had little to no power and control over the situation. These situations were not your fault and do not belong on your original list.

The same is true for being provided the "authority" to be in charge of someone or something. Being provided the authority in name only, without the associated power and control will render the person in charge impotent. They are not able to control the outcome because they lack the power to do so. Take these experiences off your "past wrongs" list.

In other situations, you may have lacked the emotional strength, knowledge, and/or intellectual capacity to know better. As Maya Angelou says, "When you know better, you do better." There are many ways people become incapacitated to step in and stop what is happening. Typically, it is because the people and the environment at the time made it seem either almost normal to do or impossible to stop. Others set the tone and established the rules for behavior in that environment. This isn't an excuse for your behavior or theirs. It's simply putting it into the context of the time. Everyone would love to judge history based on today's standard, today's environment, and what they know now, but that's not how it was then. In some cases, we were facing a traumatic experience ourselves or perhaps we were paralyzed by fear and couldn't have done any better than what we did. Whatever the case may be, understanding allows you to accept what happened, feel remorse about it, and then to practice self-forgiveness. In understanding why you could have known or even participated in something then which you find despicable now, allows you to process through it. We knew or participated because we didn't have the tools to process it was wrong. Even if we knew it was wrong, we didn't have the capacity, power, or self-knowledge to go against the grain. In these cases, you wish things would have been different. You can mourn the fact you wish you would have done something different than what you did or didn't do, but the truth is, you didn't have the emotional strength and intellectual capacity to have done something different. You can wish you had the power and control at the time, but you truly didn't. You can grieve and then forgive yourself for not having these things at the time, but they do not belong on your "past wrongs" list.

Having been vulnerable and victimized yourself, you can certainly relate. The appropriate thing to do is to feel remorse for not having the wherewithal you now have. What is unfair to you is to continue to blame yourself for what happened *then* based on who you are *now* and what you know now. That simply isn't fair. If you had an experience where yourself or someone else got hurt and you were emotionally powerless to stop it, forgive yourself. Feeling remorseful about it and wishing it would have been different is appropriate. Grieving it is normal. But being ashamed of something you lacked the capacity to control and cannot change today is unfair and not healthy. Blaming yourself isn't fair.

Let's practice grief and remorse, which starts by feeling sad it happened. That's ok and is even a good thing to do. And let's forgive ourselves because we couldn't have changed what happened. We simply didn't have the emotional power, the intellectual tools, the life lessons, and the capacity to have changed the outcome.

There are some experiences in our past in which we did have the power and control to stop something, to stop ourselves, or to stop someone or something else and we didn't. Perhaps we had the responsibility for caring for someone or something and we had the power and control to do it, but we didn't. We simply didn't. Perhaps we were high or drunk or we thought it was ok. We can't hide what we did. Hiding it

Powers	Your Fault "Past Wrongs"	Not Your Fault "Experiences to Grieve"
Power and Control	Had the power and control but didn't exercise it.	Didn't have real power or the ability to control.
Responsibility and Accountability	Had the power and control and was responsible and accountable but didn't do it.	Didn't have the ability to control or the capacity to be responsible and/or the ability to be accountable.
Authority	Had the power and control and was given and had the authority to manage the situation but didn't manage it.	Didn't have the power or authority to manage the situation.
Knowledge and Intellectual Capacity	Had the power and control and knew better and had the knowledge and intellectual capacity but didn't step up.	Lacked the power via self-knowledge and new way of thinking present today.
Emotional Strength to Respond	Had the power and control and the emotional strength to respond but chose not to.	Didn't have the power via the emotional strength to respond and/or know better.

resulted in us stuffing it deep down inside of us and it is sitting there rotting. It remains on the list of past wrongs we created. It is causing internal damage and destruction to our thoughts and our feelings and we must deal with it. Today we are a changed person. We have to forgive ourselves for what we did or for what we didn't do to stop it. Today we know better, and we pledge to do better. The chart below will help you more clearly understand which of your experiences should go on the "past wrongs that were my fault" or the "experiences to grieve" list.

There are some cases in which we did stand up and did do the right thing. We should be applauded and celebrated for speaking up or stepping in. That took an incredible amount of courage. Often however, when people speak up or step in for the right reasons, they can be met with ridicule or shame from their family, friends or others in society. It's often because they are breaking some unspoken rule rooted deeply in the family or the community. They can begin to feel bad about the good thing they've done. Instead of warm support from family, friends, and the community, they can be met with a cool reception. It can sometimes be lonely when we do the right thing. In these cases, finding like-minded friends and family members who understand and support you.

Guilt, Remorse, and Shame

The 10th Journey is focused on loving and forgiving ourselves for both the past experiences that were our fault and those that were not our fault but we blamed and shamed ourselves anyway. Before we can forgive ourselves, we need to understand and address the damaging effects of blame when it's associated with shame.

When blame and shame are deep within us, it threatens to chip away and destroy everything we have built thus far. Shame prevents us from having a healthy dose of self-esteem. It prevents us from experiencing genuine joy. It robs us of having an honest accounting of our past and future actions because shame gets inside and twists our thoughts, our feelings, and leads us to make decisions and behave in ways which are harmful to us. Therefore, to be healthy and forgive ourselves, we have to get to the bottom of our shame and root it out.

So let's define shame. Shame is the feeling of humiliation for being the victim of or engaging in behavior or thoughts we feel are wrong. There are important differences among guilt, remorse, and shame. Guilt is what you feel and acknowledge when you've done something wrong. It is usually followed by an apology and/or a consequence of some kind. If you've spoken harshly and did something which was inappropriate, admitting it is appropriate. When you *do* something wrong, you should admit guilt and feel appropriately remorseful for having done it. Shame is different from remorse. Remorse is a feeling of regret. Shame is what you feel when you *are* something wrong. When you *are* something wrong, it can make you believe the only way to eliminate shame is to eliminate you. We should never feel shame. However, some of our past experiences and the way society sees us, and the way we have chosen to see ourselves, has erroneously led us to feel a deep sense of shame.

It is acceptable to feel guilty and remorseful for something which happened in the past. Guilt is admitting you did something wrong, and remorse is the feeling of regret. The examples below are provided to better help you understand the difference.

Grieving and Letting Go

Grieving is a process. It is a healthy way of managing the experience and allowing a memory to live inside ourselves without destroying us. As a part of our grieving process, we may go through the five stages of grief including denial, anger, bargaining, depression, and acceptance. In other words, at some point we may have denied it ever happened, felt angry about it, bargained with ourselves or God about it, felt a deep sadness and depression over it, and if we complete the process, we will finally accept it happened and grieve it.

There comes a time when we must face our demons and process the past experiences which appear on the lists we've created. We have a list of the "past wrongs" which are our fault and those past experiences that aren't our fault. We need to grieve both. We must grieve what happened before we can ask ourselves for forgiveness. We suggest before you grieve and ask for forgiveness, you discuss it with your trauma

Guilt – Acknowledgement something bad happened	Remorse - Regret something bad happened	Shame- Belief that your whole being is wrong because something bad happened
Admitting I said something terrible about a friend.	Feeling bad for what I said about a friend.	Feeling shameful for being the type of person who would say such a thing.
Acknowledging I didn't get the thing done I promised to do.	Feeling bad about not getting the thing done I promised to do.	Convincing myself that only a horrible person would not get it done.
Acknowledging I didn't wash the dishes before company came over.	Feeling bad I didn't wash the dishes before company came over.	Believing I am a worthless slob who doesn't deserve to have a house or friends.
Admitting to myself my outfit today isn't the best.	Feeling bad about not changing to a better outfit.	Blaming my ridiculous, stupid, misshaped body for being shaped in such a way.
Admitting to myself I didn't do my best in sticking to my diet.	Feeling bad I didn't stick to my diet.	Thinking of myself as a loser who can't get anything right including a diet.
Acknowledging I know about the past and what happened.	Feeling bad about what happened in the past.	When I think about it, I just want to die or believe I should die and/or I don't deserve to be happy.
Admitting I know what someone else went through in the past.	In knowing, I feel bad about what someone else had to go through.	Wanting to punish myself for not changing the outcome of what happened to someone else, so I spend time punishing myself now in different ways.

therapist to make sure you are emotionally strong enough and ready to take on this Journey.

The List of Past Experiences We Need To Grieve

Take each past experience or situation we determined was not our fault and assign the appropriate feelings to it. Feel sad, feel hurt, and feel disappointed it happened. Give yourself the space and the time to cry. Cry a long and cleansing-your-heart type of cry. Cry for the pain that was caused. Cry for the loss that was experienced. Cry for the emotional damage that was caused. Cry because sometimes the world is cruel and heartless. Cry because of the years you had to endure this pain and shame. Cry because of the other person's deep suffering. Cry because what the world showed them is cruelty. Cry because perhaps that experience may have changed their life forever. Cry because you were truly helpless to stop it. Cry because no one else stopped it. Cry because others knew or didn't know or should have known. Cry because sometimes you hate people and what they are capable of. Cry because you wish you had the power and control. Cry because you didn't. Cry because of the time spent holding yourself accountable and beating yourself up about it. Cry because you wish you could go back - because you would have done something different. Cry because you know you can't go back and change things. Cry because you want forgiveness for not being enough or doing enough about it. Cry because you wish you would have known better, would have been smarter, or would have been more powerful than you were.

Cry because there is nothing else you can do except cry.

Allow your heart to feel what it feels about the situation.

When you are all cried out, let yourself know you are kind and compassionate.

Let yourself know you are powerful today.

Let yourself know from this day forward you will forever be a protector of the vulnerable.

Most importantly, let yourself know those situations and experiences were not your fault. You feel for what happened. You wish you could have had the power and control and the right mindset to have changed it.

Let yourself know if you did have the power and control you certainly would have changed the outcome. Why would you have changed the outcome? Because your true nature is to be kind, loving, and protective.

Now make the choice to move away from your heart space and move to your thoughts and your head space. Understand these experiences are *not* your fault. These burdens are *not* yours to carry. Without real power and control, you couldn't have truly changed the outcome. Those experiences are not ours to own. The guilt and/or shame we feel is not ours to carry. Those heavy burdens belong to someone else. Whether they do or don't carry the burden is not our business. What we need to understand is it doesn't belong to us. Imagine that burden being a 50-pound sack you have been carrying. It's heavy. It's backbreaking. It has been weighing on your mind and heavy on your heart. Set that burden down because it's not yours. In fact, it's disrespectful. Set that burden down and allow the rightful owner to lift it, deal with it, and carry it. In reality, no one can make someone carry their own burdens, but we can certainly relieve ourselves of those that aren't ours. When we discover we have been carrying something which isn't ours, we can hurry-up and drop that burden and say "whew! goodbye burden! I'm so relieved to finally realize it wasn't mine to carry in the first place." When we do it, we just feel so much lighter emotionally.

Write a letter to yourself explaining the past, what happened and why it happened. Write all of your feelings, thoughts, and behaviors. Tell yourself why you believed it was your fault and why and how you lacked the power and control to take responsibility for what happened. Ask yourself for forgiveness for feeling guilt and shame for something that was not your fault. Forgive yourself for confusing your compassion with fault. Forgive yourself for carrying this burden which isn't yours for so long. Ask yourself for forgiveness for living with this pain for so long. Toward the end of the letter, acknowledge your compassion, anger, and sadness about what happened. Work with your therapist to decide how you will handle the letter. Will you keep it and re-read it anytime you begin to once again own what happened in the past? Should you read the letter aloud alone or with others and then burn it so it is gone forever? The choice is yours.

We must forgive ourselves for our past. We are better today than we were yesterday, and we'll be even better tomorrow. From this time forward, whenever you have wronged someone, sit with it, examine it, understand the part you played in it and if the wrong indeed belongs to you, promptly make amends where and when you can. If the wrong isn't your fault and it doesn't belong to you don't pick up and carry the emotional burden. Let it go. It doesn't belong to you.

Finally, we need to take responsibility for what is ours and does belong to us. We know we have been engaged in some activities, thoughts, and feelings we aren't proud of. When we have done something to someone, or not done what we should have done, then we should feel an appropriate level of guilt, regret, and remorse. If there is something from the past which is our fault, we need to own it. It is ours and we 've been carrying it. It's time to lay these burdens down.

For some of us, we have less of a problem admitting when we have wronged others yet have an extremely hard time forgiving ourselves and being kind to ourselves. This Journey also asks you to work on being a good friend to yourself. A good friend is a good listener. They forgive. They care about your feelings and even though they know about many of your previous bumps and bruises they still care about you. They see your warts and they are still willing to love you. They nurture and challenge you to be the best version of yourself as possible and when you're not, they sit with you and are there for you. A good friend removes the perfect in favor of the good. Are you a good friend to yourself? Are you nurturing and kind and understanding of yourself? Think about how talented, kind, and loving you really are. Do you see the funny side, the talented side, and the loving side of yourself? Looking at the way you treat yourself, if you met yourself on the street, would you want to be friends with yourself? If your honest answer is no, then you have some work to do.

First, take ownership for the part you played in the past. Feel all of the feelings you need to feel and have the thoughts you need to have. Be careful. Whenever you see yourself beginning to shame yourself, stop. Make the choice to move your thoughts and feelings back to those of remorse and regret and out of shame. Write a letter to the person or persons who were hurt. You'll find the instructions for writing this letter in your workbook. Write about the experience as you remember it and ask for forgiveness. If there is more than one experience, deal with each one by thoroughly writing about it and asking for forgiveness. Sharing or not sharing your thoughts with the victim is up to you and your therapist. Then write a final letter to yourself. Explain why the situation(s) happened. Explain the way you feel about it today and who you are today. Ask yourself for forgiveness. When you notice your writing beginning to become shameful instead of remorseful, stop, erase it, and try again. You may have another thriver who you trust will help you craft a letter asking yourself for forgiveness. Read this letter often. Read it to yourself again and again until you feel ready to forgive yourself. You'll know when you have accepted your own forgiveness because the past will feel like a somewhat painful memory, but not one so painful or shameful you have to lock it away inside yourself.

Self-forgiveness is just that, an opportunity to forgive yourself, it's not necessary to ask or receive forgiveness from someone else. However, if there is an opportunity and desire to express your remorse and regret and apologize to the person you may have participated in harming, work with your therapist to determine if or how, and when to do this. When completing this exercise take into consideration all of the potential legal ramifications in writing down your past and sharing it with others.

Tool: Self-Forgiveness

The first relationship you have is with yourself. As we move forward in life, if you are going to be successful as a friend and a life partner, you need to be a good friend to yourself. When you are feeling "shame" identify it. If you did something wrong, give yourself permission to feel guilty and remorseful about it. If you've done something wrong, make amends by apologizing and making it right. Don't hold onto it so tightly and bury it. Don't let it fester and poison inside you. Genuinely apologize and if it's possible, make it right. If it's not possible, explain why. Once you have made amends, let it go and move on. If you feel guilt or shame about something you had or have no control over, work with your therapist to process through it and let it go. For some of us, we must practice letting it go every time it pops in our heads. Say a prayer about it and release it time and time again until you can truly let it go.

Strive for a good life, but not a perfect one. When we work to obtain perfection, we will always come up short because we will persistently compare ourselves to others. The problem in comparing ourselves to others is we tend to compare up, meaning we compare ourselves to those who we believe are better looking, more hard working, and smarter and better in almost every way. We will always come up short when we compare ourselves to others we already believe are better than us. Try not to compare, but if you do, compare apples to apples. Look at where you used to be and where you are now. Look at your current self and where you want to be. If you want to see where you've been, look at others in the group who are struggling with what you are no longer struggling with and use others' stories and perspectives to get the emotional, psychological, and spiritual lessons you need to get.

Mind-Field: Charged and Convicted

When we aren't successfully applying this Journey to our lives we will continue to charge and convict ourselves for situations which don't belong to us. Even further, many of us will convict ourselves to a lifetime of blame and shame and all of the emotional pain and behavioral problems that come with it.

The way to avoid these mind-fields is to remove those torturous thoughts from a "feeling" level to a "thought" level. Logically, go through the process we outlined in this Journey. When you want to blame yourself for the past, ask yourself if you had the power, the control, the intellectual capacity, and the authority to have changed the outcome. If you didn't, remind yourself to let it go. Continue to do this until you believe it. If you did have the power or the control to have changed the outcome but didn't choose to, forgive yourself. Each time it crops up, practice self-forgiveness. For all of the struggle you've been through in your life, you deserve someone to come along and show you grace. You have suffered enough. You deserve forgiveness. Grant it to yourself. Each time a memory crops up practice giving yourself grace through self-forgiveness.

The Transformation: *"I practice ongoing daily nurturing and self-forgiveness".*

Today, and in the future, when you make a mistake or are disappointed in yourself, if possible, work to make whatever you did right and then quickly forgive yourself and move forward. The fact of the matter is most people have strong days, and they have weak days. They have good days, and they have bad days. On the strong days you will move forward doing the right things and being the person you can be proud of. Relish in those days because those are the days in which the magic happens. Be proud. During the weak days, take care of yourself. Take good care of your heart and take good care of your feelings. Be a good friend to yourself and take it easy during these times. Do yourself a favor, during these days don't make demands on yourself. Stay in your safe space. Lick your wounds. Build yourself back up. Do the things you love to do. Watch your thoughts. Don't allow your wounds to be re-injured on those days. This is a time of nurturing and building yourself back up.

On your weak days reflect on where you were last year, or a few months ago, and compare your progress today. It's a good barometer that lets us know when you are moving in a positive direction or if you need to adjust. If you're not where you want to be, don't beat yourself up about it. Take action, start working on it, stop looking for the gold star from others who you want to acknowledge your growth. Seek internal validation for your growth and a job well done.

In this Journey we also agree to forgive ourselves for not doing or not becoming what others wanted us to do or become. We will forgive ourselves for not becoming or living up to our own expectations of where we should be in life. We will ask for forgiveness for not being the perfect person we hoped to be. We forgive ourselves for not always do-ing the right things and for making bad choices. We forgive ourselves for not being as productive and accomplished as we think we should have been. We will practice being comfortable with who we are and where we are in life. A lot of our experiences were rooted in trauma. We should celebrate that, even as someone who has experienced the debilitating effects of trauma, we made it this far. We are a marvel to behold. We are the rose that grew from concrete.

Today we practice grace. We will forgive ourselves for wherever we think we should be in life and in the various ways we haven't made it there yet. We will forgive ourselves whenever painful memories crop up and we start to fall back into old patterns of blaming and shaming ourselves. We will recognize these toxic thoughts and feelings, say a prayer, and release them back into the universe. We will forgive our-selves whenever we make a mistake and come up short. We will ask for forgiveness from others whenever we hurt them.

When someone nags you, demands you do better, guilts and shames you for a past you can't control, that's the last person you want to be around. Sometimes, that person is you. Unfortunately, everywhere you go, there you are. Being a good friend to yourself is the most import-ant thing you do in life. In filling your own bucket with kindness, love, support, and patience, and showing yourself grace through self-forgive-ness, you successfully complete the 11th Journey. Learning self-forgive-ness first will also open the door for you to truly forgive others.

This 10th Journey doesn't require daily perfection. However, if you understand the difference between guilt and shame and choose guilt and remorse for those things you've done wrong and continually let go of the things that aren't your fault, you have made progress. If you practice self-forgiveness and make amends when and where you can, you have achieved the 11th Journey. If you more clearly understand and have learned to grieve those past experiences that were not your fault, you have accomplished the 10th Journey.

11.

11th Journey: *The thriver believes they are more than their negative experiences and releases their burdens.*

11th Truth: *I release toxic energy through unburdening and untethering.*

11th Transformation: *I engage in a daily practice of unburdening and untethering.*

Trigger or Validation:
For some, the material in this Journey may be triggering. If it triggers you, reach out to your support system including those you trust and appropriate members of your Bomb Squad and/or engage in some self-care activities. For others, this information will be validating. In those cases, use the material to help validate you and affirm that what you are or have been experiencing is real.

CHAPTER 11: UNBURDENING & UNTETHERING

"Secrets keep you sick" ~AA

You have reached the point in your recovery when it's time to deeply and more profoundly understand you are more than what happened to you in your life. What happened to you helped to shape who you are today, but it is not the totality of you. Not even close.

You are unique. In all of the universe there is but one you. And all of your experiences from birth until now make up the totality of you. Those include your physical characteristics, your genetics, your personality, your habits, your perspectives, your intellect, your attitudes about things, how relationships have shaped you, your childhood experiences, adolescent experiences, adulthood experiences, what you've seen over your lifetime, the fun you've had, your talents, your creativity in certain areas of life, your passion, your goals, your unique style of humor, the way you communicate, your taste in food, furniture, intimate partners, and friends, and even the way your eye twinkles, your smile, the way you wear your hair, and a million other assets, that all put together, make up YOU.

You are even much more than your past experiences because your past doesn't have to dictate your future. Your future is yet to be written by you and could contain whatever you'd like it to contain.

Truth: *"I release toxic energy through unburdening and untethering".*

Your abuse and your victimization was an experience, but it is not the total sum of you. There were approximately 100 million sperm that had a shot at eventually becoming a human being and you swam faster and harder than any one of the others. You were strong enough even before you were born. And you made it to where you are today because you are smart, because you are blessed, and because you are favored. You are stronger and wiser today than you were yesterday. That's what happens when someone has been through hell and back. Others see the growth and wisdom in you, and they wonder how you did it. You have grown to become spectacular.

Why did you have to go through what you went through? For what purpose? The answer to that question lies with your maker and in the universe of your soul. Perhaps you were put here to be a walking testimony that good truly does conquer evil. Even though you hated what you went through, the strength and wisdom you have will serve you well in your future.

Where does wisdom come from? It comes from going through something and coming out stronger on the other side. Wisdom doesn't necessarily come with age. What's the evidence that wisdom doesn't come with age? There are thousands of very unwise, dare we say ignorant, older people right now who are walking the earth continuing to make dumb decisions. In turn, there are some very wise younger people. Wisdom comes from facing problems and processing through them. People who never get an opportunity to learn how to become wise are people who never faced their problems or made difficult decisions. Instead of dealing with their problems and adversities, they figured out ways to go around their problems, go under them and over them so they didn't have to face them and deal with them. And maybe you have done this in your past too. But in doing this work, you made the decision to go straight through the eye of the storm and you came out the other side. You carry with you the battle scars of successful battles won. You also carry the badge of honor for becoming wiser in having successfully come through it. Like the cowardly lion, you proudly wear the badge of courage for coming this far! You didn't come through it unscathed, but today you are indeed wiser and stronger.

When someone hurts you deep inside. I'm talking about a hurt which touches your very soul, you have two choices. You can work through the pain and get to a point where you practice unburdening yourself of the strong emotions attached to it -or- you can let the pain eat at you until it destroys vital parts of your being. When someone hurts you deeply, they take your power. They control you. They have the power to control your emotions. Whether they keep the power and control they have over you is up to you.

How do you know your victimizer still has power and control over you? Take a moment and think about them. Do certain emotions crop-up that can take-over and ruin your day like anger or fear or shame? As you go about your day, do you have the need to avoid certain people or places? Is there a time during the day when a memory can pop-up to ruin your day? When you have a memory, a feeling, or a person who has the power to ruin your good day, then you are no longer in control. When something or someone has that level of power over you, that's entirely too much power to have *given* away. Yes I mean GIVEN. Because no one should have the power to make you feel anything you don't choose to feel.

The 11th Journey is about taking the totality of "you" back and acknowledging every part of you. It means letting go of the pain which has been present in your life. There are five stages of grief as outlined by Elizabeth Kubler-Ross. Those are denial, anger, bargaining, depression, and acceptance. No doubt you experienced each one, except perhaps acceptance. Not acceptance that the abuse, violence, or exploitation was ok, but an acknowledgement it happened. Acceptance means you process through it and put it in your past. It's no longer front-and-center controlling your world. Acceptance is akin to unburdening and untethering.

Unburdening and untethering is a choice and a consistent practice. The more you do it, the less you'll have to do it overtime. Unburdening means to lift the heavy emotional weight on your shoulders and throw it to the ground because it is no longer a burden you have to carry. Untethering is to untie the ropes or chains that tether you to something, someone, or a set of thoughts and feelings. Unburdening and untethering is the practice of letting go of the power which the abuse or exploitation had over you. Some people try various techniques to do this. Some do this by forgiving their abuser or exploiter. Not because they deserve to be forgiven. In fact, most who forgive their abuser never even tell them. Some thrivers also choose to forgive others who knew what happened and could have provided protection but didn't.

Why are you forgiving your perpetrator or forgiving the person(s) who didn't protect you? Because forgiving them is not about them, it's about empowering YOU. Forgiving is not forgetting. Forgetting is to try and pretend it never happened. Forgiving also does not necessarily mean you accept them back into your life. When you forgive, you allow light to come into your life and your soul. You free yourself from the burden that violence, abuse, and exploitation brought into your life. Forgiving means not allowing the burden to be ever present in your life to wound you whenever it feels like it. You become free. You begin to trust those who are trustworthy. You begin to truly live and love your life. You begin to see this is something which happened to you, but it's not the total you.

Instead of forgiving, some people prefer to "unburden" themselves from the emotional energy it takes to hate. They will never forgive, but they can release the energy associated with hate. It takes an incredible amount of energy to hate someone, and hate takes a toll on the health of the hater. That's why Martin Luther King said, "*Hate is just as injurious to the hater as it is to the hated. Like an unchecked cancer, hate corrodes the personality and eats away its vital unity. Many of our inner conflicts are rooted in hate. This is why the psychiatrists say, "Love or perish." Hate is too great a burden to bear.*" Some prefer to unburden and release the energy associated with hate.

Finally, some let go by trying to understand their perpetrator. They try to empathize with what their perpetrator's life may have been like, the situations they may have encountered, and experiences they may have gone through to make them who they were when they abused, exploited, or were violent. For some, when they are able to humanize them and understand, that can let go of the hatred.

However you decide to unburden yourself is your choice as you are now an empowered thriver who is in the best position to determine your course of action. Decide what feels and fits best for you. Then when you're ready, take the 11th Journey.

However, we don't want to confuse unburdening with letting your abuser or exploiter walk free. Unburdening the negative energy which hate brings and seeking procedural justice in the courts are different things. If we desire justice we should seek justice. Some will find the strength to move forward and seek justice for what happened to them. Some victims, survivors, and thrivers with evidence and fortitude choose to prosecute. They work past their fears to stand up against their perpetrator(s). They believe their perpetrator(s) should stand accused and be convicted for what they've done. In seeking out and receiving procedural justice for a crime committed against them, they feel vindicated. They feel as though they have gained some self-worth back. When they receive justice, they feel as though society stands with them and against what has been done to them. They also believe their perpetrator should have their freedom taken, while they have an opportunity to heal and reclaim their life. Others can't or don't want to prosecute. They just want to move on and get on with the business of healing. Whether or not you choose to prosecute or can prosecute, the process of unburdening and untethering remains a critical Journey in your recovery.

Tools: Unburdening and Untethering

How do you unburden and untether? First, you clearly define what that means for you. For some people a component will mean prosecuting their perpetrator. For some it will mean forgiving their perpetrator. For others it will mean not to forgive, but to let the energy associated with hate go. We have to remember that healing is about you, not them. Healing doesn't require you prosecute or forgive them, it only requires you let go of the strong emotions associated with it which burdens you. Some people prefer to work with their therapist to learn to lay their burdens down and let go of the energy and power they are giving to their past negative experiences. Some prefer to meditate on the process while learning to let go. Others write letters to their victimizers, say a prayer, and burn their letters. Your workbook will give you some good examples of ways to let go. What's important to know is letting go is not an event, but rather a process. The more you do it, the easier it will become.

Your goal is to get to a place where your past abuse or exploitation is a scar you have, but not an open wound. Unburdening yourself of the strong emotional pain like anger, sadness, regret, and grief, takes time and practice. You'll have some bad days and some good days. The goal is overtime the good days begin to outweigh the bad days. A good book to read to help you with this is "Caring Enough to Forgive" by David Ausburer. Another is "Forgiveness: 21 Days to Forgive Everyone for Everything" by Iylanla Vanzant. Also, you may want to work with your therapist on unburdening and moving past your abuse and exploitation.

Why do People Victimize Others?

There are various reasons why others victimize. Oftentimes a person abuses because they were victimized. The saying is "hurt people, hurt people". Many times, the abuse a perpetrator acts out is connected to their own previous abuse. Some victimizers who were victims themselves made a choice that they would grow up to be the victimizer and not the victim. Some victimizers grew up to have boundary issues, control issues, or experience excessive fear. Some abusers lack empathy, they have a personality disorder, or they have sociopathic or psychopathic tendencies and lack the empathetic and caring feelings we have. Finally, some abusers grew up where they witnessed violence in the home and/or they grew up in a home where a parent(s) was not emotionally available because of drug or alcohol abuse or an untreated mental illness. Finally, someone may become abusive out of frustration, lack of opportunities, and a lack of coping skills.

Mind-Fields: Complicit and Corrosive Thoughts and Behaviors

When you don't free yourself from the burden of contempt you feel for your abuser, you become complicit in the continued hurt you feel. In essence, you have joined with your abuser to hurt YOU. Why would you ever choose to be on their side against you? Instead, make the decision to choose you. Choose your life. Choose to have a happier life by letting go of the burden. Surrender the emotion so you can live free.

Whether you can understand why your victimizer did what they did or not, shouldn't make a big difference on whether you let go of the hate or not, because your forgiveness is not at all about them. It's all about you. Your hatred for them, eats you alive. Hatred takes a lot of energy to produce. When you hate, you overexert your body in negative ways. Hate will cause your blood pressure to go up. The stress from hatred will cause ulcers and your hair to thin. How long can you hold onto hatred without it affecting your long-term health? When you allow darkness to seep into the core you, your whole world changes. It weaves its way throughout your life and your attitude about life will reflect it. It is corrosive. You see the world and the people in it as potentially evil. You navigate through the world with this belief and everything you feel, think, and believe reflects this. A person who holds this hatred in their heart is not a pleasant person to themselves and is often not a pleasant person to be around for others.

Transformation: *"I engage in a daily practice of unburdening and releasing".*

Some people who walk through these Journeys and get to the 11th Journey realize they experienced some or all of the elements of Post-Traumatic Growth (PTG). PTG is a positive transformation which can happen following trauma. It was developed by theorists Tedeshi and Calhoun in the 1990s who published articles on people who endured a traumatic event, psychological struggle, or adversity and experienced positive growth.

There are five areas in which someone might grow emotionally or psychologically following a traumatizing event. Those include personal strength, new possibilities, positive growth, appreciation of life, and spiritual change.

Personal Strength

The first is personal strength. Thrivers who experience PTG understand they are stronger than they thought they were. They begin to feel as though they can handle difficult situations more than they thought they could. Because they discovered they are personally a stronger human being, they may put more effort into the activities they are engaged in and put more effort in their relationships. They feel they have learned to rely on themselves more.

New Possibilities

Because of what a thriver has gone through, there is a shift in life perspective. They think of life differently than they did before. New possibilities emerge either because of the experience and/or as a result of a new way of thinking about life and their future. There is a shift in their priorities and a shift in their values. They may be willing to forge a new path, develop new interests, or work on changing what needs to be changed in their life.

Personal Growth

Those who experience PTG may have a deeper sense of compassion for others who suffer. They may relate and connect with people more than they did before. Because of their own experience, they may have the ability to see other people's pain and their need for help. They understand the importance of getting professional help and/or reaching out and gaining social support when they need it.

Appreciation for Life

Some thrivers appreciate each day because they realize because they lived through what they have, they can truly survive anything. They practice gratitude and are grateful for their life, the people in it, and the things they have. They may believe and say things like, "I am grateful to have made it this far".

Spiritual Change

Someone who experiences PTG may seek to better understand themselves, the world, and what's beyond the world. They contemplate life and may seek a greater spiritual connection. There is a deeper meaning to life for them and/or a stronger spiritual faith. They may look for love, meaning, and connection. Questions like, "Why did this happen to me?" and "How can I use what happened to me to be of use to others?", "What really happens when you die?" or "What would have happened if someone's life were different?" are questions they more deeply contemplate.

When someone experiences PTG, their perspective shifts. They learn they can count on themselves more and what they value becomes clearer. When someone experiences PTG will they live a charmed life? No. They will have good days and bad days. That's what the life of a thriver is made of. Thrivers have good and bad days. The difference is that thrivers have the emotional tools to deal with the bad days. Because they have suffered, they know more than anybody the bad days are numbered and soon there will be good days again. They know emotional pain is temporary and they have the tools and the support to weather the storm. What they learn through their experience is to recognize and use the lessons they have to process and get through the troubled times. Someone who has experienced and worked through trauma has seen what the bottom of life looks like, and they learned to appreciate and be grateful when life is good.

Use this Journey not only to unburden the traumatic experiences of your past but use it daily and weekly in your present. Forgive those who trespass against you on a daily or weekly basis. When someone angers you, violates your boundaries, upsets you, belittles or demeans you, or double crosses you try to practice forgiveness. Process the experience. Learn from it. Don't hold onto the anger. Don't let anger turn into resentment. Process it and handle it with a level of maturity. Remember to teach people how to treat you and then let it go. Give it over to your higher power or to the universe. You are not meant to carry such a heavy burden. Keep the lesson learned but let go of the negative energy. Untether yourself from these negative thoughts and negative people. Practice letting go and unburdening yourself often. You are being lifted to a new elevation. You are not meant to carry burdens which weigh you down and keep you down. Genuinely and wholeheartedly - let them go.

12.

12th Journey: *The thriver carries and passes on this new way of thinking, feeling, and behaving throughout all their affairs.*

12th Truth: *I understand by giving back I maintain my health and well-being.*

12th Transformation: *I know my choice to help others helps me.*

Trigger or Validation:
For some, the material in this Journey may be triggering. If it triggers you, reach out to your support system including those you trust and appropriate members of your Bomb Squad and/or engage in some self-care activities. For others, this information will be validating. In those cases, use the material to help validate you and affirm that what you are or have been experiencing is real.

CHAPTER 12: GIVING BACK

"Even after all this time, the Sun never says to the Earth, 'you owe me'.
Look what happens with a love like that. It lights the whole sky."
~ Unknown

T he 12th Journey is about carrying your new way of thinking, feeling, and behaving throughout all your affairs. You might do this by speaking and presenting to audiences, by writing and publishing, by mentoring victims or survivors, or by simply being the best person you can be to your loved ones. Even though it is important to share your story to those that need to hear it, it's even more important to share your recovery journey in group with others. They need to hear your wisdom. They need to see what is possible for them.

The way you live your life is totally up to you, but in the spirit of Martin Luther King Jr, "You've been to the mountaintop" and looked over. You can see the way to live your life. You can choose to implement the lessons you've learned, or you can choose to continue to be greatly affected by what happened in your past. The choice is yours. That is what empowerment is all about. It's about making choices.

- In the 1st Journey you learned you need to be aware and expect recovery. You learned no one is going to save you but you, and so you courageously took on the challenge.
- In the 2nd Journey you focused on gathering your Bomb Squad aka the formal support system you needed to help guide you through the rest of the journeys.
- In the 3rd Journey you delved deep into your trauma in order to better understand it while you worked to identify and began to handle your triggers.

- In the 4th Journey you focused inward to listen to and change your internal self-talk, challenge your core beliefs, and recognize your schemas.
- The 5th Journey led you to increase your external safety and establish good healthy boundaries.
- Through the 6th Journey you investigated your past and conducted an open and honest self-evaluation so you could clearly see where you came from and could put plans in place to lower the risk factors ahead of you.
- In the 7th Journey you confronted and worked on your trust issues.
- The 8th Journey had you pursue healthy and supportive relationships and encouraged you to distance yourself from toxic ones.
- The 9th Journey challenged you to let go of some unspoken commitments you've made and dysfunctional loyalties which didn't serve to benefit you.
- The 10th Journey focused on self-forgiveness, and
- The 11th Journey had you release your burdens and practice forgiveness of others.
- Finally, this Journey asks you to carry the lessons and tools from the Survivor's Journey with you and pass them along to others.

Truth and Tools: Gift of Giving

"I understand by giving back I maintain my health and well-being".

Any ugly secret is toxic. It sits inside our hearts in loneliness and shame. It is a burden we carry which often feels heavy and at times steals our joy. Our trauma story is a part of us. When we hide it, we can feel like we are sharing only a part of ourselves. We feel ingenuine. A part of us lives in the darkness because our trauma story lives in the darkness. We associate what happened to us to be something we should continue to feel ashamed about. When we keep our story to ourselves, we may continue to blame ourselves or worse, minimize the story and our victimization because we don't value ourselves. Or we just want the memory of the story to go away but it won't go away because it is a part of our past experience.

For some thrivers, telling our trauma and recovery story helps us release our burdens and we feel better about ourselves and our futures. When we tell our trauma and recovery story and we hear understanding and empathy back from our listeners, we feel validated and connected. When others tell us and show us they are listening, we feel valued. When others validate our story was indeed horrible, and they are grateful we survived, we feel supported. It reminds us that we have accomplished something meaningful in surviving and then thriving.

Each time we tell our story we release a bit of shame and self-blame. It's like a teapot which begins to build up steam and boil, it needs a place to release the steam into the atmosphere and let it go.

There is darkness and loneliness in shame. When others hear our struggle, they struggle just for a moment, along with us. Their struggle brings light to us. Telling our story helps us see how others celebrate our survival. When we see others are genuinely concerned for our well-being, we feel connected. When others can't believe how well we are doing today, it reminds us about how far we have come and validates we really are thriving across many aspects of our life.

Just like any other profound accomplishment, when someone else sees what we have been through and where we are today, there are lessons to be gained by them. When an audience acknowledges in a formal presentation that your experience was real, you have indeed suffered, and you thrive today, they are validating a few important facts. First, you indeed survived and thrive and are ready to move forward in life. This is called a Rite of Passage. All over the world there are various forms of these rituals called Rites of Passage. When a teen graduate's high school, there is a Rite of Passage ceremony where the teen walks across the stage in front of family and other loved ones to receive their diploma. This ceremony formally acknowledges to the world this person is now an adult and can be launched onto the next stage of their life. Another Rite of Passage may be a marriage where a ceremony is performed to tell the world this couple made a life-long commitment of love to each other. Other familiar ceremonies may include baptisms, bar mitzvahs, confirmations, quinceaneras, college graduations, retirement parties, and funerals to name a few. These ceremonies formally identify various life transitions.

Second, in addition to helping you, what telling your trauma and recovery story does for others is it gives others permission to acknowledge their own story and perhaps even tell their story. It gives them permission not to hold on to the shame associated with their own story and to release their own burdens. It gives them permission to seek validation for having survived their own experience. Finally for others, it is through your story that they will learn to connect with who they really are and what they value. By telling your story, you give them an opportunity to learn valuable lessons embedded in their own story. As they celebrate you, the words you use to tell your story moves past the chest wall cavity to their heart and past the blood brain barrier to their mind to speak straight to the soul. When you tell your story, you are speaking a language which transcends all time and space and for that brief time, you are speaking the language of God, Allah, Jesus, Mohamad, Moses and The Great Spirit because you are speaking to the spirit of humankind, which is to love and not do harm to any breathing, loving being.

It doesn't get any more real than when you appeal to someone's heart through a story. Whether it is an audience of one or an audience of hundreds or thousands, your message will resonate with those who are open to receive it.

Those who choose not to tell their stories in a formal way in front of an audience can experience that same Rite of Passage when they tell their story to a safe and special friend or family member. In doing so, they release their demons so the thriver can experience a lifted burden in knowing someone else knows their story and instead of being repulsed by it, they empathize. They share the sadness and validate that you have indeed survived and gone on to thrive. It can be cathartic. Cathartic means to experience and express strong emotion and to receive psychological relief from it aka the feelings of healing.

Not telling your story continues to burden you with a past which is so psychologically troublesome it short circuits your ability to adequately process it alone. And because you have devalued yourself in the process, you are not the best person to process through the trauma alone. There is an old saying in law about a person who decides to represent themselves in a criminal court of law. The saying is "he who is his own lawyer, has a fool for a client." In Survivor's Journey groups we say, "he who decides to process his own trauma, has a fool for a therapist." That is why it was important to see a trauma treatment therapist and why it is important to also tell your story. To release your burdens you need to, at the very least, tell your whole story to your therapist. While taking this Journey, we also encourage you to tell your story to at least one more trustworthy person. In sharing your story, you practice trust as well as allowing at least one other person to know the complete story. Your trauma story is not the complete you, but it was an experience or series of experiences which put you on the path to recovery and your recovery is the most important part of you.

Today you walk with a certain confidence which is empowering to others. They see your light and they want to know how you got from there to here. It is your responsibility to show others the path to thrivership. We ask that you pass it on and give back to others who need to hear the message. Some victims are lost, and they need the Survivor's Journey so they can experience recovery. Don't hoard it. Pass it along generously.

You've spent a long considerable amount of time focusing on yourself and your recovery. This was an important time for you and likely one of the first times you have loved yourself so much. We are so proud of the time, attention, and love you gave to yourself. Now you know what true love can look like. Giving to others is self-fulfilling because you can take pride in helping someone else to receive the gifts you have received.

Sharing Your Story

By now we're sure you have either shared your story, been asked to share, or have contemplated sharing your story. Some thrivers experience a healing effect when they share their story. They connect with their audience to appreciate the love and support they receive during and after sharing. They teach someone else to understand and empathize instead of stigmatizing others. The audience learns compassion. Sharing your story also takes the experience out of your head where only your interpretations were prominent and places the story in an objective context. While the audience is listening, it helps the presenter to realize their own growth in a more profound way.

There are several ways to share your story. Some will be asked to share their story to a formal audience. The presentation topic might be domestic violence, gangs, child abuse, sex trafficking, commercial sexual exploitation, or other forms of abuse. When a thriver presents, it can be life changing for some in the audience. Having interviewed many people about how they got involved in anti-trafficking work or other forms of social justice and human rights type of work, it was most often because they heard a story. The power of story can propel some in the audience to change their life and focus on helping others. The late rapper Tupac Shakur, said *"I'm not saying I'm going to change the world, but I guarantee that I will spark the brain that will change the world."* You may be the person who places that spark in the brain of someone in the audience who goes back to create programs for others, develop policies and laws that protect others, or who changes their life or life's work to help others.

A thriver may share their story to an audience of Survivor's Journey members at a group meeting. When you think of sharing your story with other wounded and traumatized members on their journey, it is considered a testimony. A testimony is defined as "evidence or proof" or an accounting of the truth. Giving your testimony to victims, survivors, and other thrivers, becomes a powerful way of showing others they can do it to. Letting them know where you were, where you are now, and what you still struggle with emotionally, mentally, spiritually and in your relationships with others is highly valuable and meaningful to other members. This gives them hope. Is your life perfect today? No, but you've chosen the good over the perfect and learned to be ok with it. Your testimony can change someone's life for the better. Just like you received the messages you needed, it's your turn to carry the message forward as a living, breathing example that you are the rose that grew from concrete, you did rise from the ashes like the phoenix, and you are stronger and more powerful than ever before. Share the truth, that you continue to struggle, but now you have the tools to overcome your struggles. But more than overcome, you have hopes and dreams which you are putting into action. Share that you put in the daily work to maintain your emotional, mental, physical, and spiritual health. You don't sit on the sidelines any longer and just let life happen to you, you take the reins, and you make it happen.

Finally, you can choose to share your story with one individual at a time. Often there are opportunities and teachable moments which present themselves. Take advantage of these moments to share your story with someone so they might have the opportunity to challenge themselves to seek out better health and well-being. The opportunity may present itself right after a violent occurrence in someone's life. The opportunity might also present itself on a quiet day when it seems the person's heart is open to listening. Whatever the case may be, if the opportunity presents itself, give the gift you have to someone else.

Not Sharing Your Story of Trauma and Recovery

Some of you would prefer to keep your recovery to yourself and that is absolutely your right as a free and empowered person. You control your own life, and you are empowered to conduct it in any way you see fit. We respect your decision and applaud your desire for confidentiality. When we say, "carries this new way of thinking, feeling, and behaving throughout all of my affairs and passes it on", it is very relevant to interpret this to mean you carry the wonderful and evolved you forward in all of your affairs and you pass on all the lessons and skills you have learned along the way to others. You can certainly do this without telling your personal story. Do this by living by example.

Other Ways of Giving Back

Sharing your story is not the only way to give back. Becoming a Survivor's Journey group facilitator is great way to give back. By taking the training and becoming a certified trainer you will be eligible to host weekly groups yourself. There is no better way to give the gifts you received than to give one or two hours a week running your own group. Giving back is a way to continually validate your own growth because in others you consistently see where you used to be emotionally, psychologically, and more. Not only that, helping others is fulfilling. Helping others helps you. It is the rent you pay for your own continued success because it reminds you of how easy it is to slip back into old ways of thinking, behaving, and feeling.

Giving back feeds the soul. Donating your time while you are a survivor is therapeutic. Being involved in increasing awareness, prevention related activities, engaging in fundraising, and/or directing other victims and survivors to agencies and service providers they want are all good ways of giving back. Also encourage survivors to become engaged in these activities. However, attempting to help someone learn the lessons and achieve the tools they need to recover internally should be done by thrivers, otherwise it will be like the blind leading the blind. It's not possible to share something with someone which you simply don't have yet to give. If neither knows the direction, both will end up lost. The tools a victim or survivor brings to the helping space are the tools they learned while traumatized. Trauma mixing with trauma breeds toxicity. Because you physically survived your experience doesn't mean you are automatically equipped to help others emotionally recover. Quite the opposite. The energy a victim or survivor has should be spent on their own recovery, not someone else's. In the same vein, a thriver running a Survivor's Journey group is still working and practicing daily. They are still going through various Journeys themselves, going deeper and learning more each time. That's what makes a thriver the perfect facilitator. The day they don't have a journey to travel is the day they become an expert at life and no one is an expert at life. Survivor's Journey facilitators can relate to members of the group because they see the value in continuing to grow and do their work.

Giving Back without Being Victimized

A part of your ongoing healing and recovery is to help others, but please do so without being revictimized. Remember to take time for yourself and not push yourself into a relapse or a sickness. Pay attention to any emotional or physical triggers causing you stress and may cause you to give too much, to your own detriment. Never compromise your own recovery.

Sharing, supporting, and giving back without being revictimized, used, and exploited is key, particularly when you are working with others who are still close to the fire or in the fire. You'll have to decide what you can handle. Bring the "adult" you into the equation and make a rational, honest decision about what you handle emotionally, mentally, and psychologically. And never put yourself into a situation where you could physically be hurt. You are not a police officer and it's not your job to enter situations reserved for other professionals, like the police. Seek guidance and mentorship when necessary.

Giving back to someone should come as a breath of fresh air. If you are dreading it, then you are not in the head space or heart space to do this work. *That is ok.* Knowing your truth and empowering yourself to say "no" is ok.

Finally, donating, volunteering, and working in an agency who cares for survivors is another way to give back. Helping to sponsor and support a Survivor's Journey group in your area is particularly helpful and is a way of endorsing the program and providing an opportunity of healing to others.

Today, you have the power to choose internal joy. On the days you are happy, celebrate them because you deeply understand what it's like to experience the opposite. Joy and happiness are gifts, celebrate them. When you are not experiencing joy or happiness, you have the understanding that these feelings are temporary. You have the tools to process through them. You have the resources to lean on both your informal (healthy friends, family members, neighbors, or co-workers) and formal supports (Bomb Squad) when you need help to get through something.

You have changed your life for the better. When you doubt it, go back into the Survivor's Journey group and check your reality. Look at the group members. You can see where and how much you have grown. Sit in and listen. When you hear their stories, issues, and circumstances you might be thinking of ways in which you would handle it. Why? Because you have the tools and the mindset to take on their challenge and handle it. As they struggle through the Journeys, you can see your past struggles in their current struggle.

Are you fully recovered and will never need a Survivor's Journey group again? We hope so, but life keeps happening. And because our tools can get rusty overtime and lessons are lost, we may need to come back. Because we go out in the world and have experiences, we may have some negative experiences which challenge us. But the difference is now we have a wonderful resource. There is one thing you have learned and that is to reach out when you need it. Reach out to your informal support system. Reach out to your formal support system. Think of your Survivor's Journey group as your extended family. Reach out and participate in the Survivor's Journey groups again for as long as you need them and as long as you feel supported.

Use The Survivor's Journey for Any Problem

The Survivor's Journey can be used for almost anything you are struggling with. If you are struggling with something that frustrates you, think of that problem, that need, or that frustration and focus on it as you work the 1st Journey. Focus on it as you work through the 2nd Journey. Think of it as you work through Journeys 3 through 12. The Survivor's Journey will work in addressing almost any internal problem you might have because the foundation of each Journey is to understand your truth, to use the tools given, to work with your Bomb Squad, and to create the transformation you desire.

People in recovery in Alcoholics Anonymous and Narcotics Anonymous groups say that drugs and alcohol are both cunning and baffling.

Without working the program, drugs and/or alcohol will find a way back into their lives. When it comes to trauma and dysfunction, your mind will figure out a way to silence your protest against getting involved with dysfunctional people, places, and things that aren't good for your mental and emotional health and well-being. Understand that you have developed these patterns of behaving, thinking, and feeling for a very long time and without you fighting for your recovery every day, getting you to go back to your old vulnerable ways is like giving candy to a baby.

> *"I remember getting away from my second physically violent relationship. I finally figured out that I needed to work on myself and my self-esteem. I vowed to never be abused again and I wasn't. However, instead of connecting with highly dysfunctional boyfriends, I began to connect with highly dysfunctional female friends. I hadn't changed. I just adapted. Once I realized this, I not only got rid of my dysfunctional friends, but I also distanced myself from dysfunctional family members. When I craved a little craziness in my life, I turned on a dysfunctional reality show to get my fix."* ~Celia

Are you ever cured? You may process and successfully work through your previous trauma(s), but because it was a part of you, you may be susceptible and vulnerable to involvement in unhealthy relationships and/or battle with your self-esteem. Just like someone with diabetes, you'll have to always monitor your health and make sure you are emotionally healthy. That means you'll have to monitor the things you say to yourself and what you think of yourself. You'll have to stay aware of who you hang around because you will begin to pick up their attitudes. If they are dysfunctional, it will be that much easier for you to slip back into dysfunction. You'll need to strategically choose your intimate partner and your best friend and monitor your contact with unhealthy friends and family. You'll want to make sure you eat healthy, get enough rest, practice meditation or mindfulness, and engage in the physical exercise of your choice, whether it be walking, yoga, or some form of physical exercise. It is critically important you devote some energy to engaging in meaningful work and/or volunteer activities which help others. You feel best when you are helping other people. Finally, balance is the key. Pour into yourself as much as you pour into others.

Relapse

While this Journey focuses on giving back, we also acknowledge the potential for relapse. What does relapse look like for Survivors? Relapse occurs when we become complacent in our recovery. A relapse is any experience allowing you to fall back into your old ways of thinking, feeling, and behaving. Relapse for survivors comes in many forms. You'll know it when you begin to get stuck in your thoughts, persistently replaying negative situations, thoughts, or feelings about yourself or others. In AA they call it engaging in "stinkin-thinkin". It may show up back in your life when you throw caution to the wind and no longer implement the lessons or tools you've learned, and you end up back in a negative head or heart space. Perhaps you relapse because you find a way to justify why it's ok to ignore the warning signs or excuse someone's dysfunction who may lead you back into a hurtful and traumatizing situation. Maybe you develop persistent and negative feelings again about yourself. It may appear once again in your behavior as you start engaging and investing time in harmful activities or making commitments to someone or something bad for you. Anytime you experience a relapse, come back to Survivor's Journey groups. There can be no shame in your game. Life is not perfect. Shit happens. Recovery is important. Come back and work the Journeys.

Anytime you relapse and go back to your old ways for even a day or a few hours or you go back to using drugs or abusing alcohol, distancing yourself from healthy others, isolating yourself, or throwing caution to the wind and not practicing the lessons or tools from the Journeys, you run the risk of slipping back into dysfunctional patterns. Getting involved with unhealthy people, places, and things is likely because you lost hope, or the opposite could be true, and you believe you are cured or can cure others. Realize you need to regain awareness by coming back into the program and revisiting the 1st Journey about awareness and expectation. Travel this Journey again. Attend the groups. Read the journeys again. Do the old exercises again. Also, there are always new exercises you can ask for and complete which align with each Journey. Begin to heal yourself again, and again, and as many times as you need it because you are worth it, your life is worth it. Your dreams are worth it.

Love-Based Life vs Fear-Based Life

These Journeys to recovery have been all about loving yourself and living a love-based life instead of a fear-based life. Living a love-based life means gaining both the realization and motivation to be unafraid to love yourself enough to seek out and achieve all you want out of life. Living a love-based life means love, instead of fear, is the basis through which your life is lived. Decisions and life transitions are determined based on love. It doesn't mean a life is absent of fear, it means fear is not the dominant force through which your life is lived. One of the main character elements of a life guided by love is courage. Courage is being afraid but moving forward anyway. Bring your courage, integrity, strengths, and endurance you showed to survive to achieve any goals you have.

Living a love-based life means you develop your life goals and go after them. What does success mean to you? For some it means being financially successful. They put their financial success upfront, they find a mentor, and devise a plan to achieve the level of income they need to afford the luxuries in life they desire. They are willing to work hard for them. For others, a goal may be to be in a loving relationship and/or having a loving family. For some it may mean achieving their goals of going back to school, opening their own business, or working their dream job. And yet for others it may mean all of these things and more. When you live a love-based life, the possibilities are endless because you dare to dream and are willing to work hard on yourself and your dreams to make them come true.

Those who choose to live a love-based life typically lead a more fulfilling life because they are courageous enough not to just survive, but to thrive. It is realizing you can live a life designed by you which is most thrilling and fulfilling. So, for a moment, sit back and just dream about all the things you would like to become a part of your life and who you are. Many of those things are possible when you love yourself and are willing to put in the hard work to make your dreams become a reality.

Living a fear-based life will always hold you back. Fear encourages you to kill your hopes and silence your dreams. Fear will keep you from even being able to think about doing something else with your life. It keeps you from considering and exploring possibilities. Fear will criticize everything you do. It will even call you "stupid" for even thinking about such a thing. Fear has company; doubt, anxiety, and negative self-talk. And if all that fails, fear will ramp itself up into self-hatred and all-out panic to be sure to kill your dream. Fear is the ultimate hater because if fear can get you to tell yourself, "no" then there is a 100% guarantee you won't even try. On the other hand, in living a love-based life, you understand you may hear someone say, "no" to you, but (1) you got as far as to ask, and (2) because that person engaged with you, their initial "no" might be on its way to "yes" once you strengthen your weaknesses and revisit your dream.

Mind-Fields: Counting

As you give back to others, make sure you do it with a closed fist. We don't mean come in with an attitude ready to fight, we mean come into the helping process not ready to count every single thing you did for someone on your fingers. Anytime you open your hand to count how many times you've helped someone and how much help you provided, you are concerned about yourself with the help being more about you. If you want to be acknowledged and thanked and given a virtual gold star for the work you did, choose a setting and a job where you can get that type of feedback and reward. Giving back as a part of the 12th Journey is something you do from the heart. It certainly does help you, but it also helps to take "you" out of the equation by focusing on someone else. When you turn around and make it all about you, you defeat the purpose.

Sometimes when we help others and they haven't properly thanked us or paid us back, we can get so frustrated we take it out on them or someone else. Because we have found our self-esteem, someone is really going to pay if they don't treat us right. Inadvertently, what you end up teaching and mentoring for the person you intended to help had the opposite effect. They learned you need to be paid back in the form of a "thank you" for everything you did. It reinforces to them all people really are out to get their own needs met. They conclude that you really aren't genuinely concerned about them and their well-being. Your need for recognition trumps their need for love and support.

Anytime you get frustrated because you helped someone and they didn't thank you, think again about why you are doing what you are doing. It's not for you or about you. It's about them. What you get from it is a chance to pay back what you were given and to see how far you have come.

Take the Survivor's Journeys with you through life. Once you complete the Journeys, continue to come to the group as a matter of choice or whenever you need. Because you are now a thriver and have completed the Journeys, it doesn't mean you are a perfect human. Indeed, you are not. Arrogance and ego have no place here. We are all human and as humans we make mistakes, and we need each other.

Making The Survivor's Journey a Continuing Practice

Survivor's Journey groups are open to anyone wanting to recover from an emotional or physically violent trauma. Many people may find it comforting to continue to attend Survivor's Journey groups and continue to work in their workbook and on themselves. Continuing to attend groups is good practice.

If you are struggling in one particular area, you can work through the 12 Survivor's Journeys with just that issue in mind. For example, many people still struggle with trust even though they have worked on trust in the 7th Journey. You may have reached enough of a level of trust that you believed you could move forward onto the next journey. By the

12th Journey you realize you are ready to tackle trust again and go a little deeper on the issue of trust. You may go through all the journeys just with the goal of working to obtain a deeper level of trust in yourself and in others. The issue of relationships, as discussed in the 8th Journey, is another difficult area to master because each new relationship may be challenging with different issues to manage. If you still struggle or would like to dive deeper in a particular area, all you have to do is add the issue of your choice to your Journeys.

Here's an example of using "trust" as the issue you will work on throughout all the Journeys:

- *1st Journey:* The victim comes to believe they are not living a life of choice and freedom, but a life filled with mistrust
- *2nd Journey:* The victim answers the call and assembles the team
- *3rd Journey:* The victim works through trauma and consistently combats the issue of trust
- *4th Journey:* The Survivor wins the internal battle to trust themselves
- *5th Journey:* The survivor recognizes and minimizes external threats and increases external safety around the issue of trust
- *6th Journey:* The survivor engages in an open and honest self-examination to understand trust and mistrust
- *7th Journey:* The survivor learns to trust and engages those who are trustworthy
- *8th Journey:* The survivor pursues healthy and trustworthy relationships which includes trust
- *9th Journey:* The survivor honors spoken and unspoken commitments which support them and helps them learn to trust
- *10th Journey:* The thriver understands life is good, not perfect and continually nurtures and forgives self
- *11th Journey:* The thriver believes they are more than their negative experiences and releases their burdens associated with mistrust
- *12th Journey:* The thriver carries and passes on this new way of thinking, feeling, and behaving throughout all their affairs.

Transformation: The Chain Reaction: Your 12 Promises

"I know choosing to help others helps me".

Have you ever watched a fuse that is lit? Sometimes, there is a chain reaction where one process makes something else happen and so forth. One process makes another process ignite. The bomb that goes off affects everything around it. We think of a bomb as breaking things apart or tearing them down. Some bombs are used very productively to break through things. When we need to destroy walls and tear down old buildings, we use bombs. A life transformation is a break-through to another, more wonderful and more fulfilling life. One that, before the Survivor's Journey, you could only dream of living.

If you carefully and specifically work the 12 Survivor's Journeys, you will experience a life transformation and will fulfill the 12 promises you make to yourself.

- *Promise #1:* We use our truths and tools to guide our life transformation and we experience joy.

  When I understand my truth; that I was divinely made to live a life full of lessons, life truths, and life transformations; I experience joy. I know I am forever evolving, becoming wiser, and growing emotionally. I now know happiness comes and goes, but I choose joy because joy is internal. No matter what happens, I can find the joy in life because I practice gratitude and grace. I remember that I am grateful to be alive and why I am grateful. I show myself and others grace in that grace is unexpected and undeserved love. I don't do it because someone has earned it, I do it as a matter of daily practice.

- *Promise #2:* We work from the inside-out to achieve the life we truly want to live.

  I know my work is internal. No matter what I do for a living or what my external life looks like, working from the inside-out means as I work to achieve internal joy, internal satisfaction, and emotional health, I am living the life I truly want to live. Even if my ego isn't happy with my external circumstances, my soul is satisfied.

- *Promise #3:* We have healthy boundaries and learn to trust ourselves and others that are trustworthy.

  Trust is built on faith. It's the belief someone is trustworthy. I understand a level of trust is critical to a healthy relationship, and I have learned to selectively trust those who are trustworthy. I am more comfortable trusting because I learned to have healthy emotional and physical boundaries and to control who I trust and what I trust them with.

- *Promise #4:* We have the formal supports we need to create the informal supports we want.

  I have learned to use my Bomb Squad, aka my formal support system, to help me select and navigate my informal support system of friends, family, co-workers, and life partner. Both are supportive in different and valuable ways to me.

- *Promise #5:* We handle difficult situations with grace because we are in control of our emotions.

  I know how to regulate my emotions. Before I lose emotional control, I sit and reason through what happened and what I'm feeling. Instead of my emotions guiding my reactions and decisions, my decisions will guide my reaction and response.

- *Promise #6:* We are no longer internally vulnerable because we have internal healing.

  I am no longer easily wounded because I choose when and with whom I'll be vulnerable.

- *Promise #7:* We regularly escape or avoid life's traps, and we know the difference between life's luxuries and life's trappings.

  I have been awakened to life's traps and I avoid them. I know the difference between life's trappings and life's luxuries, and I enjoy the luxuries in life when I can.

- *Promise #8:* We live a love-based life and through love, we achieve.

  I know the difference between living a love-based life and a fear-based life. Whenever possible I try to live a love-based life.

- *Promise #9:* We lead a life of freedom powered by our will, our voice, and our choices.

  I am internally free today because I am empowered to make choices over how I will feel, think, and behave. The power of my will, my voice, and my choices are stronger today.

- *Promise #10:* We no longer allow trauma and shame to control our lives.

  Trauma was a part of my life experience, but today it is only a part of my past experience. It is not the totality of me. As I carry the memory of my life experiences, I also remember the trauma, but trauma doesn't control my life. I control my life. Shame doesn't control what I think, how I feel, or what I choose to do or not do. I control those things.

- *Promise #11:* We fully love ourselves, love others, and are loved.

  As quiet as it is kept, I feel proud of myself, and love who I am because I know I am amazing, strong, and wise. Others recognize it when I share my story. I am admired because of my courage, my outstanding achievements, and my noble qualities. I return the love tenfold when I help others start and stay on their journeys.

- *Promise #12:* We never again experience the control of a lover, a drug, a system, or an institution.

  I am free because I will no longer allow someone, something, or some place to control me. I will never compromise my self-esteem, give over my voice, or give up my power of choice in life again. Those in my company will be internally strong enough to allow me to be me. We will share because we make a choice to share our lives, not because one has to control the other.

Someone else needs to travel the journey. Pass it on and let someone else know their life can also change.

The Survivor's Journey Chart of Journeys

	Journey	Chapters
1st Journey	The victim comes to believe they are not living a life of choice and freedom, but a life filled with internal traps and external trappings, but this can change.	Chapter 1: Awareness & Expectation
2nd Journey	The victim answers the call and assembles the Team	Chapter 2: Courage & Connection
3rd Journey	The victim works through trauma and consistently combats their triggers	Chapter 3: Self-Discovery
4th Journey	The survivor wins the internal battle to gain an inner voice that supports them	Chapter 4: Internal Safety
5th Journey	The survivor recognizes and minimizes external threats and increases external safety	Chapter 5: External Safety
6th Journey	The survivor engages in an open and honest self-examination to understand the past	Chapter 6: Self-Examination

Truths	Tools	Mind-Fields	Transformation
	Awareness & Expectation	Circumstances and Consequences	I have the power to choose to change my life.
I can't live the life I want to live without help.	Courage and Connection	Complacence and Collusion	I work with others to regain my power, choice, and voice.
Trauma is the source of my pain	Self-Discovery	Clenching and Clawing	I consistently combat my triggers and heal from trauma.
I have the power to control and change my internal thoughts and feelings about myself.	Internal Safety	Catering and Clashing	My inner voice loves, embraces, and supports me.
I know having unhealthy boundaries increases my vulnerability and decreases my safety.	External Safety	Choosing and Cheating	I maintain emotional and physical boundaries and am safer.
My past explains my present but doesn't dictate my future.	Self-Examination	Creating and Constructing	I know how I got here and where I want to go.

	Journey	Chapters
7th Journey	The survivor learns to trust and engages those who are trustworthy	Chapter 7: Trust
8th Journey	The survivor pursues healthy and supportive relationships	Chapter 8: Healthy Relationships
9th Journey	The survivor honors spoken and unspoken commitments that support them.	Chapter 9: Disobedience
10th Journey	The thriver understands life is good, not perfect and continually nurtures and forgives self	Chapter 10: Self-Forgiveness
11th Journey	The thriver believes they are more than their negative experiences and releases their burdens	Chapter 11: Unburdening & Untethering
12th Journey	The thriver carries and passes on this new way of thinking, feeling, and behaving throughout all their affairs.	Chapter 12: Giving Back

Truths	Tools	Mind-Fields	Transformation
Trust is demonstrated in action, not words.	Trustworthiness	Conviction and Corruption	I trust people who are nurturing and trustworthy and I remove those who are toxic.
Unhealthy relationships keep me sick.	Healthy Relationships	Cynical and Constrained	I build and sustain healthy and nurturing relationships and support systems.
I honor commitments that support and benefit me.	Healthy Beliefs, Obligations, and Loyalties (BOLs)	Compliance and Control	I honor healthy commitments and those who support my growth.
I engage in daily self-forgiveness	Self-Forgiveness	Charged and Convicted	I practice ongoing daily nurturing and self-forgiveness.
I release toxic energy through unburdening and untethering	Unburdening and Untethering	Complicit and Corrosive	I engage in a daily practice of unburdening and releasing.
I understand by giving back I maintain my health and well-being.	Gift of Giving	Counting	I know choosing to help others helps me.

PART III:

The TNT Way

What is the Survivor's Journey and Purpose?

The Survivor's Journey leads participants through internal Journeys along the continuum of recovery from victim to survivor to thriver. Through The Survivor's Journey, you learn your personal truths which allow you to heal from your trauma. Within each Journey, there are certain truths which need to be revealed. Internal tools are given to help you reveal the truths and move you toward transformation. There are 12 Guided Journeys. Members take each Journey using 12 tools to adopt 12 truths and to experience 12 guided transformations to address trauma.

What is TNT?

TNT stands for Truth and Transformation. It is only by understanding a certain set of truths that we can use the tools we are given in each Journey to experience a series of transformations. Because a series of truths and transformations are at the core of what takes place in recovery it is our core process.

What's the Difference Between TNT and the Survivor's Journey?

The process of recovery is through truth and transformation aka TNT. The book and the groups are called "The Survivor's Journey".

What Do You Mean by "Truth" and "Transformation" in TNT?

Growth through the use of TNT means a commitment to address your trauma and grow emotionally, mentally, physically, socially, and spiritually into the person you want to be with the life you want to live. We believe in the power of "Be-Do-Have." Once you "become" the person inside, you want to be, you will "do" the things you want to be doing and will "have" the life you want to have (Covey, 1989). "Be-Do-Have" happens by both learning and telling the truth and creating life transitions and transformations.

You are truth-worthy. A large part of the healing process is first understanding our truth and standing in it. Many of us would rather skip our truths, deny them, cover them up, and pretend we are someone else or that something else really happened instead of our truth. Before transformation can begin, we have to face some truths which lead us to understand our experiences and know who we truly are. Even some therapists we visit or friends and family who care about us will allow us to slide by our truths and not face them. They will become a partner in our lies about ourselves and our experiences and what these experiences have truly done to us. Only by understanding your truth and speaking your truth, can you heal.

Transformation is the creation of lasting and meaningful change in our lives. Change can lead to transformation, but change is different from transformation. Change alone can be superficial. Changing your external behaviors is a positive Journey in the right direction and can lead to transformation, but transformation is changing the internal core beliefs, feelings, and thoughts. Some people say change is hard, but change is not the goal. Transformation is the goal. Change is like going on a diet, while transformation is creating a lifestyle of healthy eating habits. As you work to change, you grit your teeth and white knuckle through it, hating it all the way and counting down the days until it can be over. Why do you hate it? Because it's not really you. Transformation is making healthy lifestyle changes in the way you eat. It is introduced slowly. You change the way you think about food, the way you feel about food, and ultimately make choices that grow to become fulfilling for you. You begin to like the healthier choices you make. You appreciate the transformation taking place. You're not "on a diet," you "are a healthy eater." Healthy eater becomes your identity. It's not something you do, it's who you are. If someone asks you why you look so good, you wouldn't say "I'm on a diet," you would say "I'm a healthy eater," because that is your identity. You've transformed into a healthy eater. The same thing is true for someone who wants to play the piano or wants to learn to swim. They can change their behavior to practice the piano every day or practice swimming once a week, but until they behave in the manner which suggests they are a piano player or a swimmer, they are still practicing. Until the moment their behavior matches their "feeling" and "thinking" about piano or swimming they are still in process. When they behave, think, and feel it, they have transformed into a piano player or a swimmer. They refer to themselves as such, they believe it, and because of their transformation, others believe it too. Thus, transformation requires a change in our thinking, feeling, and behavior. In fact, many of the biggest psychological theories therapists use help their patients change their thinking, feeling, or behavior, or a combination of those. Why? There is a theory called "cognitive dissonance." It means thinking, behaving, and feeling must come in-line and be in-unison with each other. For instance, if I snatch an old lady's purse while she is walking down the street, that behavior is clearly bad. I don't want to consider myself to be someone who would do that to a frail old woman. I don't want to think of myself as someone who would hurt someone weaker than I am or that I might have taken her purse which contained necessary medication she needed or that I might have taken the money from her purse she needed to pay for her senior living apartment. That is something a horrible person does. So, I make up logical reasons why I'm not a horrible person. I tell myself it's really her fault. "If she wasn't swinging that purse while she was walking, then I wouldn't have snatched it." Or it's really her fault because she shouldn't have brought her purse anyway. "Old ladies get robbed. She should have known better than to bring her purse with her." Or "Why was she walking on that street anyway? Someone was going to do it; it might as well have been me" and so forth. With this reasoning, I can convince myself it's not really me who is wrong. I'm a good person. It's really her who is bad, or it really is just the way of the world. I need to "feel" and "think" I'm a good person, so I need to justify why I did a bad thing.

What therapists know is if they can disrupt the way you "think" about something or "feel" about something or the way you "behave", they have a chance to help you create the change you want to see in your life. It will force you to bring your thinking, feeling, and behavior in-line and in-unison with each other.

What we do in Survivor's Journey groups is work on all three - behavior, thinking, and feeling - so that transformation can occur. To create the changes you need in your life, requires the use of tools we provide through the Journeys.

What are the Survivor's Journey Tools?

We view victims as being chained and enslaved in their experience, not through the use of literal chains, but by invisible yet very real internal chains, making it nearly impossible to escape and be free. In Survivor's Journey groups, we use specific tools to help you break the chains and craft the life you want. When you have the tools, it is completely possible to heal from your experiences of abuse, violence, and/or exploitation. When you understand your truths and are ready to change your thinking, behavior, and feelings, your life can take a dramatic turn for the better. The tools we provide in each Journey of the process helps each member break each link and take each Journey in their recovery process which leads to their personal freedom.

Who is Most Appropriate to Take the Survivor's Journey?

Victims of child abuse and neglect are suitable to take the Survivor's Journey. Child sexual abuse refers to the involvement of a child (person less than 18 years old) in sexual activity which violates the laws or social taboos of society and which they do not fully comprehend, do not consent to, or is unable to give informed consent to, or are not developmentally prepared and therefore cannot give consent (Center for Disease Control and Prevention, n.d).

Individuals who have been victims of sexual assault aka sexual contact or behavior which occurs without the explicit consent including forced sexual intercourse, forcible sodomy, child molestation, incest, fondling, and attempted rape (U.S. Department of Justice, n.d) are appropriate to take the Survivor's Journeys.

Victims of sexual exploitation or commercial sexual exploitation in which there is another party who benefits monetarily, socially, or politically from the sexual exploitation of another, and in which the victim is placed in a position of vulnerability, differential power, or trust for sexual purposes are suitable and can benefit from the Survivor's Journeys.

Victims of domestic violence/intimate partner violence are suitable for Survivor's Journey groups, no matter how recent or how much time has passed. Victims who have been under the control of anyone where they have suffered a level of trauma which still effects them today will find value in attending Survivor's Journey groups.

Those who have been affiliated with gangs and suffered trauma as a result are appropriate for the Survivor's Journeys. Trauma occurs when gang related beliefs and activities become incompatible with the member's mental and emotional sensibilities. When gang membership or affiliation is harmful emotionally, mentally, and spiritually, it is victimizing and can be traumatizing.

Many victims involved in Survivor's Journey groups find it hard to identify with just one experience. It is common for victims to have experienced more than one form of victimization and trauma. Often victims have suffered early childhood abuse, some have experienced sexual assault, and some may have experienced sexual exploitation.

Trauma is in the eye of the beholder. This means each person's traumatic experience is their own, qualified only by them. How deeply they were affected is subjective, the measure of which can only be quantified by them. If you have suffered and have been victimized and desire recovery, the Survivor's Journey may be right for you. However, there are various Survivor's Journey groups which are exclusive to the type of trauma suffered. Find the right Survivor's Journey group for you.

What are the 12 Survivor's Journeys?

The 12 Survivor's Journeys are summarized below. For some, each Journey may take a day or a week. For others it may take weeks, months, or years. Once one Journey is mastered, the next is taken.

- *1st Journey:* The victim comes to believe they are not living a life of choice and freedom, but a life filled with internal traps and external trappings, but this can change.
- *2nd Journey:* The victim answers the call and assembles the team.
- *3rd Journey:* The victim works through trauma and consistently combats their triggers.
- *4th Journey:* The survivor wins the internal battle to gain an inner voice that supports them.
- *5th Journey:* The survivor recognizes and minimizes external threats and increases external safety.
- *6th Journey:* The survivor engages in an open and honest self-examination to understand the past.
- *7th Journey:* The survivor learns to trust and engages those who are trustworthy.
- *8th Journey:* The survivor pursues healthy and supportive relationships.
- *9th Journey:* The survivor honors spoken and unspoken commitments that support them.
- *10th Journey:* The thriver understands life is good, not perfect, and continually nurtures and forgives self.
- *11th Journey:* The thriver believes they are more than their negative experiences and releases their burdens.
- *12th Journey:* The thriver carries and passes on this new way of thinking, feeling, and behaving throughout all their affairs.

What are the Similarities and Differences Between Traditional 12-Step Programs and the 12 Survivor's Journeys?

Much like Alcoholics Anonymous or Narcotics Anonymous, people involved in Survivor's Journey groups come together to discuss, learn, and grow. Similarly, there is a process to follow. In the case of AA there are 12 steps and in the case of the Survivor's Journeys, there are 12 journeys. Other similarities include having 12 Pillars similar to AA's 12 traditions. While both focus on recovery, unlike a traditional 12-Step program, Survivor's Journey groups are trauma-informed and focus on addressing trauma.

How Should I Use the Survivor's Journey Book and Workbook?

As a member of a Survivor's Journey group, you should obtain a Survivor's Journey book to read and a Survivor's Journey Workbook. The workbook comes with some self-reflection exercises, challenges, and areas to write your thoughts. If you run out of activities or fill your workbook with your thoughts and reflections, your facilitator will have many more reflection exercises to provide you which will allow you to process and go deeper into working each Journey until you believe you have mastered it.

What are the Survivor's Journey Tools?

We view victims as being chained and enslaved in their experience, not through the use of literal chains, but by invisible yet very real internal chains, making it nearly impossible to escape and be free. In Survivor's Journey groups, we use specific tools to help you break the chains and craft the life you want. When you have the tools, it is completely possible to heal from your experiences of abuse, violence, and/or exploitation. When you understand your truths and are ready to change your thinking, behavior, and feelings, your life can take a dramatic turn for the better. The tools we provide in each Journey of the process helps each member break each link and take each Journey in their recovery process which leads to their personal freedom.

Who is my Survivor's Journey Group Facilitator?

In the Survivor's Journey, we offer four types of group facilitators. We have facilitators who are Ally Facilitators meaning they may be lay people who have been trained to facilitate Survivor's Journey groups. A facilitator may be a Peer Facilitator, meaning they received Survivor's Journey training and have lived experience as a survivor of trauma. A group facilitator may be a Professional Facilitator, meaning they have a degree in one of the helping professions like social work, mental health counseling, nursing, and so forth and have been trained to facilitate Survivor's Journey groups. Finally, a group facilitator may be a Therapeutic Facilitator which means they have a masters or doctorate in social work, psychology, clinical mental health or similar and are trained to facilitate groups. Only those who are trained and certified to implement the Survivor's Journey program may facilitate Survivor's Journey groups.

How Long Should I be Involved?

Survivor's Journey groups are open to you for as long as you need to be involved. There can be no limit on transforming one's life. Taking this Journey is not easy, but you're not taking it alone. Your health and your well-being are worth it. If it becomes too much you can leave the group and come back to a group at a later time or access a new group to continue your work.

Taking the Survivor's Journey may mean a group member may come in and out of groups and may remain a member for several years. For instance, it's unlikely someone will come to a group meeting where Journey 8 regarding "trust" is being discussed and instantly learn everything they need to know about trust. They may self-assess and self-reflect on how the issue of trust has presented both barriers and protections in their life, sort out all the issues associated with trust, distance those in their lives who are not trustworthy, and begin to bring into their lives those who are trustworthy. If trust is the major issue they seek to work on, they may be involved in working on trust for as long as they need to in order to build the trust they need to interact in healthy ways with loved ones.

What Types of Survivor's Journey Groups Can I Join?

To increase the probability that group members relate and connect to one another, a trained Survivor's Journey facilitator may choose to host "women-only" groups, "men-only" groups, "trans-only" groups, "gay-male" groups, and so forth. The facilitator may also choose to facilitate a group based on similar lived experiences i.e., those that have been victims of child abuse or neglect, sex trafficking, domestic violence or intimate partner violence, sexual assault, and/or those currently or previously involved in a gang. We should also remain cognizant that some who have experienced one form of victimization have likely experienced other forms.

Group facilitators should make sure they advertise the type of survivor most suitable for their group and should work to avoid having a survivor show up to a group and feel alienated or be rejected from the group.

Is Survivor's Journey Designed to be Delivered in a Group Format Only?

The Survivor's Journey is designed with a group format in mind but may be implemented via one-on-one work. It is easily adaptable for one-one-one work with a trained Survivor's Journey facilitator.

Example: If a Survivor's Journey group meets on Wednesday evenings and 'Client A' can't join on Wednesdays, 'Client A' should be provided one-on-one Journey focused work, which is providing the same information and materials provided in a group setting but adapted to an interpersonal setting with the facilitator. The same is true for a client who prefers one-on-one work, a client who would be toxic to a group of survivors, or a client who might not otherwise be able to take advantage of a group setting.

What are the Survivor's Journey Group Rules?

There are only a few hard and fast group rules for Survivor's Journey Groups. Group rules are different from the 12 Pillars of the Survivor's Journey presented later. The group rules for Survivor's Journey groups are provided below:

1. Everyone has the right to use their voice to communicate their feelings, thoughts, opinions, and struggles. No one should be condemned for using their voice. However, when speaking, the focus should always be on themselves and their experiences. Participants should begin a sentence with "I" instead of "you." For example, "I feel confused about...." "I am thinking about..." "Yesterday I decided to...". Even when they are attempting to help someone else, they might say, "When I had a similar problem, I...."

2. No advice giving or problem solving should take place by others in the group. We find survivors sometimes believe they can solve other people's problems but have a hard time solving their own. All energies should be spent resolving our own issues.

3. Confidentiality is important in Survivor's Journey groups. If a discussion happens outside of group, it should occur between a Journey member and their therapist and should be limited to the participant's experience.

What is a Survivor's Journey Bomb Squad?

The Bomb Squad is YOUR team of people who are there to help you. This is the team of people you need around you to help you fully heal. In the 2nd Journey, we will ask you to gather your team and regularly meet with them. We DO NOT recommend you take Journey 3 without having your Bomb Squad in place. At a minimum, you'll need a trauma treatment therapist on board. This information is presented to you in detail in Journey 2 in preparation to pursue Journey 3.

What is The Chain Reaction?

Have you ever watched a fuse that is lit? There is sometimes a chain reaction where one process makes something else happen and so forth. One process makes another process ignite. The bomb that goes off affects everything around it. We think of a bomb as breaking things apart. Some bombs are very productively used to break through things. When we need to destroy walls and tear down old buildings, we use bombs. A life transformation is a break-through to another more fulfilling life.

If we carefully and specifically work the 12 Survivor's Journeys we will experience a life transformation in which:

1. We will use our truths and tools to guide our life transformation.
2. We will work from inside out and achieve the life we want to live.
3. We will have healthy boundaries to learn in order to trust ourselves and others and will be trustworthy.
4. We will have the formal supports we need to create the informal supports we want.
5. We will handle difficult situations with grace because we are in control of our emotions.
6. We will no longer be internally vulnerable because we have internal healing.
7. We will escape from our traps and avoid life's tricks.
8. We will live a love-based life instead of a fear-based life.
9. We will lead a life of freedom powered by our will, our voice, and our choices.
10. We will no longer allow trauma and shame to control our lives.
11. We will fully love ourselves and have loved-filled relationships with others.
12. We will never again experience the control and abuse of a lover, a drug, a system, or an institution.

Our Suggested Format for Survivor's Journey Group Meetings:

1. Begin by quoting the Survivor's Journey prayer:

Please take these chains and free me from my internal prison. Take the pain and replace it with joy. Take my existence and replace it with life. Take my sorrow and replace it with happiness. Today I live by choice, not by chance; I make changes, not excuses; I am motivated, not manipulated; I am useful, not used. I choose self-esteem, not self-pity; I trust others who are trustworthy; I am not bound by others, but I have boundaries; I eliminate from my life those who offer me despair and disrespect. I work toward healing and put my energies into my freedom and recovery.

2. Read the 12 Journeys or
3. Read the 12 Pillars or
4. Read "The Chain Reaction".
5. New members introduce themselves.
   a. Each member should introduce themselves by saying, "Hi, I'm (name), and I'm looking to live free," or "Hi, my name is (name), and I'm looking for freedom," or "Hi, I'm (name), and I'm reclaiming my power, choice, and voice."
   b. Members should welcome any new members to the group by saying "Welcome, we are happy you are here."
6. Announcements
   a. Any announcements should be made which pertain to the Survivor's Journey information and activities, information and activities occurring in the community related to the Survivor's Journey, or that promote health and freedom.
7. Any potential bombs which are about to go off?
   a. This is the part of group where a member can discuss any specific problems (bombs) they might be having which need the immediate attention of the group.
8. Group Meeting
   a. The group meeting may consist of *any* of the following:
      i. Reading and discussing a section of Part I or Part II of the Survivor's Journey
      ii. Reading and discussing a section of one of the Survivor's Journeys, Pillars, or Chain Reactions.
      iii. Discussing a workbook reflection assignment
      iv. Discussing anything related to the Survivor's Journey.
9. Close with commitments
   a. Go around the group and have each member mention what they will be working on this week related to their

recovery. Below is an example of what a group member might say. This is not an exhaustive list:

    i. Read and write in my Survivor's Journey workbook
    ii. Work on a Journey
    iii. Read a chapter in the Survivor's Journey
    iv. Search for a member of my Bomb Squad
    v. Meet with a Bomb Squad member (e.g., trauma treatment therapist)
    vi. Talk to my children or share with a loved one about...
    vii. Meditate, go to yoga, etc....

The Search for Freedom

"Ye shall know the truth, and the truth shall set you free" ~ John 8:32

Whether we consciously know it or not, freedom is something most people are searching for. Simply getting your needs met is not living a life of freedom. Achieving real freedom is having "control" over our own lives. Control means to have autonomy, agency, and choice over most things. No matter where you live, freedom is a human right.

An animal who is trapped, and understands it is trapped, will chew its own leg off because that's how important freedom is. Freedom is so important, when a human being breaks a law, society decides that taking their freedom away is the most devastating consequence imposed on that individual. Yet freedom is a thing which is so relative, many people think they are free when they aren't. There are three levels of freedom. The freedom from something, the freedom to do something, and the freedom to be something. In group, we work to help you achieve all three.

Why BELIEVE?

Belief is fundamental to recovery. You need to believe you can recover. You need to believe you can live the life you want to live. You need to believe you can be happy. You need to believe there is justice in the universe, even if you don't see justice on earth for what happened to you. Believing will help you understand there is something or someone more powerful than anyone who will right the wrongs despite the laws of man, and this is critical to your healing. Calling on the universe to support you is the difference between healing mentally and emotionally and healing the soul.

Spiritual healing is deeper than what any case manager or therapist could ever help you with. It's a deeper healing than even you could do by yourself for yourself. It's connecting with your soul. Your soul is the other part of you and it's the deeper part of you. It's the one, as Gary Zukav in the book "Seat of the Soul" put it, that is deep inside you, that looks out at what is happening and what has happened to you and understands your heart and your genuine self. The soul is the real you. The soul is devoid of ego and doesn't care what you wear or what you look like or how successful you appear to others. The soul is you and it understands how awesome and wonderful you are because it knows who you really are. The kind, loving spirit that exists in you, and your need to love and be loved genuinely. It understands how funny and sweet you are, and your capacity to love and to want to trust others. And it understands why you use the ego to protect it.

In your recovery, we ask you to connect your soul to the One. Because at times your soul needs the strength of more than 100 men to help you. Who is more powerful than 100 men? Who has the strength and capacity to love you more than anyone ever has? It's the One who loved you first and it's the One who loved you when you believed no one else would or could love you again. Your creator loves you no matter what you did or didn't do, who you were or weren't, and no matter who you are today and who you'll be tomorrow.

Believing in the healing power of a higher power settles the soul, quiets the ego, and feeds the spirit. We call it "spirituality", "the Creator", "the One" or your "higher power". You may call it "God," "Allah," "the Great Spirit," "Brahman," "Devas," "Shen," or more.

Spirituality is the belief in something bigger than yourself. The difference between spirituality and religion is in spirituality you define your relationship with your higher power. In religion someone explains your relationship with your higher power. Some prefer to be spiritual; some prefer to be religious, and some prefer to have both in their lives. Whatever the case may be, call in the One who is there to help you heal and who has the power to heal you.

As a spiritual person, you don't need to believe in a God or Allah per se, you can choose to believe in the universe, evolution of life, and the principles and ethics of humankind. As a spiritual person, you may also choose to believe in God or Allah.

Learning the Survivor's Journey Pillars

Survivor's Journey groups are organized around 12 Pillars. These Pillars provide the lens and context for how Survivor's Journeys groups must operate. The 12 Pillars are a recognition of the framework surrounding Survivor's Journey groups. These 12 Pillars represent our beliefs and ways of being. They provide guidance on the structure, stance, and perspective of the groups, group facilitators, and members involved.

Pillar #1: The Truths and The Transformations are the Core of the Program

We are truth-worthy. We seek the truth in understanding who we are, what we've been through, and how to heal and move forward. Through truth, we use the tools provided to do the work necessary to heal and recover. Transformation is the result of our hard work. When we use the tools provided by the Survivor's Journey program, we can transform our lives in ways which are healthy for us.

We could say that truth is our understanding, tools are what we use to do the work, and transformation is the result. When we view it through the paradigm of change, we are moved from "Being," or standing in our truth, to "Doing" the work necessary, and "Having" what we need to transform our lives.

When we suffer abuse, exploitation, or violence, our power (to do or act) and agency (to be self-directed) is taken and used against us and for someone else's benefit. We can't fully recover when we aren't self-directed to act in our own self-interest. When we know our truth, we can learn to use the tools provided to us to create life changes we want.

Translation: Who you are, what you do, and what you have in your life is a product of your hard work. You are either working on improving your life or working on destroying your life. There is no in-between. Learning your truth may set you free and set you up to begin working on the life you want to live.

> *Example: "I finally realized the type of person I kept picking was abusive and controlling. I wanted to be loved so bad I have literally gone to jail for this person. That put being with my kids in jeopardy because of our fights and I finally went to jail because of some shit they did. I don't need to be loved that bad. I can do bad by myself. And I'm realizing I don't have to be by myself forever. I'll meet somebody that's good for me, once I'm good for me."*

Pillar #2: Using Survivor's Journey "Tools" and Working Through the Mind-Fields is the Path to Recovery

Tools come in various shapes and sizes and have a variety of uses. Some tools are used to combat internal demons and help members process and regulate their thoughts and feelings. Some tools are used to help members externally navigate interactions and relationships with others.

Tools help you become empowered to successfully direct your own life and help you exercise your power, choice, voice, autonomy, and agency over your thoughts, feelings, and actions. The manner in which the tools you are provided are used is relative and is shaped by your experiences, cultural background, spirituality, education, and socio-economic status.

Taking control of your own life also means gaining and using the support of others to guide you in the right direction. Your new support system walks beside you until you are ready to walk on our own. In taking the Survivor's Journey, you learn to move from dependence and co-dependence to independence and then inter-dependence.

Recovery not only requires using the Survivor's Journey tools, but it also requires working to defuse the mind-fields. Victims' lives have been akin to a series of mind-fields they don't even recognize exist. Without proper recovery, victims walk through their life repeatedly stepping on hidden bombs they didn't know were there. In the Survivor's Journey world, we call these Mind-Fields. Many people go through life unaware of the mind-fields. They simply believe they have no control over their life and their life just doesn't work out the way they want it to. Others are aware of their own personal mind-fields, but instead of addressing them, they actively work to avoid them by going around them, under them, or ignoring them. But instead of going away, these mind-fields show up in other areas of our life. While we provide you with the tools to work each Journey in your recovery, we also discuss the mind-fields associated with each Journey and what happens if or when you don't work the Journey in a way which is productive and supportive to your recovery. Your recovery involves using the tools and defusing the mind-fields which threaten to prevent you from successful recovery.

Translation: Just like you need tools to fix your car, you need tools to better handle your life.

Example: "Instead of going off like I usually do, I learned that the reason I would go off is because I wasn't really mad, I was hurt. So, I learned to just walk away until I calm down and think about what is going on with me. Then I come back and try to talk about my feelings. It has really worked with my kids. I actually feel like a better parent."

Pillar #3: The Absence of Violence, Abuse, and Exploitation is not the Presence of Recovery.

The absence of violence, abuse, and exploitation is not the presence of recovery. Similarly, no longer being abused and being free are not the same. The absence of victimization from your abuser means you are no longer subject to victimization from them. However, the victim carries the trauma from the abuse and/or exploitation with them. Because of the pattern of vulnerability, without recovery, the victim will likely experience repeated patterns of violence, abuse, and exploitation. Internal and external freedom through recovery is the goal and it takes hard work. Being free is a state of being and takes daily internal and external work to both achieve and maintain. Recovery leads to freedom. Our goal, through the Survivor's Journey, is for you to experience internal and external freedom.

Translation: Just because you are no longer (fill in the blank) doesn't mean your life will get better and you are healed. You still have work to do to repair the internal damage that was done.

> *Example: You worked hard to get away from him, or it, or them, only to find yourself in the same or similar situation sometime later. This makes total sense. If nothing has changed with you on the inside, then you are likely to repeat the same or similar patterns of destruction in your life.*

Pillar #4: Recovery is Relative and All Patterns Have Exceptions

Recovery is relative. Everyone will not recover at the same rate and across all Journeys of recovery. It took many years for certain patterns to develop, and it may take a longer time for issues to be resolved. Give yourself grace and allow yourself to do the work you need to do. Keep coming back to group for weeks, months, and years, each time growing more and more until you feel healthy and healed.

A member may go through the Survivor's Journey process and really grasp the idea that having healthy boundaries (Journey 8) is important, or the member might spend a considerable amount of time focused on establishing healthy boundaries. There is no set time frame. A member can continue to focus where they need to focus for as long as they need to focus there. They will know when they feel, think, and behave in a healthy manner. The same thing may be true for "trust" (Journey 7), or "self-forgiveness" (Journey 10), and so forth. Members should work through the Journeys over and over until they have mastered each Journey. If a member feels old patterns creeping back in, they can come back into group and work through them. Survivor's Journey members are always welcome and nonjudgmentally supported.

Translation: Ain't no shame here. You are always loved here without judgment. Anytime you are out in the world, and you get your life rope tied up in knots again, we will help you untie it by doing the work. So anytime you need to sit your ass down and do your work, sit your ass down with us. We love it because we love you. We got you fam.

> *Example: Janice worked the Journeys over and over. She felt much better and even got her kids back. However, she continued to struggle and self-sabotage parts of her life. She discovered she never really felt and practiced self-forgiveness. She reached back out and began attending Survivor's Journey groups again to go deeper working all of the Journeys, using the idea of "self-forgiveness" within each Journey.*

Our common patterns of dysfunction are the focus for recovery. When we focus on our collective struggle instead of our individual differences, we can support each other. In reality, we all have different stories which are unique to us. Whatever the individual circumstance and unique story, the outcomes from trauma are similar. We suffered psychologically, emotionally, spiritually, physically, and socially. We lost ourselves, our health, and our sense of safety, and we are working to gain it all back. If your experience wasn't exactly the same as someone else in the group, it's ok. We are all working on recovery, and we may all be on different paths, breaking different patterns in our recovery process. There is no one right way of doing the work. When we focus and fixate on the individual differences in our experiences and recovery process, we lose the point of our collectiveness, which is to support each other through our recovery.

Translation: I promise you boo, no one else's trauma and experiences are more important than yours at this very moment in this very hour. Let's put the focus on you and the work YOU have to do. You are powerful, and you can do this. But have you ever heard the saying, "picking shit with the chickens"? It means to nitpick everything or to pick apart every little thing to the point where there is no longer a point. Quit looking for the differences between us. If someone has a different path or focus for their recovery, it is THEIR path and focus. We do not invalidate someone else's experience or path and take that away from them. So very kindly and very bluntly we say, shut the hell up and allow someone else to have an experience or a perspective that is different from yours. Regaining your own power back DOES NOT mean to take power from someone else. Chill the fuck out and put the focus back on working on yourself. Love on yourself instead.

> *Example: Sherry was trafficked by a pimp who sold her on the streets in Boston. He set a quota for her to meet every night. When she didn't meet that quota, she was tied up to the back porch and made to sleep there all night without a blanket or coat. Cindy and her boyfriend were addicted to heroin. Cindy would trade sex with drug dealers in order to get heroin for herself and her boyfriend. Sherry dismissed Cindy's experience, thinking this was just a case of two junkies looking for ways to pay for their drugs. Sherry said, "Cindy's experience is in no way an abusive or exploitative situation. Cindy should just go to drug treatment and stop wasting time in a group for survivors." What Sherry came to learn was that both suffered trauma while trading sex to meet their needs. Sherry's need was to not have to face the wrath of her traffickers by showing back up without having made her quota for the night. Cindy's trauma was in having to trade sex to meet her trafficker's demands, aka the drug. Both had the common experience of feeling degraded, being controlled, and suffering long term trauma as a result.*

Pillar #5: Experiences of Trauma are in the Eye of the Beholder

The trauma a victim may have experienced is in the "eye of the beholder". This means there isn't an objective gauge we can use to determine one person's experience of trauma was significantly more harmful than the next person's experience. Full recovery is not possible if we begin to evaluate and quantify whether one person's trauma was more severe than another's, or if someone is worthy of recovery at all. The trauma and effects of trauma is within the individual, and it is no one's right to tell the traumatized individual how traumatized they should or should not be. Focus on your trauma and recovery, and honor and respect your sister or brother's trauma and recovery journey.

Example: One person who was French-kissed by an uncle as a child may have suffered just as much trauma as someone who was penetrated by an uncle. Both are incredible acts of invasiveness.

Translation: That's just plain weird to focus on the fact you believe your trauma was worse than someone else's trauma, or theirs is worse than yours. Instead of focusing on them, how about focusing on YOU. You don't have the energy to focus on someone else. You need all your energy directly placed on you. You deserve to focus on YOU and not someone else. Or if you think your trauma isn't worthy of your full participation and focus, think again. You are worth your focus. Your trauma is real. Tell that part of your brain which is minimizing what you've been through to fuck off. You ARE worthy and your trauma is real, and we support you in placing your attention on it and working through it.

Pillar #6: Power and Privilege is Part of the Problem and the Solution.

We recognize power and privilege is embedded in what happened to us. We as women, LGBTQ populations, people of color, foreign born, developmentally disabled, and those living in poverty, are disproportionately affected because we are more likely to be stigmatized by society. We suffer oppression and discrimination, which makes us vulnerable, while the powerful continue to blame the powerless. We are often blamed for our own victimization. We fight to receive legal, social, and economic justice and full human dignity and human rights.

We recognize both power and privilege are embedded in our recovery and we fight to remove the range of negative issues plaguing the movement from implicit bias to invisibility and discrimination.

Translation: Racist, sexists, homophobic, and other assholes who are biased see people who are different as less deserving and less worthy of having full human dignity and human rights. Some people, who claim to want to help end violence, are unconsciously deciding who is worthy and deserving of their help. If you encounter any of this in the professionals or agencies who claim to want to support you, don't quit working on your recovery. Sometimes we recover because of and sometimes we recover despite of. Whatever the case may be, continue to recover.

Example: Jackie is a black woman, aged 32, who works the streets in a moderately sized city and was arrested for solicitation. Jackie was abused by her father at age 12, suffered domestic violence from ages 16 to 23, became addicted to drugs and stayed in active addiction from 22 until now. Jackie was arrested working the street. She was charged and convicted of solicitation. She received three days in jail and was given a fine of $250 dollars. The conviction is on her record. This might hurt Jackie's chances at future jobs, but no one considers it. Jackie has suffered trauma and finds it difficult to reconnect with conventional society, but no one bothered to learn Jackie's history, her earlier abuse, her current trauma, or her active drug addiction. Because no one provided Jackie support, when released Jackie returned back to the streets to resume her life until she was arrested again.

George is a customer who was just arrested for attempting to solicit. He is offered the opportunity to attend a "John School" program where he will spend one day learning about prostitution, HIV, and some of the life experiences of the women he is choosing to solicit. The goal is to convince George not to solicit women on the street. The program will also test George for HIV. It's partly to let George know when he engages in this behavior, his health is at risk. He will, in turn, put his family's health at risk. If George completes his program, his record will be cleared. George will be able to go on with his life because no one wants George's record to be stained. It might cause him shame and problems in his life, his job, his family, and his reputation.

In the first example we can see Jackie has really suffered through some negative experiences and needed support which she didn't receive. However, George was given the benefit of the doubt and a potential second chance.

Pillar #7: Both Internal and External Change is Required for Sustained Recovery and Healing.

Creating internal change is critical to recovery, but is not enough. Negative outside influences will work against recovery, to undo all of the achievements obtained. Therefore, external change is also needed, including the distancing of negative others and bringing closer those who are nurturing and supportive. This also includes spending time in pro-social settings with healthy others.

Translation: You can't just change yourself on the inside and live in a fucked-up environment with fucked-up people. You also can't live in a great environment with all the beauty and external material trappings of life and remain fucked-up inside. You have to work on and fix both. In other words, don't put some window dressing on a house that is fucked-up inside. And don't move your beautifully redesigned interior house to sit on top of a swamp next to a toxic landfill.

Example: Julie had been a victim of child abuse from age 3 to 7 before she went into foster care. She was abused by someone in the foster home from age 14 to 15 before she got the courage to tell someone. By age 19 she was finally on her own. Her foster parents helped to financially get her through college. She was lucky and landed a great job which paid her well enough to move to the sub-

urbs. She had a great home and drove a nice car. She was viewed by her former case worker and the entire child welfare system as one of their success stories. Her foster parents were proud. Her friends were amazed at how far she came in life. Julie had realized the American dream, but inside Julie was broken. She pretended she was happy, but she was extremely depressed and was on medication for depression and anxiety. She found it difficult to sleep at night and would frequently have flashbacks of what happened to her when she was younger. She kept trying to ignore the past, hoping the past would stay in the past. Julie was introduced to Percocet® and loved how they made her feel inside. She quickly progressed past Percocet® to use heroin. Everyone was shocked when Julie died from a heroin overdose. Julie is in great company with Kurt Cobain, Shock G, and others who seemingly by outward appearance, had it all. Julie is a great example of someone who did the external work, but not the internal work needed to be happy and live the life she wanted.

Pillar #8: Partnership is Needed for Whole Person Recovery

Not only should we create positive internal change and have positive informal supports around us like friends, family, neighbors, and co-workers, we should establish partnerships with professionals who help us recover. The best life outcomes for any human being are to have a village of positive supports around them, hence the saying, "It takes a village". When we don't have a naturally existing positive village, we have to create one. Therefore, our partners in recovery should include our trauma treatment therapist, our AA or NA sponsor, our case manager, and our Survivor's Journey group of survivors and facilitators, to name a few. If we want to see how healthy we are, just look at our village. When we fail to have a village around us, we are subject to taking missteps which cost our emotional health. Therefore, we must always have a positive village of supports around us.

Translation: If you want to know how healthy you are, look at who you hang around right now. Are they messed up? Are their lives messed up? The old saying is true, be careful who you hang around because you will pick up their behaviors, patterns, and attitudes. Purposefully spend your time with positive, supportive people that can show you how to live life.

> *Example: Cheryl kept trying to leave her husband over and over, only to be beaten up again. Every time she tried to leave, she would get stressed out, depressed and would stay. She felt like she just didn't have the willpower nor the resources to leave. In reality, Cheryl was strong enough, but she needed support from others to be successful. Once she received the emotional support and resources she needed, she was able to leave and not go back.*

Pillar #9: We Decrease Bureaucracy and Increase Recovery

In Survivor's Journey groups, we are not as concerned with the official labels assigned to victims of violence, abuse, or exploitation by governments and laws. Those who have been victimized, abused, or exploited are welcomed. The Survivor's Journey is designed for you.

Pillar #10: We Recognize That We Bring Drama from Trauma

When we bring our drama as a result of the traumas we suffered, we lose focus of the Survivor's Journey purpose and process. In fact, drama has been such a large part of our lives, some of us feel alive when we are involved in drama. As it is happening, we believe we are right and we are justified. We become "right" fighters, thinking instead of sharing, learning, and growing, we have to debate, argue, and win. We do it for lots of reasons, some of which may have to do with the warped way we've learned to see the world and people in it. It may be because of our previous abuses or societal stigma where we learned to fight to get what we need. It may be because we are seeking the attention we so desperately need. It may be because we are learning to wield our newly found power and independence. It may be because people are beginning to get close to us emotionally and we feel threatened. Whether we are working to avoid vulnerability, engaging in manipulation, misleading the group, or mis-understanding the situation, we are using our time to damage our group process, our growth, and our support system. We are fighting against our recovery. Whenever you are a part of any drama, reflect on it. Meditate on it. Process with the facilitator or your therapist or someone with sound advice. Come back into group. Your recovery is more important than drama.

Translation: Stop, reflect, reevaluate. What part did you play in this drama? Don't worry about what someone else's part was. What was your part? Ok, then genuinely make amends and learn from it.

> *Example: Have you ever heard the saying, "One monkey don't stop no show"? That means if there is one person, aka "monkey," in your group who is annoying you, they shouldn't stop you from gaining all of the recovery knowledge, jewels, and pearls of wisdom you need to grow, change, and live the life you want. Never let one more person stop you from achieving everything you want and need in life. Throughout your life, you let too many people stop you from achieving what you wanted to achieve in life. They took power and control from you. Let's not do that anymore. That way of responding should be dead to you now. Try a different response and one which is finally in support of YOU.*

Pillar #11: Confidentiality is Critical to Recovery

Information shared in a Survivor's Journey group should stay in a Survivor's Journey group. It's important survivors learn to trust because trust is a part of the recovery journey; therefore, confidentiality is important to recovery. If a discussion about group happens outside of group, it should occur between the member and therapist and should be limited to only the member's experience in group. What we do in group is serious business to the members who are doing their work. Part of your recovery involves integrity, or being a person who honors their word and holds another person's information confidential.

Translation: What is said in group should stay in group. Someone else's journey, issues, and experiences are not our business to share outside of group with anyone. Be a person of your word. It's rude to say one thing and do another. Honor your tribe.

> *Example: One of the men in group revealed the name of the person who sexually assaulted him. He described the attack. Someone in the group happened to know the attacker, but never saw him be violent. They have never been victimized by him personally and they find him to be a fairly good guy. They know him to be a hustler, but he's just doing what he needs to do to survive, like a lot of people. The fact that the person in the group is spreading lies about him doesn't seem right and makes them mad. They decide to tell him about the lies the man in the group is spreading.*

In the scenario above, it seems as though the man who is mad has taken it upon himself to judge a situation he truly knows little about. Because he knows the attacker in one context doesn't mean he knows for a fact how he treated the man in group. He decided to dishonor and disrespect his fellow men in recovery. He does not understand the serious consequences which might come from the decision to break confidentiality and talk about what happened in group. The man who broke confidentiality should be immediately removed from group. The group should process what it means to rewound someone who is working on recovery. They should also decide when or if the member should return to group. If not, the facilitator may decide to regularly meet with this person individually and/or to connect them with other services.

Pillar #12 Recovery is Our Only Purpose

Facilitators and organizers should not use Survivor's Journey groups or the Survivor's Journey name to further their political or religious agenda outside of the Journeys and Pillars of The Survivor's Journey. The purpose of The Survivor's Journey is recovery from violence, abuse, or exploitation.

The Survivor's Journey is a guided 12-Survivor's Journey Program, period. We bring truth which cuts through the self-blame to create transformation. If someone follows the Journeys, they will experience recovery and their lives will change. That is the purpose and only purpose. The Survivor's Journey brings powerful knowledge from the fields of psychology and sociology to bear, along with the belief in something universal, loving, and supportive to heal wounds of the mind and heart.

Translation: Don't twist us up in some pro or anti-political or religious agenda you have. We are about recovery only.

We end this book with a simple quote from a woman who transformed her life from victimization, poverty, and oppression, into a globally recognized poet laureate. Dr. Maya Angelou said:

"Do the best you can until you know better.
Then when you know better, do better."

ABOUT THE AUTHORS

Celia Williamson, PhD is a Distinguished University Professor that has worked on the issue of human trafficking and vulnerable populations for 30 years. Lisa Belton, MSW is a master level social worker also engaged in helping vulnerable populations. Both have experienced violence and trauma and work on their recovery.

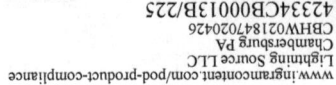